MY ENEMY'S
ENEMY

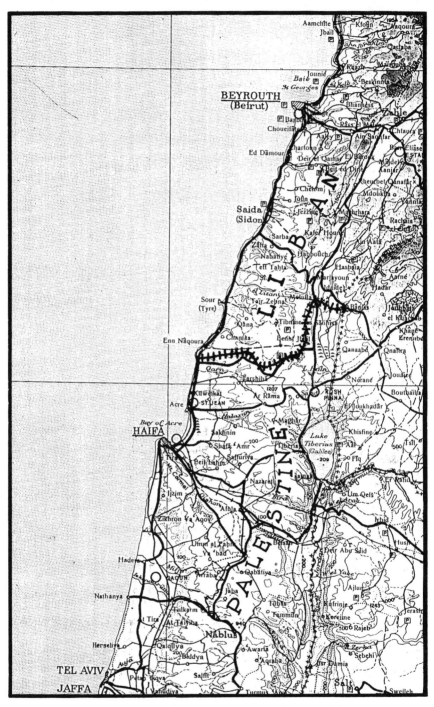

British map of northern Palestine/southern Lebanon, 1942. Courtesy of the Department of Geography, Tel Aviv University.

MY ENEMY'S ENEMY

LEBANON IN THE EARLY ZIONIST IMAGINATION, 1900–1948

Laura Zittrain Eisenberg

 WAYNE STATE UNIVERSITY PRESS   DETROIT

Library of Congress Cataloging-in-Publication Data

Eisenberg, Laura Zittrain.
My enemy's enemy : Lebanon in the early Zionist imagination,
1900–1948
/ Laura Zittrain Eisenberg.
p.   cm.
Includes bibliographical references and index.
ISBN 0-8143-2424-X (alk. paper)
1. Zionism—History. 2. Jewish Agency for Palestine—History.
3. Lebanon—20th century. 4. Maronites—Lebanon—History—
20th century. 5. Jewish-Arab relations—1917–1949.
I. Title.
DS149.E533   1994
320.5′4′095694—dc20
93–45499

Designer: Joanne E. Kinney

CONTENTS

5

PREFACE

In June of 1982 I traveled to the northern Galilee with the Israeli army hot on my heels; and two days after my arrival, the army rumbled past me and into Lebanon. Finding myself in the midst of a military mobilization and on an invasion route constituted a shocking and sobering reminder that what is academic in one part of the world is reality in another. My scholarly interests and physical proximity to the front combined to create an intense professional and personal curiosity about events unfolding across the border.

Throughout that summer I spoke with Israeli journalists, civilians, and soldiers in an effort to learn what they understood their country's interests in Lebanon to be. In the years since then, I have followed closely both the drama of Israel's continuing involvement in Lebanon and the wealth of scholarly literature emerging on that topic. It is my observation that most analyses of Israel's interests in Lebanon treat the entrenchment of the Palestine Liberation Organization in southern Lebanon in the early 1970s as the catalyst for serious Israeli attention to that country. While this is accurate in a narrow sense, Israel did not wait twenty years to discover her northern neighbor. Preliminary research revealed that remarkably little has been written about early Israeli interests in Lebanon, and that there is, indeed, a long and colorful history of Zionist-Lebanese relations worth exploring. I set for myself the task of unearthing the historical antecedents of Israel's policy toward Lebanon, taking as my focus Lebanon's place in the general scheme of pre-state Zionist foreign policy and the specific

7

problems and opportunities that Lebanon presented to the early Zionists. My intention was to fill an important gap in the understanding of Israel's relations with Lebanon and provide a historical context in which to consider continuing Israeli interests in Lebanon. On a wistful note, the course of events described here reminds us that there was once a time when Zionists looking for a quiet border, friendly relations, and perhaps even a political accord considered Lebanon, of all the Arab countries, to be the land most promising.

This study is based on archival research, with the bulk of relevant documents residing in the Central Zionist Archives in Jerusalem. The most illuminating material on the topic of Zionist policy toward Lebanon appears primarily but not exclusively in the files of the Political Department of the Jewish Agency. Reports sent back to Jerusalem from Agency representatives in Beirut are full of observations about the political climate in Lebanon and suggestions for further Zionist activity there. Agents submitted purportedly verbatim transcripts of discussions held with both common and high-ranking Lebanese and passed along for comment a myriad of proposals, offers, and schemes with which they had been approached.

By regrouping stray letters and memos from different files it is possible to reconstruct the significant correspondence between members of the Jewish Agency and some of the most prominent representatives of Lebanese political and religious life. Both content and tone indicate the comfortable familiarity and even affection that developed between the two sides. Letters from Lebanon preserved in the original French or Arabic permit the Lebanese to speak for themselves and provide a clear sense of the encouragements and inducements that helped shape the images of Lebanon formed by the Jewish Agency.

One can follow the debate about Lebanon and the minority alliance question in the minutes of the meetings of the Jewish Agency Executive and internal memos of the Political Department. Reports commissioned from the research staff are valuable not just for the information they convey about a specific subject but as indicators of what topics particularly interested the department at any given time. Statements drafted by department members for public consumption are good examples of Agency efforts to mold public opinion in favor of Zionist positions or control the damaging effects of enemy propaganda. Supporting documents along these lines also exist, to a lesser extent, in the Israel State Archives, Jerusalem; the Weizmann Archives, Rehovot; the Ben-Gurion Archives, Sede Boqer; the Haganah Archives, Tel Aviv; and the Archive for Jewish Education at Tel Aviv University. I have also drawn upon the press of the period.

Other sources include the memoirs and diaries of individuals, both Zionists and non-Zionists, whose Middle East activities touched upon the combined topics of Palestine and Lebanon. Whenever possible, I followed up on the written record by interviewing the players themselves. Former Jewish Agency officials Eliahu Elath and Ya'akov Shimoni were especially helpful. I found other political and academic personalities also easily accessible. The most striking interviews, however, were those with a number of elderly people who have lived all their lives along the border with Lebanon. I visited the kibbutzim of Hanita, Ein Gev, Kfar Giladi, and the town of Metulla and spoke with former spies, smugglers, fighters, farmers, and pioneers whose memories of time spent in Lebanon in the 1920s, 1930s, and 1940s and of their relationships with Lebanese neighbors gave me an important perspective on my topic very different from the one derived from a study of documents alone.

That my sources are overwhelmingly Zionist reflects no intentional bias or sloppiness on my part. The current conflict in Lebanon prohibits archival research there at this time. Lebanese with close ties to the Jewish Agency generally left no written record of their Zionist connections and would be even less likely to discuss the subject today. Given these conditions, I carefully chose Zionist policy toward Lebanon as my focus and not Zionist-Lebanese relations per se, which would suggest an equal balance between Zionist and Lebanese documentation. One can hope that when the conflict in Lebanon is resolved, historians will be free to look for the missing Lebanese pieces to the Zionist-Lebanese puzzle.

I did travel to France to consult the archival holdings of the French Foreign Ministry and the French High Commission in Beirut. Material there both confirmed and fleshed out the picture of French Mandatory attention to Zionist-Maronite affairs which I had originally drawn from Zionist and Lebanese sources. Relevant documents reside in the Archives Diplomatiques du Ministère des Affaires Étrangères, Paris, as well as in the Centre des Archives Diplomatiques de Nantes, Nantes.

Precision demands that two terms that dominate the discussion be clearly defined at the outset. "Zionism" here denotes a political movement whose ultimate aim was the establishment and development of a sovereign Jewish homeland in Eretz Yisrael, or Palestine. A Zionist consciously supported this cause. In this study, "Zionist" policy or personalities are generally those of the official Zionist representation in Palestine, the Jewish Agency. "Zionist" and "Jewish" in the context of this study are often (but not always) synonymous, as will be clear from context.

The Maronites are an eastern Catholic sect and one of many different Christian denominations in Lebanon. As such, "Maronite" and "Lebanese Christian" are not technically synonymous. The Maronites are the largest single Christian community in Lebanon, representing half of all Lebanese Christians, and have monopolized political and economic power for generations. Walid Khalidi contends that the long-running internal Lebanese conflict is not between Christians and Muslims as such but, rather, between Maronite and non-Maronite Lebanese.[1] By virtue of their numbers, organization, aggressiveness, and heightened sense of group identity, however, Maronite interests are best described as simply Christian and most non-Maronite Christians with Christian political priorities generally follow the Maronite line. For the purposes of this study, Christian Lebanese interests are indeed represented by the term "Maronite," unless otherwise noted.

ACKNOWLEDGMENTS

A number of people and institutions contributed to the successful completion of this project, and I am happy to thank them all.

I am grateful to the director and staff of the Central Zionist Archives in Jerusalem for their tireless assistance. The archivists at the Israel State Archives in Jerusalem, the Weizmann Archives in Rehovot, the Ben-Gurion Archives in Sede Boqer, the Haganah and Israel Defense Forces Archives in Tel Aviv, and the Archive for Jewish Education at Tel Aviv University also deserve my gratitude, as do the staffs at the Archives Diplomatiques du Ministère des Affaires Étrangères at the Quai d'Orsay in Paris, and the Centre des Archives Diplomatiques de Nantes, in Nantes.

Special thanks go to the following agencies and institutions, which funded or otherwise facilitated my education, research, and travel abroad: the Horace H. Rackham School of Graduate Studies at the University of Michigan, the United States Department of Education, the National Foundation for Jewish Culture, the Foreign Language and Area Studies Fellowship Program, the Center for Near Eastern and North African Studies at the University of Michigan, and the Moshe Dayan Center for Middle Eastern and African Studies at Tel Aviv University.

I owe a particular debt of gratitude to Neil Caplan and Meir Zamir, who gave generously of their time and expertise with careful readings of the manuscript, and to colleagues who otherwise helped shepherd this project through publication with criticism, suggestions, and provocative musings, among them Hemda BenYehuda Agid, Jacob Lassner, Yosef

Olmert, and Kenneth Stein. Abba Eban, Elchanan Oren, Yehoshua Porath, Kamal Salibi, and Arye Shalav graciously consented to meet with me and probe the issue of Zionist-Lebanese relations from their own particular vantage points. Former Jewish Agency officials Eliahu Elath, Yehoshua Palmon, and Ya'akov Shimoni shared hours of precious memories with me.

Todd Endelman, Juan Cole, Zvi Gitelman, and Raymond Tanter of the University of Michigan provided excellent guidance as I began this undertaking. Rudi Lindner, in particular, impressed upon me the power of the written word and taught me the importance of knowing the historian behind the history. Itamar Rabinovich provided invaluable direction during my research year in Israel. Asher Susser proved especially helpful on numerous occasions and I thank him for his interest and patience. The strengths of this book reflect all these scholars' wise tutorage, while the shortcomings are the product of my ingenuity alone.

I must also express my appreciation to Arthur Evans, Kathryn Wildfong, and all the good people at Wayne State University Press, who walked me through the publishing process with good guidance and good humor.

I am grateful for the encouragement of family members and friends who rallied to my side with emotional and technical support when my computer failed. My cousins Hanan and Nimrod Ben-Ze'ev and Chanah Tzur welcomed us to Tel Aviv, and special thanks are due Chanah for her tireless research and unfailing enthusiasm in support of my endeavor. I am happy to have fulfilled my parents' expectations in completing this book. This project has taken nine years from start to finish, and I thank my husband Michael for his patience in living with both of us. He is more familiar with Zionists and Maronites than any dentist needs to be. My final thanks go to Rebecca and Hannah. Their bright smiles and cheerful "Mommy!" remind me that I am many things: among them, mother, historian, wife, teacher, daughter, and friend, and that each is important. If I have learned to look for complexities in the personalities I encounter in the study of history, perhaps these little girls will have taught me the most important lesson of all.

— 1 —

A Harmony of Interests
or Discordant Objectives?
Lebanon in the Early
Zionist Imagination

DURING THE PERIOD of the British mandate over Palestine, Zionist policy toward Lebanon, as conceived and pursued by the Jewish Agency, was motivated by the conviction that Lebanon differed significantly from other Arab entities and that mutually rewarding relations with it were all the more possible for this reason. Lebanon's uniqueness lay in the powerful Maronite Catholic community, first among its many ethnic and religious factions.

Lebanese Christians have a proverb suggesting that once the Muslims do away with the Jews, they will turn on the Christians: "After Saturday, Sunday." Another adage often cited with regard to intergroup relations in the Middle East is, "My enemy's enemy is my friend." Together, these two maxims suggest that an alliance between the Christians of Lebanon and the Jews of Palestine might have benefited both sides. In fact, the Maronite Catholic community in Lebanon and the pre-state Jewish community in Palestine (the *Yishuv*) maintained an intensive, decades-long relationship alternately characterized by quiet periods of pleasant exchanges and fitful attempts to produce a politically effective alliance.

The Maronite-Zionist relationship dates to the early years immediately preceding the European mandates over Lebanon and Palestine. Zionist curiosity was naturally piqued by the demographic and political oddity that was Lebanon, an Arab country with a sizable non-Muslim population enjoying political predominance. Zionists found their initial contacts with members of the leading Maronite sect encouraging. Faced with

13

nearly monolithic Muslim/Arab opposition to their activities in Palestine, many Zionists believed that the existence of a strong and apparently friendly non-Muslim community in Lebanon offered a better chance for good relations with that country than with any other Arab country.

As the Zionists came to know their Maronite neighbors better, the similarity of the circumstances in which the two communities found themselves became clear. The Lebanese Christians were losing numerical superiority to the Muslims and feared losing political superiority, as well; the Zionists sought to overcome their numerical handicap in Palestine vis-à-vis the Muslims and aspired to political dominion. The Maronites jealously guarded Christian autonomy, and some even toyed with the idea of establishing an independent Christian state in Lebanon. They watched with special interest Zionist efforts to establish an independent Jewish state in Palestine. Many Maronites and Zionists agreed that the two minorities, similarly beset by large numbers of Muslims resisting their respective claims, shared a natural harmony of interests.

The desire to translate these shared concerns into meaningful political advantages led individuals in both communities to suggest the concept of an "alliance of minorities." This strategy called for Lebanese Christians and Palestinian Jews to join forces and coordinate economic and political resources in confronting their common enemy and pursuing their similar national aspirations. Ideally, other non-Muslim and non-Arab minorities in the Middle East would join the Christian-Zionist partnership. The wide range of shared economic and political interests between Christian Lebanon and the Yishuv, the warm personal relationships that developed between leading Maronites and Zionists, and the Zionists' absolute isolation in the region certainly made the alliance-of-minorities concept a logical one for Zionist foreign policy makers to explore.

But was the minority alliance idea a logical policy to pursue? Despite debating the concept many times, the Zionist leadership never decisively accepted or rejected a pro-minority policy; and without a hard test case to prove or disprove its efficacy, the idea persisted. Fluctuating support for the minority alliance proposal and intermittent efforts to advance it characterize the evolution of Zionist thinking about Lebanon during the mandate era. Although Zionist strategists hoped that the Muslim Arab states would eventually acquiesce in the establishment of a sovereign Jewish entity in their midst, they were not adverse to looking elsewhere for regional support should mainstream Arab acceptance not materialize.

It is useful to consider why Lebanon became a topic of Zionist interest when it did, how the nature of that interest set the tone for early Zionist thinking about Lebanon, and in what ways Lebanon seemed possibly more receptive to Zionist overtures than other Arab countries. It is easy to sense the enthusiasm with which Jewish Agency delegates in the field recorded the many ways in which Lebanon seemed ripe for fruitful relations with the Yishuv and the Zionist movement. Clichés quickly developed along the lines that Lebanon was a "window in the wall of Arab enmity," a "flash of light in the darkness of Arab opposition," or an "island in a vast Muslim sea." But before being swept away on a wave of hyperbole, it is necessary to consider those factors that inhibited any potential Lebanese receptivity and acted as a brake on the Zionist-Lebanese relationship.

The Jewish Agency's Political Department tried to weigh the unusual opportunities Lebanon presented against the constraints and then to es-tablish broad directives for a realistic Zionist policy. Different individuals within the department placed varying degrees of importance on the posi-tive versus negative aspects of Lebanese receptiveness. This study exam-ines the impulse behind the minority alliance approach and, to the extent that it was ever implemented, its successes and failures.

Toward a Zionist "Foreign Ministry"

The Zionist movement at the turn of the century had no official place in the international community of nations. With its leadership and constit-uency scattered among Europe, America, and Palestine, it struggled to de-termine policy toward the Arab countries surrounding the proposed Jewish national home. Essentially, a handful of individuals charted the course of Zionist relations with the Arab world, each bringing different perceptions and priorities to the task.

In the early years of the mandate, a series of Zionist organizations conducted relations with the Arab world. In the year following the 1917 Balfour Declaration, Britain approved the establishment of a Zionist Com-mission to look after Jewish affairs in Palestine. Under Chaim Weizmann's direction, the commission served as a liaison with the British, organized the Jewish community, undertook relief for Jewish refugees, and saw to the reconstruction of Jewish settlements in the wake of World War I. Barred by local British military authorities from purchasing land or bringing in significant numbers of Jewish immigrants, the commission focused on communal and economic work within the Yishuv. Some members per-ceived possibilities for political activity among the Arabs, however, and in June of 1920, Weizmann's colleague at the commission, David Eder, pro-posed the creation of a formal Arab Bureau.[1]

In 1920, a British civil administration replaced the military adminis-tration in Palestine and granted a wider latitude of activity to the Palestine Zionist Executive, which replaced the Zionist Commission that same year. Weizmann responded enthusiastically to Eder's idea for a department to manage Zionist-Arab relations and inquired as to a proposed program and budget.[2] For much of that decade, the controversial Chaim Kalvarisky headed the Zionist Executive's Office of Arab Affairs.[3]

Kalvarisky used his position to further the contacts he had made among the Arabs on his own initiative. Many Zionists opposed his practice of making generous gifts to Arab notables for, as one detractor claimed, "no specific purpose but only that they should be generally useful" to the Zionist cause.[4] That critic, Col. Frederick Kisch, head of the Palestine Executive, disapproved of Kalvarisky's system, since "it either involves a life commitment or else it invariably means bitter trouble when one terminates such a salary." The dire economic straits in which the executive consistently found itself made such a policy especially questionable. Members of the executive feared that only a miracle would save the organization from bankruptcy and lamented that a lack of funds had forced them to abandon many important undertakings. Wrote Kisch in 1928, "I am not using too extreme an expression if I say that we are trying to keep body and soul together."[5]

In 1929, the Palestine Executive became the expanded Jewish Agency for Palestine and adopted an even wider scope of activities. While the Jewish Agency Executive in London maintained contact with politicians and officials of the colonial and foreign offices there, the Agency in Palestine formulated and implemented the daily decisions of state building. Distinct departments for labor, immigration, economic matters, and so on existed; and foreign policy, such as it was, emanated from the Political Department. Each department boasted sections, with the Political Department's most active being the Arab Affairs Section and the Middle and Near East Section. By 1937, the Peel Commission found that the Jewish Agency constituted a complete administrative apparatus amounting, in effect, to a government existing side by side with the British mandatory government.[6] Of the two, however, Britain commanded the primary attributes of state power (e.g., foreign policy making) and occasionally hampered the Agency in its more ambitious activities.

Like its predecessors, the Agency and its Political Department suffered from an ongoing lack of funds and trained personnel. Without the manpower or money necessary to sustain contacts, the Agency could not aspire to a serious foreign policy. Chaim Arlosoroff, who became director of the Political Department in 1931, complained about the many opportunities missed due to the lack of relatively small amounts of money. He worried that the inability to pursue contacts would ultimately prove dangerous, because it would "reveal our utter inability for action" and asserted that without special funds it was "superfluous to speak of any political work in Palestine and the neighboring countries which might deserve the name."[7] Only by pressing into service young Palestinian Jews already studying in Arab countries and willing to work for trifling pay did he succeed in ensuring a regular flow of information between the department and important Arab capitals.

The staff of this embryonic foreign ministry was committed to its task but inexperienced in high-level diplomacy, its top leadership notwithstanding. Chaim Weizmann, president of the World Zionist Organization and the Jewish Agency, certainly took an interest in Zionist relations with the Arab countries. A cautious man, he pursued Zionist aims by appealing to his wide circle of prominent British acquaintances. As the mandate progressed, Weizmann's faith in the British and willingness to compromise with them took him further and further out of step with the increasingly bold demands of the Zionist movement. In his greatest hour, he secured the Balfour Declaration in 1917; but by the 1940s, he was aged and sickly, unable to grasp the great changes overtaking Zionist thinking. One year before Israeli independence, Weizmann still opposed the 1942 Biltmore Program, in which the Zionist movement formally committed itself to the goal of a sovereign Jewish state. He was a respected international figure, and Arabs naturally often addressed themselves to him. But younger men in the Zionist mainstream determined the daily decisions and operations of the department. His voluminous correspondence shows that in his later years he continued to lobby vigorously on behalf of Zionist interests, but the evidence suggests minimal correlation between his activities and the actual conduct of policy by the department. Weizmann's name came to have more weight in the conference rooms of Europe than influence among his Zionist colleagues.

David Ben-Gurion, chairman of the executive of the Jewish Agency, personified the bold and activist Zionist school that finally led the Jews to statehood. A learned man, he was also stubborn, difficult, and authoritarian. Political Department records and his own diaries indicate that he did not involve himself with the details of daily policymaking and specific operations. His interests were overwhelmingly military. Nevertheless, the department undertook no significant activities without his knowledge and approval. Ben-Gurion believed that the courage, daring, and strength of the Jews themselves would create the Jewish state, regardless of international commissions and resolutions. He did not believe that the Arabs would quickly resign themselves to Jewish sovereignty but was prepared to accept decades of Arab hostility until the future Jewish state's superior strength (of which he was certain) finally convinced the Arabs to reconcile themselves to its existence. He devoted himself to security issues accordingly and left diplomacy to others. He gave his blessings to the Political Department's efforts but occupied himself with preparing the Yishuv for Israel's violent birth.

In 1933, assassins murdered Chaim Arlosoroff, and Moshe Shertok (Sharett) became head of the Political Department, assuming responsibility for the conduct of Zionist foreign policy for the remainder of the prestate years.[8] An intelligent, diligent man, he carefully read the mountains of paperwork generated by the department, marking each document with his distinctive "M.S." and jotting comments in the margins. With Ben-Gurion's concurrence, he made the decisions that shaped the daily management of foreign policy. Personally devoted to Ben-Gurion, Shertok was himself "Weizmannist" in orientation. He saw the Jewish national renaissance in the context of the flow of world history and evinced more concern than Ben-Gurion with international opinion. He had lived for two years in an Arab village as a child and his fond familiarity with Arabs and Arabic gave him a fuller image of Arabs as proud, reasonable people and a greater faith in the power of direct negotiation. Shertok's son suggests that his father's perception of Arabs as dignified human beings influenced the scope of policy options in that he automatically dismissed those grand designs which sought to transfer Arabs from place to place for political reasons or otherwise treated them as if they were objects.[9] Ben-Gurion and Shertok often complemented one another, but when their thinking diverged, Shertok proved too weak to mount serious opposition to his formidable boss. Although no idea became policy over his objections, Ben-Gurion's preoccupation with security and military matters generally gave Shertok free rein in the Political Department.[10]

The department maintained a modest staff in Jerusalem and a small cadre of roving ambassadors in the field, but the two agents most directly involved with Lebanon were Eliahu Epstein (Elath) and Eliahu Sasson.[11] A young Russian immigrant to Palestine, Epstein studied at the American University of Beirut from 1931–1934. He earned pocket money there as a freelance reporter for the Reuters news agency, the Hebrew daily *Davar*, and the *Palestine Post*, and as one of the enthusiastic young Palestinian Jews first pressed into service for the Jewish Agency by Arlosoroff. Epstein proved to be a sociable young man who made many friends among the students, faculty, notables, politicians, and religious people whom he met as a student and journalist. Although he matured into one of Israel's finest diplomats, his early work in Beirut often reflected a youthful naïveté. He studied Arabic but preferred to conduct interviews in French or English, and his long reports from Lebanon read more like term papers than concise bulletins to a harried staff back in Jerusalem.

The department's reliance on young moonlighting agents occasionally constrained good policy. In November of 1932, Epstein enthusiastically reported that George Naccache, a Maronite editor, wanted to visit Palestine to gather information for positive articles about the Zionist endeavor. Since Naccache had requested that Epstein accompany him, however, Epstein informed his colleagues that this important visit would have to wait until the end of final exams and the start of Christmas vacation at the university![12] He obviously enjoyed his time in Lebanon and maintained a lively correspondence with his many Lebanese acquaintances after he left.

An initial amateurism notwithstanding, Epstein's many contacts in Lebanon served the Jewish Agency well. In 1934, he returned to Jerusalem to head the Political Department's Middle and Near East Section, in charge of contacts with neighboring Arab countries.

Whereas Epstein looked at the Arab world with an outsider's perspective, Eliahu Sasson was born there. The son of a prominent Jewish family in Damascus and educated at St. Joseph's College in Beirut, Sasson felt most at home in the progressive political circles of Arab society. Arabic was his native tongue, and he was briefly active in the Arab Nationalist movement prior to immigrating to Palestine.[13] Sasson headed the Arab Affairs Section of the Political Department, which orchestrated relations with the Palestinian Arabs; but his contacts among the most prominent Arabs in the Levant kept him involved with Zionist policy toward Lebanon and Syria. With the reorganization of the Political Department in 1943, he assumed responsibility for Agency activities in those two countries. Sasson approached his work in a systematic, professional manner, and his colleagues credited his eastern orientation with giving him special insight into the Arab world.[14] Sasson's letters stimulated debate and his voice was an influential one. He pushed the department to develop a consistent foreign policy toward the Arab nations and looked for ways in which mutual interests in developing the region might overcome the political differences dividing the Yishuv and its neighbors.

In charting Zionist activity within the Arab countries, these individuals worked with colleagues in the Political Department and other Agency departments, consulted leading personalities in the Jewish private sector, drew upon ongoing experiences in the field, and relied on their instincts. While certain broad themes guided their activities, "policy" as such was more a series of ad hoc reactions to opportunities as they unfolded, rather than a systematic program of preferred activities. Denied complete freedom of action by the British authorities and lacking sufficient resources, personnel, and experience, the Political Department labored to conduct Zionist foreign policy.

ZIONIST POLICY TOWARD THE ARAB STATES

As unique as Zionist thinkers imagined Lebanon to be, it was still a predominantly Arabic-speaking country and an integral part of the Arab environment surrounding the Yishuv. Zionist activities there thus fell within the rubric of general Zionist policy toward the Arab world.

The Jewish Agency approached the Arab world with the aim of advancing the threefold task of creating, defending, and populating the Jewish national home in Palestine. A primary goal was therefore to end Arab opposition to the national home or, failing that, to win great power support for the establishment of a Jewish entity despite Arab opposition. Zionists searched for a single, recognized Arab leader with whom to negotiate and whose commitments would not be nullified by opposing sectors of Arab opinion. The Agency looked for this leader beyond the confines of Palestine. It did not consider Palestinian Arabs a distinct nationality but, rather, constituents of the larger Arab world. A basic ingredient of Zionist diplomacy thus became that it was sufficient to develop local economic and social relations with the Palestinians, while reserving political relations for a leader of the wider Arab movement outside Palestine.[15] This thinking led the Agency to try and circumvent the Palestinian Arabs, who were proving almost unanimously opposed to Zionism. At different times it seemed that Emir Faisal of the Hejaz or Transjordan's Emir Abdullah might be such a leader. Zionists reasoned that someone with a broader view would be more likely to grant the Jews concessions in tiny Palestine than a local activist for whom Palestine was the only frame of reference.[16]

Chaim Weizmann expressed this perspective in a 1937 letter concerning negotiations between some Zionists and their Palestinian friends, whom Weizmann described as good people, but unable "to deliver the goods."[17] Instead he enthused over Jewish Agency contacts with the governments of Syria, Lebanon, and Iraq. According to Weizmann, by neutralizing anti-Zionist elements within those governments, the Agency could "obtain their good offices in order to influence the Palestinian Arabs." Weizmann surmised that positive results were possible, largely because those countries were coming to realize that the Jews "might be helpful to them." He concluded that cooperation with the Arabs of the neighboring countries might win friends for the Zionists in the Arab world, relieve some of the pressure in Palestine, and isolate Palestinian extremists completely hostile to a Jewish presence.

Agency overtures often took the form of a proposed "exchange of services." Zionists hoped that some pan-Arab leader would recognize the Jewish claim to Palestine and use his influence to persuade the Palestinians to accept an accommodation with the Jews. In return, the larger Arab world could expect to benefit from Jewish capital, technical skills, and international political support.[18] Initially Zionists directed a similar approach toward the Arabs in Palestine but quickly realized that no leader of significant standing would forfeit an independent Arab state of Palestine in exchange for a higher standard of living within a Jewish state of Palestine. David Ben-Gurion presented this line of Zionist thinking, focusing on the non-Palestinian Arabs, in his testimony before the Peel Commission of 1937. He stated his belief that the Zionists would reach an agreement with the Arabs outside of Palestine, who would then "bring their influence to bear on the Arabs of Palestine to come to terms."[19] He argued that the promise of Jewish intellectual, financial, scientific, and organizational assistance would ultimately convince the non-Palestinian Arabs that their own best interests lay in an accord with the Zionists.

This concept found its way into ostensibly non-political arenas. In conjunction with other Zionist associations, the Jewish Agency published *Palestine and the Middle East*, an economic magazine concerned with regional industry, trade, and agriculture. The Agency regularly sent copies to influential persons in Syria, Lebanon, Iraq, Turkey, Iran, Saudi Arabia, Kuwait, and Yemen. The journal concentrated on the economic *accomplishments* of Jewish Palestine and the unfulfilled *potential* of the Arab world, clearly suggesting that if the Arabs made peace with the Yishuv, the Zionists would share with them the secrets to making their deserts and economies bloom.[20]

The exchange-of-services approach underestimated the depth of Arab nationalist sentiment and failed to attract serious Arab attention. Most Arab leaders genuinely opposed the Zionist enterprise. Those tempted to respond lacked the influence necessary to deliver on their end of a bargain. The exchange-of-services theory encouraged some Arabs to "look on the Zionists as a cow to be milked."[21] They came with projects in need of funding, hinting that their new party or newspaper might be less hostile to Zionism. To the extent that money was available and these projects dovetailed with efforts to improve its image in Arab political and press circles, the Zionist cow sometimes obliged.

The failure of the exchange-of-services proposal to produce an Arab-Zionist agreement led the Zionists down an even more circuitous path. Difficulty in finding a strong Arab leader through whom to circumvent the Palestinians prompted the Agency to try to negotiate around the Arabs entirely by reaching out to non-Arab or non-Muslim countries more on the periphery of the Arab-Zionist conflict arena, such as Turkey, Iran, and Ethiopia, and to minority communities such as the Druze, Shi'a, Circassians, the Kurds of Iraq, and, of course, the Maronites.

Although often warmly received, Zionists in search of a quick fix to the Palestine problem looked even further afield and appealed directly to the mandatory and other Western powers. A curious outcome of the deep involvement of outside forces in the region was that both Jews and Arabs often perceived that they had more to gain by turning to exterior forces than to each other. Each hoped to persuade the great powers to impose a solution that the other would never voluntarily accept. Toward this end, Zionists lobbied long and hard to persuade the British to apply the Balfour Declaration firmly and force the Arabs to accept the existence of a permanent Jewish national home.[22] Zionist organizations cooperated fully with investigative commissions dispatched to the region under British, American, and United Nations auspices, and sent emissaries abroad to press their case before foreign governments and constituencies. Chaim Weizmann in particular focused his political activity on personal acquaintances in the British and French governments. Zionist thinking held that what the Arabs would not accept willingly, the great powers could force them to accept grudgingly.

The campaign for Jewish sovereignty engendered another basic policy goal, that of securing physical control over as much of Palestine as possible, thereby extending the de facto boundaries of the future Jewish state. Land purchasing and settlement organizations such as the Jewish National Fund and the Palestine Land Development Company were affiliated with the Jewish Agency and political considerations certainly played a role in the acquisition of land.[23] Land purchase issues only involved the Political Department when the prospect of buying property beyond the borders of Palestine arose.

Jewish settlements reinforced Zionist control over territory purchased. Another broad policy aim was thus the security of Jewish residential, agricultural, and industrial sites. The Jewish Agency appealed to the British with only limited success and Zionist security came to rely on both officially sanctioned and underground Jewish paramilitary defense forces. The Political Department participated in the battle for the safety of the frontier outposts by pressing authorities in Palestine and those across the border to prevent Arab attacks.

The third aspect of the mission to create, defend, and populate the Jewish state made Jewish immigration (aliyah) to Palestine another basic policy premise. This entailed the dual project of promoting aliyah among Jews in the Diaspora and manipulating British quotas to make possible their immigration. British antagonism toward a continuous Jewish influx into Palestine resulted in a substantial Zionist program of illegal immigration. The Haganah (Jewish self-defense force) and the Agency's Immigration Department worked together to smuggle Jews into Palestine.

The Political Department conceived and conducted its activities in pursuit of these fundamental aims. Officials did not expect any single campaign to bring about the creation, defense, and population of the national home, but aimed to perpetuate an atmosphere and relationships that would permit their collective efforts over time to achieve these Zionist goals. Toward this end, the department invested great energy and finances in creating active connections within the Arab world.[24]

It is difficult today to imagine the ease with which Zionists made and maintained contacts in the Arab countries prior to 1948. Palestinian Jews traveled freely throughout the Arab world, studied in Arab countries, and conducted business with their Arab counterparts. Correspondents from the Hebrew press and Jewish Agency officials routinely met with prominent Arab leaders of all political persuasions.[25] With the exception of those in Saudi Arabia, the major cities of the Fertile Crescent welcomed Jewish wayfarers. Some Jewish contractors working on British projects during World War II served as Zionist conduits to the Arab world. David HaCohen, of the leading Solel Boneh firm, established close ties with many Lebanese and consulted regularly with the Jewish Agency as to the development of those relationships.

Expectations as to what might come of these contacts ranged from the modest to the ambitious. The Agency valued such relations even if the only outcome were an exchange of views in a coffeehouse. The openness of its society made Lebanon an easy place in which to gather intelligence and allowed the Zionists to keep abreast of internal Lebanese intrigues and circumstances relevant to their own cause. Jewish Agency employees checked in regularly with a lineup of informants, some of high standing in their communities, most in return for financial remuneration. By nurturing ties with Epstein's wide circle of acquaintances among Lebanese newspaper editors, religious leaders, influential personalities in the government and opposition, notables, and intellectuals, the department kept its finger on the pulse of the Arab world and created for itself a fuller image of the environment in which it operated. Anxious to be heard, as well as to hear, the Agency hoped that an ongoing exchange of views might persuade some key Arab players to moderate their opposition to Zionism. Occasionally, a well-placed contact was willing and able to affect a slight gesture favorable to Zionist interests. Eliahu Sasson took a special interest in closely monitoring the Arab press and tried to induce Arab editors to adopt a moderate, if not sympathetic, stance on the Palestine issue.

Agency representatives tried to cultivate ties with different factions in the Arab world in an effort to prevent the crystallization of a united anti-Zionist stance. They promoted the concept of pluralism whenever possible, reasoning that the less homogeneous the region, the more easy the integration of yet one more tiny group. Ideally some of these extensive contacts would pay off in Arab acceptance of the Jewish national home and a formal Arab-Jewish entente. While few Zionists permitted themselves such optimism, the Agency did press for a related but supposedly more realistic goal. Once the Zionist movement accepted, in principle, the partition of Palestine, the Political Department conducted its activities with an eye toward encouraging prominent Arabs to speak out for partition and the establishment of a Jewish state. Such Arab leaders would have to have come to the conclusion that partition was the only solution to the bitter battle in Palestine and that it served the Arabs' own best interest to accept partition, rather than condemn themselves to interminable conflict with the Jews. Agency operatives found that while many of their contacts privately endorsed partition, few were willing to do so publicly.[26]

Despite general Arab rejection of Zionist claims in Palestine, its success in establishing relations with leading Arab personalities encouraged the Political Department in its endeavors. Moving freely throughout the Arab world, its agents observed firsthand the rifts and factions that riddled the Arab countries, each with its own, not necessarily Palestinian, priorities. This persuaded the Zionists that the Arab opposition was not an impenetrable monolith and that, with the right approach, they could achieve a modus vivendi with the Arab countries. Besides the obvious benefits of regional peace, the Agency hoped that ties with those countries might bring Arab pressure on the Palestinian Arabs to acquiesce in the establishment of a Jewish homeland in some part of Palestine.

Lebanon as the Focus of Zionist Attention

Objectively there was no question that Lebanon was unique among the Arab states. But debate over Lebanon centered on the question of whether Lebanon's uniqueness demanded a policy different from that applied to other Arab countries or merely suggested that the standard Zionist approach enjoyed greater chances for success there.

There is a strange symmetry between the arguments of those who celebrated the particularity of the Lebanese case and those who found in Lebanon's differences equally formidable obstacles to Zionist-Lebanese relations. As we shall see, many incidents in Zionist-Lebanese relations reflected both approaches. The perplexing choices Lebanon presented to Zionist strategists boiled down to the question, Did Lebanon's uniqueness promote or inhibit an understanding with the Yishuv?

Zionists on both sides seized first upon the unusual demographics that made Lebanon the only pluralistic state in the Arab world. Optimists pointed to the lack of a homogeneous, Muslim bloc. They believed that Agency policy should take as its basis the existing confessional system in Lebanon and work from there to encourage the development of political pluralism in the truest sense: the genuine acceptance of people of different attitudes, customs, cultures, and faiths and the belief that they are all entitled to full and equal rights. Such a phenomenon would clearly be to Lebanon's advantage and would also legitimize the national existence of yet one more people in the region, the Jews. If this undertaking proved too ambitious, optimists still saw in Lebanon's highly factionalized society an unusual opportunity for striking up friendships. With so many groups, there were bound to be several interested in what the Zionists could offer.[27] The more cynical reasoned that even if the genuine acceptance approach failed, rival factions would be open to external assistance, and the Agency could decide with whom to ally. That divisions were drawn along religious lines also augured well for the Zionists, since the well-worn adage "My enemy's enemy is my friend" seemed to suggest that Christian communities fighting off Muslim domination would find the Palestinian Jews natural allies.

Pessimists contended that the uneasy nature of Lebanese pluralism actually acted against a successful Zionist-Lebanese relationship. Highly fragmented, the Lebanese political system spoke with many voices. Although the Agency might ally with one or more groups, no faction could speak for the country of Lebanon or commit Lebanon as a whole to a pro-Zionist policy. These Zionists doubted the efficacy of any one Lebanese partner and objected to a policy whose success hinged upon one faction's conclusively imposing its will upon all the others, something that Lebanon had resisted for generations. True, it was a society easily penetrated; but it was doubtful how jumping into the quagmire of Lebanese sectarian politics would benefit the Zionist cause or whether the shifting sands of inter-Lebanese rivalries could be a firm foundation for Zionist policy.

Both Zionist views held a perception of Lebanon as a country where economic interests took priority over ideology. Zionists overwhelming shared the impression that everyone in Lebanon could be bought and that if the price were high enough, issues like pan-Arabism, anti-Zionism, and the commitment to a wholly Arab Palestine would not impede Zionist-Lebanese relations. Those Zionists inclined to see great promise in Lebanon wanted to appeal to what they saw as a highly developed sense of self-interest among the Lebanese, whom they believed to be particularly susceptible to the exchange-of-services theory of Zionist-Arab relations. These optimists argued that the Lebanese resort industry's dependence on Jewish tourism and the dependence of the Lebanese economy on markets in Palestine would propel Lebanon toward increasingly closer relations with the Yishuv. They believed that business and profits would offset periodic calls for an anti-Zionist boycott, which would clearly be detrimental to important sectors of the Lebanese economy.

Pessimists agreed that economics outweighed ideology for the vast majority of Lebanese but held that financial interests actually inhibited Zionist-Lebanese relations. They doubted that Lebanon would risk jeopardizing lucrative economic relationships with the rest of the Arab world for a formal relationship with the Yishuv, especially after the Arab boycott of the Yishuv tightened in 1945. No matter how profitable that relationship might be, there would still be only one Jewish state, which could not possibly make up for all the business Lebanon stood to lose in the Arab world. While some Maronite factions, in particular, showed great interest in harnessing Zionist capital for their own benefit, the question remained as to their ability to persuade their countrymen and the Palestinian Arabs to mitigate their opposition to Zionism. Another economic drawback to Lebanese-Zionist cooperation was the threat of competition between the two sides. A Lebanese businessman told a Zionist friend, "What is there for us to do with you Jews? We are good merchants and you are good merchants. We need the more primitive Arab societies and they need us. There we can make a good living."[28]

It was also no secret that the "Greater Syria" plans emanating from Damascus similarly threatened the future of Jewish Palestine and the integrity of independent Lebanon. Syrian nationalists and pan-Arabists regularly proclaimed their belief that Lebanon constituted a natural part of Syria and that Palestine was really southern Syria. They aimed to unite these areas under the rule of one Arab leader and the best that the national minorities could hope for was limited autonomy.

Optimistic Zionists saw the Greater Syria threat as yet another force driving the Christians (and other non-Arab or non-Muslim communities) into the Zionist embrace. Whatever measure of independence they had or aspired to in a small, fragmented Lebanon would surely be diminished when they were but specks in a large, Muslim Syria. For its own part, the Zionist movement was not interested in leaving the Jewish national renaissance to the whims of an Arab ruler. Pro-Lebanon Zionists urged the Agency to play on the Greater Syria threat as a means of strengthening the bond between the Yishuv and Christian Lebanon.

Skeptics looked at the Greater Syria issue in another light. Syria was the seat of Arab nationalism and anti-Zionism, sentiments easily exported to Lebanon. They knew that much of Lebanon's Muslim population supported the "reunification" of Lebanon with Syria, which meant, once again, that at best the Zionist "bond" would be with only specific Lebanese factions of dubious influence. Syrian interest in Lebanon translated into considerable Syrian influence in Lebanon, and Syria would surely object to any attempted separate Lebanese-Zionist accord.

The Political Department staff included individuals of both the pessimistic and optimistic persuasions vis-à-vis Lebanon, all of whom contributed to the attitudes developing in Jerusalem about the neighbor to the north. In charting its Lebanon policy, the Political Department started with the premise that Lebanon was unique among the Arab states and was even of one mind as to what factors made it distinct. Whether those factors made Lebanon friendlier to Zionism or just hostile for different reasons, however, was a matter of personal interpretation. It is within the context of this debate that the department set broad policy goals specific to Lebanon.

Lebanon seemed to offer special opportunities for pursuing the fundamental Zionist program of creating, defending, and populating the future Jewish state. The perception of a "natural harmony of interests" with the Maronites and shared economic interests with the rest of the Lebanese population suggested that finding prominent persons who would disassociate themselves from the general anti-Zionist attitudes of the Arab world was a realistic goal. Agency people wooed important Lebanese with ideological, political, religious, historical, or strategic arguments, depending on an individual's orientation; supplied statistics attesting to the achievements of the Yishuv, reinforced by personal tours; and used the exchange-of-services argument to appeal to both national and personal self-interest. The effort to reduce anti-Zionism focused on the Lebanese press and later on curbing Palestinian Arab influence on Lebanese public opinion.

In exchange for suitable compensation from their side, the Zionists hoped to strike a bargain by which Lebanon would recognize Jewish claims in Palestine. This could strengthen the Zionist hand in several ways. The remote chance existed that Lebanese support for the Jewish national home would raise the concept of an accommodation with the Zionists to a realistic plane in the Arab world and make it more acceptable. The Agency also believed that a pro-Zionist Lebanese stance would impress the Western powers. By producing evidence of Arab support for the establishment of a Jewish state in Palestine, the Agency hoped to convince the international community that such a state could find acceptance among the Arabs, thereby soothing international concern that a pro-state policy would inevitably mean Arab rejection and war.

The campaign to establish the Jewish state also tried to capitalize on the respect Lebanon enjoyed in the West as a Christian haven in the East. Zionist thinking held that while the great powers were wary of new concepts, the prospect of a sovereign Jewish state would be more palatable to them if they accepted Christian Lebanon as a precedent for Jewish Palestine.[29] It thus became policy to encourage militant Maronite nationalist and even separatist trends and to propagandize on behalf of the maintenance of Lebanon as an independent Christian country.

The general principle of securing Jewish control over as much of Palestine as possible applied to Lebanon to the extent that property along, or just across, the Lebanon-Palestine border was for sale. The basic goal of establishing and protecting Jewish settlements prompted the Agency to use its connections in Lebanon to ward off harassment of northern Jewish outposts by Arab irregulars crossing into Palestine from Lebanon.

Zionists understood that the Galilee's usefulness depended upon the full exploitation of the natural resources of northern Palestine/southern Lebanon. By 1920, Zionists already had detailed plans for the development of the Galilee's water. When the final boundary between Palestine and Lebanon left important hydrologic factors on the Lebanese side of the border, the need to find a Lebanese partner, private or governmental, with whom to exploit the region's water resources for the benefit of both Lebanon and Palestine became standing policy.

The Agency was similarly interested in establishing commercial relations with Lebanon. Besides offering immediate financial rewards, these ties also served the larger goal of binding important sectors of Lebanon and the Yishuv closer together and strengthening those common interests which could possibly offset Arab pressure on Lebanon to adopt an anti-Zionist posture. Epstein, in particular, used his contacts to encourage exchanges between social, athletic, medical, professional, and academic institutions as means of fostering personal relationships between Lebanese and Palestinian Jews and combating negative Zionist images in the Lebanese imagination.

The basic Zionist goal of encouraging immigration also posed specific policy implications for Lebanon. The Political Department was not responsible for immigration per se; but in the course of its dealings with the Lebanese Jewish community did exert some effort toward encouraging younger Jews to come to Palestine. The department expressed concern for the safety of the Lebanese Jews, but purposely did not exploit its contacts with that community to advance policy.

Lebanon thus seemed particularly well suited to mandate-era Zionist activity. Results on the ground were mixed, however. Some Zionist operations succeeded on an immediate level, such as establishing close relationships with highly placed Lebanese or encouraging economic ties between Lebanon and the Yishuv, but did not yield the loftier results of precluding anti-Zionism in Lebanon or persuading the rest of the Arab world (or even all of Lebanon) to accept impending Jewish sovereignty. Some efforts never found an audience, while others enjoyed an enthusiastic response in certain Lebanese circles. The department could not decide whether Lebanon's uniqueness made it more receptive to Zionism than the other Arab states or just hostile for different reasons. As relations progressed with an especially friendly faction of the powerful Maronite community, however, opinion began to lean toward the thesis that Lebanon offered particular promise for a Zionist-Arab understanding.

THE MINORITY ALLIANCE OPTION

Unable to reach a consensus as to the implications of the Lebanese situation for Zionist activity, the Political Department established no specific policy and no strict program of action. Individual department members emphasized different priorities and exercised different methods of operation based upon their personal interpretations of Lebanon's receptivity to Zionism. More sophisticated goals notwithstanding, when presented with an opportunity for action, the department reverted to a bottom-line policy of "making friends and neutralizing enemies."[30] Debate ensued, however, as to the best method for accomplishing this.

The alliance-of-minorities proposal proved one of the more tantalizing and controversial options. As prospects for a peaceful settlement with Muslim Arabs grew more remote, the vision of a partnership with Lebanese Christians grew more appealing. Zionists had to weigh probable risks against possible rewards. There was the danger of putting all the Zionist eggs in a Maronite basket of dubious strength and untested durability and the likelihood that a clear anti-Muslim and anti-pan-Arab policy would irrevocably sour any chance of a larger Zionist-Arab accommodation. But there were advantages to ending Zionist isolation in the region and there was the possibility that together Christians and Jews could stave off Muslim domination and perhaps induce the Western powers to intervene on their behalf.

The Maronite camp was similarly torn between taboo and temptation. Siding with Zionist intruders against their own Arab brethren was taboo, and public knowledge of such collusion would result in immediate political delegitimization. Nonetheless, the temptation to use perceived Zionist resources in the struggle against their Arab rivals remained.[31] The department's interest in promoting pluralism naturally led to an exploration of ties with non-Muslim and non-Arab minorities, and the notion that it was possible to do business with the Maronites was generally accepted. But what should be the nature, terms, and extent of that business?

Proponents of a minority-based policy fell into two groups. One was a tiny band of authors, artists, and poets on the extreme fringe of the Revisionist Zionist movement. Based in Paris, they proposed that a "mosaic of minorities" should govern the Middle East. Their logic was both confused and confusing and fellow Revisionists disregarded their political fulminations. Ostracized by the Zionist mainstream, this circle had no influence on Zionist policy. Only the prominence of members such as the poet Yonathan Ratosh and Ari Jabotinsky, son of Ze'ev Jabotinsky, won this club any attention—and only then for its artistic output. For the purposes of this study, this group is quickly dismissed because of its absolute irrelevance to Zionist political life.[32]

Others who favored a strong pro-minority policy did not belong to an organized circle with a distinct doctrine but were, rather, individuals who concluded that pushing the Maronite-Zionist relationship would best serve Zionist interests. These same individuals, Eliahu Epstein being the most prominent within the department, optimistically perceived in Lebanon's distinctive character a greater receptivity toward Zionism. The minority alliance concept was not an illogical one to consider. A summary of the arguments for and against a policy based on a network of alliances among regional minorities illustrates the compelling nature of both sides' reasoning and explains why the department found it so difficult to rule decisively one way or the other.

Proponents of a Zionist-Maronite alliance often advanced the "beggars-can't-be-choosers" dictum, arguing that in the face of implacable regional opposition the isolated Zionists were in no position to be turning away friends. To those who protested that an accord with the Muslims was of more value than an accord with the Christians, they responded that Zionists could not afford to sacrifice the certainty of agreements based on narrow interests with a small group for the uncertainty of a general, regional settlement with many Arab countries with many demands.

That the Maronites themselves initiated the Maronite-Zionist alliance idea encouraged these Zionists. As early as 1913, Maronites already expressed support for Zionism and proposed the formation of a Jewish-Christian bloc to counterbalance the preponderant Muslim presence in the region.[33] In 1919, Nejib Sfeir, a Lebanese Maronite activist, approached Weizmann with a proposal to divide the region by denomination: Lebanon for the Christians, Syria for the Muslims, and Palestine for the Jews.[34] In November of 1931, Sfeir contacted the Jewish Agency again with a plan for coordinated Maronite-Zionist activity. Shertok had met Sfeir in 1920 and upon his reappearance noted that

> he has aspired throughout all these years to create a Christian-Jewish front directed toward that same distant future in which Hebrew Palestine will be able to conclude a treaty with Christian Lebanon: a treaty between two weak nations against a strong, common enemy.[35]

Shertok took Sfeir to meet with Chaim Arlosoroff, then head of the Political Department, who recorded in his diary both Sfeir's absolute conviction that Muslim rule constituted a mortal danger to the minorities in the Middle East ("The echo of Christian massacres from sixty or seventy years ago still rings in his ears") and the man's impatience with the department's stated inability to finance his plans to organize the Maronites in an alliance with the Jews. Sfeir's departing suggestion was that if the Agency were really so poor off, it had best lower its sights and aim merely to secure the Jewish position as a regional minority, to which Arlosoroff noted caustically, "What a clever fellow!"[36] Nevertheless, Sfeir's argument apparently continued to ring in *his* ears; for three days later, he wrote that despite anti-Jewish sentiment among the Palestinian Christians,

> we cannot afford to forgo a chance that in present circumstances the Christian minorities should look to us as their natural ally. There is at the moment any number of reasons for assuming that the tendency toward such an alliance is growing. I know very well that it may be a double-edged weapon, and I do not, of course, think of any proclamations or declarations of such an alliance. But in view of the fact that at present we are entirely isolated and cut off from any non-Jewish forces in this and the neighboring countries, I think we should not neglect such possibilities.[37]

In 1933, Arlosoroff still favored the idea of a special relationship with the Maronites and dispatched Victor Jacobson to Beirut for the purpose of laying the groundwork for more systematic Zionist activity there in the future. Arlosoroff instructed Jacobson to emphasize in his discussions the "natural community of fate" of the inhabitants of Palestine and Lebanon, since

> whatever the future of a Federated Arab State in the inlands of the Middle East may be, these two coastal provinces appear to be parcelled out by history for a destiny of their own. . . . As time goes on, the Lebanese Christians must come to cherish the idea of an alliance with a preponderantly Jewish Palestine which would strengthen their power of resistance against Moslem aggression or domination. There are Lebanese people of a relatively high political intelligence and education who have already expressed such thoughts. It is now the most opportune time to develop these ideas in direct touch with the influential people there without, of course, gratuitously accentuating the antagonism between our aims and Moslem aspirations or further arousing their animosities.[38]

Arlosoroff's letter expresses two sentiments common to those who favored a close relationship with the Maronites. The first is the belief in a natural harmony of interests between Jews and Christians and the second is a perception of Christians as Western, sophisticated, civilized, and superior to Muslims. Also clearly enamored of the Maronites, Eliahu Epstein credited them with doing "more than any other section in the Arab world to further the development of modern Arabic language, literature, and science," while describing the Arab states as backward and corrupt.[39] Chaim Weizmann revealed a similar sense of Judeo-Christian superiority in a friendly missive to the influential archbishop of Beirut, Ignatius Mubarak, in which he registered his fond belief that positive relations between "the two progressive peoples of the Middle East," namely the Jews and the Christians, would benefit the whole Eastern Mediterranean.[40]

While the Jewish Agency evinced sporadic interest in the concept, the Maronite church had a clear policy of promoting understanding among the minorities, and its most steadfast proponents were the patriarch, Antoine Arida, and Archbishop Mubarak. Throughout the years, the Jewish Agency received unsolicited declarations of support and fervent pleas for a Jewish-Christian entente from Maronites in the highest religious and political seats in Lebanon, all of which served to encourage the perception that a minority alliance was feasible.

Support for this line of thinking emanated from the Lebanese presidency. President and Maronite Emile Eddé repeatedly assured the Agency that the Jews and Christians, as the "two Occidental nations" in the region, had a special role to play that necessitated their close cooperation, and even went so far as to declare that "Jewish and Lebanese [read 'Christian'] cultures are both superior to that of the Arab neighbors and both are struggling for the same goal—to build a constructive bridge between eastern and western culture."[41] His successor, Alfred Naccache, another Maronite, darkly warned a Zionist visitor: "It would not go well for any minorities in an Arab dominated state. The Maronites and the Zionists are in exactly the same position."[42] Naccache maintained that the Quran imbued Muslims with the need to be oppressive and resort to force and complained that the "Arabs" (read "Muslims") were never satisfied with their full share but always wanted more, even though there were certain governmental positions with which they "could not be trusted." The implication was that Jews and Christians could trust one another and were culturally better prepared to hold and exercise power.

Supporters of a Maronite-Zionist alliance never tired of enumerating similarities between the two sides. The list of common features usually began with the fact that both peoples boasted cultures firmly rooted in the West and were struggling to assert themselves in the face of Muslim opposition. The Maronites envisioned Lebanon as a haven for Christians in the Arab world, just as the Zionists envisioned a Jewish haven in Palestine. The success of the Zionist venture depended on substantial immigration from the Jewish Diaspora, and the Maronites sought to strengthen their position by wooing back Christians who had emigrated over the years. The two communities excelled in commerce and finance. Familiarity with Islam and the second-class (*dhimmi*) status it prescribed for "People of the Book" (Jews and Christians) left both groups feeling similarly threatened, as did the pan-Arab and Greater Syria movements. Maronites followed with interest Jewish efforts to resurrect their national consciousness in Palestine. Among Zionists, there existed an "instinctive sympathy" for the Maronites, another non-Muslim community in their political midst desirous of protecting its national consciousness from Arab nationalism.[43] These commonalities suggested the natural harmony of interests which figured so prominently in the thinking of the alliance-of-minorities school.

Purists eagerly extended the minority alliance approach to the Druze, as well. David HaCohen, Eliahu Epstein, Aharon Chaim Cohen (Agency intelligence), Itzhak Ben-Zvi (chairman of the Joint Bureau for Arab Affairs) and Abba Hushi (head of the Haifa Workers Council) enjoyed particularly close relations with leading Palestinian Druze and, through them, sought influence among their Lebanese brethren. Palestinian Druze visited Lebanese Druze villages, at the Agency's behest, to argue in favor of Druze-Zionist cooperation. Negotiations concerning a possible Druze-Zionist alliance, along the lines of the proposed Maronite-Zionist alliance, progressed to draft pacts at various times.[44] With Chaim Weizmann's support, Nejib Sfeir arranged a 1938 meeting between a skeptical Eliahu Sasson and several Lebanese Druze leaders, who proposed a Druze-Maronite-

Zionist alliance.[45] Cohen eloquently expressed the pro-minority view when he wrote:

> This is the way—to establish specks of light and inspiration within the dark Arab ocean around us. . . . Maybe tomorrow we will be able to consolidate them into one bloc that will be inspired by us and will strengthen our position. Only actions such as this will raise our image in the eyes of the major Arab governments and force these rulers to take us into account as one of the principal factors in the Near East.[46]

The opposing school of thought based one of its main reservations concerning a minority alliance on simple arithmetic. Together, the non-Muslim and non-Arab minorities still constituted a minority in the overwhelmingly Muslim Arab Middle East. It followed, accordingly, that security in the region ultimately required of the Zionists an accommodation with that majority. Represented within the department by Moshe Shertok and Eliahu Sasson, this group comprised those individuals generally pessimistic about any special Lebanese receptivity toward Zionism. They did not necessarily reject nurturing special bonds between Maronites (or Druze) and Jews but opposed structuring policy around those relationships.

These Zionists doubted both the will and the ability of the Maronites to deliver on their end of any minority alliance bargain. Politically and demographically, the Maronite star was setting. During the course of the period under review, the higher Muslim birthrate steadily overwhelmed their numbers; France withdrew the support that guaranteed Christians predominance in the country; and the Maronite community fractured along clan lines. If the Zionists worried that no one group could speak for Lebanon, they were even more dismayed to discover that no one Maronite group could speak for that community. Michael Hudson describes the Lebanese arrangement as a classic balance-of-power system made up of many groups, none strong enough to control the entire system.[47] Perceiving the same thing, pessimists questioned the value of an agreement with just one faction of just one group.

A similar argument held that Maronite participation in this power-sharing system precluded a Zionist alliance. The legitimacy of the Maronite position in Lebanon grew out of a long tradition of guarded Christian-Muslim cooperation, formalized by the Lebanese constitutions of 1926 and 1934 and especially by the National Pact of 1943. Would the Maronites actually risk shattering the long-standing but fragile deal with their Muslim compatriots, which kept them in power? The Lebanese Christian diplomat George Hakim answered with an emphatic *no* and lectured Epstein that no Lebanese Christian government could afford to do anything

but seek the closest cooperation with the Muslims. "If the Maronite Patriarch were tomorrow to be made the Head of the Lebanese state," said
Hakim, "the need to safeguard the security of the Maronite community
and of the other Christians in the Lebanon would make of him the same
kind of 'pan-Arabist' as most of the responsible Christian leaders in the
Lebanon are at present."[48]

By putting a twist on the much-lauded litany of similarities between
Jews and Christians, one could also argue that a potential rivalry between
the two groups superseded any impulse to join forces. During the 1920s
and 1930s, for example, merchants in Beirut evinced a fear of regional
competition from the growing port in Haifa. Fouad Ajami maintains that
in the 1930s and 1940s, the Lebanese Christian bourgeoisie actually saw
the Zionists as a threat inasmuch as "both wanted to appeal to the West,
both thought of themselves as enclave societies in a culturally alien world,
and the Lebanese business community feared that a dynamic Israel would
outstrip it economically and be more successful in its appeal to the West."[49]

Nationalist sentiment ran high within the Palestinian Christian community, and some Jews could not ignore the prominent role played by Lebanese Christians in the ideological development of Arab nationalism. Butrus al-Bustani, a Maronite, was among the first to contend that the Arab
nation was a political entity encompassing both Christians and Muslims
and to which both could be loyal. Many Christian Arabs "became sincere
Arab nationalists precisely because they saw this as an areligious creed
through which Islamic primacy might be neutralized"; and some Jews worried that out of a desire to be more Catholic than the pope, so to speak,
many Maronites might be inclined to be more "Arab"—and thus less ac-
commodating to Zionism—than their Muslim Arab countrymen.[50] As the
thirties wore into the forties, most of the Christian Arab press in Lebanon
adopted actively anti-Zionist positions. The most articulate and eloquent
of these Christian journalists was Michel Chiha of *Le Jour*.[51]

Skeptics also recalled the role Catholicism played from time to time
in perpetuating anti-Semitism and cautioned against embracing the Maronites too closely. While the Jewish Agency enjoyed friendly relations with
prominent Maronite leaders, reports from the field noted anti-Jewish sentiment among the Christian masses, including the Maronites. One of the
more detailed accounts held that

> this hatred is a traditional hatred: the primitive Christian believes what he
> hears about us from his childhood in his house, school, in the church and in
> his village, [namely] that we crucified Jesus and that Judas was one of us, too.
> For this reason one shouldn't be surprised that a deep hatred toward us is in
> his heart.[52]

The report predicted that as long as the Maronite rank-and-file were hostile toward Jews, a Zionist-Maronite alliance was impossible: the Maronite leadership would ultimately decline to sponsor a pro-Zionist program unpopular with its constituency, and it would be too easy for Zionist enemies to "arouse within the Christian masses suspicions and additional hatred against us and undermine any agreement." The report's author despaired that the Lebanese churches were not even offering prayers for the suffering Jews of Hitler's Europe as churches elsewhere around the world were doing, and noted that when he spoke to friendly Lebanese Catholics about initiating such activity, he saw only "fear in the faces of my interlocutors, lest activity like this arouse hatred against them, or lest the Muslims use this issue against them."

This realistic Christian fear that open cooperation with the Zionists would provoke Muslim wrath also suggested to some the impossibility of a full-fledged Maronite-Zionist alliance. Even those Maronites actively seeking such an alliance impressed upon the Agency the need to keep joint activities secret until that day when the Christians had consolidated their power and were able to withstand the force of Muslim outrage. Those wary of a pro-Christian policy doubted that this day would ever arrive and questioned the benefit of a secret relationship in the meanwhile. Nevertheless, the department routinely urged Zionist groups not to publish friendly correspondence exchanged with Maronite friends—for instance the congratulatory notes sent to Emile Eddé upon his election as president of Lebanon in 1936, to which he responded warmly. The Agency was anxious not to handicap the new president and counseled keeping "expressions of friendship which we receive from Arab circles . . . to ourselves, because every publication turns the enemy parties against our allies and makes their friendly relations with us a burden upon them."[53]

Shertok did not believe that the Maronites (or other minorities) would commit themselves publicly to an alliance with the Zionists. "These circles know their weakness and their fear of the Muslim majority," he argued before a meeting of the executive; and while they might express a desire to come to an agreement, "no political alliance will come of it because they will not go public. . . . They are not in a hurry to openly appear as allies of the Jews."[54] Since one of the goals of Agency activity in Lebanon was to offer the world evidence of Arab support for Zionism, a secret romance with the Maronites did not appear to serve Zionist interests.

Sasson also advised keeping the Maronites at arm's length, even while accepting the hand they offered in friendship. In his estimation, all the Arabs interested in close relations with the Agency to date were more than willing to gain from an alliance but reluctant to give anything in return. Sasson recommended creating friendly personal relations for the time being but issued a warning about the Druze—applicable to the Maronites as well—that an Agency campaign to force a formal alliance could "give birth to hopes and exaggerated cravings, . . . cost us a lot of money, and in the end cause much disappointment and bitterness."[55]

Having disposed of the Maronites as suitable allies, this school made short work of the other groups mentioned as possible partners as well, such as the other Christian denominations, the Shi'a, and the Druze. These communities, (so the thinking went) were used to being minorities and had no illusions of transforming their narrow communal existences into national ones. None of these groups possessed the influence or ambition to wield power on a national level, and many of their constituents ideologically identified with the Arab nation. Although negotiations and relations with the Druze occasionally proved helpful along the border with Lebanon, only the Maronites could compete for national leadership; and it had already been argued that despite this, they were still unable to commit themselves to an alliance with the Zionists.[56]

Minutes of the Jewish Agency Executive meeting of 20 May 1936 shed light on the minority alliance debate, the uncertain policy toward Lebanon, and the place of that policy in the context of larger Zionist concerns.[57] Discussion about prospects for a peace settlement, Syria, and the European powers dominated the conversation. Ben-Gurion proposed a Jewish Palestine in federation with the Arab countries; and one discussant suggested a program of reaching out to the region's disaffected minorities, particularly the Maronites in Lebanon, as an alternative. In the ensuing discussion most of the pros and cons delineated here arose. More instructive than the discussion itself, however, is that the executive did not address the idea as intently as it did other matters. Debate about the minorities faded with neither a conclusion nor a resolution to research the prospect further. In fact, conversation about Lebanon ended when one attendee expressed a desire to "speak about more practical matters" and abruptly changed the topic. The relatively good relations between Lebanon and Palestine often meant that the subject of Zionist policy toward Lebanon received short shrift as the Jewish Agency grappled with other, more critical priorities.

CONCLUSION

The Jewish Agency repeatedly failed to carry the Lebanon debate to conclusion and never decided upon a specific course of action. Within the Political Department, both sides in the minority alliance debate marshaled compelling arguments without ever forcing a definitive ruling from the department one way or another. Theoretical reasoning aside, only actual experiments with prospective Lebanese partners could prove or disprove the efficacy of a Zionist-Maronite alignment. Did Zionist experiences in Lebanon during the mandate era support the theses that Lebanon was particularly receptive to Zionism and that a special Zionist-Maronite relationship could serve Agency goals? Did the likelihood of a positive response to this query change over time? The following examination of the record of Zionist interaction with Lebanon in the years between the turn of the century and Israeli independence will attempt to answer these questions.

— 2 —

EARLY ZIONIST-MARONITE
ENCOUNTERS

INTEREST IN THE natural resources of the Galilee and a growing sense of possible political and economic opportunities among the Lebanese characterized the early period of Zionist attention to Lebanon. Ambiguity as to the exact site for Zionist activity initially drew Zionist attention to Lebanon. The imprecision, even irrelevance, of geographical expressions such as "Palestine" and "southern Syria" to the actual territory of the eastern Mediterranean coast left open the question of the scope of Zionist activity.

Prior to World War I, the Ottoman administration divided the region into a series of distinct districts (*vilayets*) and sub-districts (*sanjaqs*). "Palestine" simply did not exist as a political or administrative entity. "Lebanon" referred to the immediate area of Mount Lebanon, so "southern Syria" presumably meant southern Lebanon and/or northern Palestine, between which there was no boundary. The Palestine-Lebanon border region was subsumed within the Vilayet of Beirut, a narrow strip running the length of the coastline from just south of Antioch to just north of Jerusalem.

"Eretz Yisrael," the Hebrew expression for the biblical Land of Israel as promised to the Jews by God, proved similarly vague in terms of twentieth-century geography.[1] Was Eretz Yisrael synonymous with Palestine, or did it include areas in Lebanon, Syria, and what became Transjordan? Was the Zionist program to colonize and rebuild Eretz Yisrael within its biblical boundaries, or was Zionist activity to be limited to that part of Eretz Yisrael which fell within the confines of the area which later became

British-mandated Palestine? Where did Palestine end and Lebanon begin? Was southern Syria actually southern Lebanon, or northern Palestine? It is understandable that early Zionist explorers occasionally found themselves investigating sites in southern Lebanon for potential Jewish settlement. The resources they discovered and the people they met there shaped their perceptions about Lebanon.

EARLY ZIONIST INTEREST IN LEBANON

Encouraged by the nebulous border in the Galilee region, early Zionist strategists considered Lebanon, especially the southern portion, an arena for potential Zionist settlement. Chaim Weizmann toured Lebanon in 1907. Initially unimpressed, he nonetheless perceived "colossal" potential there and decided to reserve judgment until he completed his trip.[2] Two-and-a-half weeks later, he was back in Haifa, anxiously seeking support for several small industries he wanted to establish in Sidon, specifically a soap-boiling plant, a lemon-processing factory, a distillation plant, and an olive oil factory. By cooperating with Atid Enterprises, newly founded by Russian Jews, Weizmann estimated that the Zionists could create in Sidon a single olive oil company to control the entire oil industry of the country. He concluded his enthusiastic proposal with the observation that "Saida [Sidon] is a good place in every respect. The raw material is available, there is a harbour, it is favorably situated, capable of development, and has a Jewish population."[3]

Property for sale around Sidon also attracted the attention of other Zionists. The Hibbat Zion (Lover of Zion) movement was a network of Jewish nationalist clubs that emerged in the Russian Pale in the 1870s. The Odessa branch maintained an office in Beirut charged with purchasing land in Eretz Yisrael for Zionist immigrants from Russia. In 1908, this group became particularly excited about a farm for sale in the Sidon/Nabatiye region, which they considered the northwest border of Eretz Yisrael.

The leaders of the Beirut Hibbat Zion office glowingly described the property as a precious jewel with enormous agricultural, political, and strategic potential. They believed that this property would give the Zionists a firm foothold in that part of Eretz Yisrael which fell within Lebanon and a starting point from which to create a chain of Jewish settlements, linking it with that part of Eretz Yisrael which lay to the south. They identified the owner as a wealthy Christian from Beirut with considerable land holdings in southern Lebanon, also available for purchase. Enthused one Hibbat Zion agent:

> Every man has his fateful hour and now is the fateful hour to seize the land. . . . It would be a sin on our part if we miss it. We must gather every resource in

our power to effect this purchase. . . . We will not cast from our hand this
treasure, this wonderful gem, which could be for us a key to a strong position
in the heights of Lebanon so dear to us.[4]

The Ottomans passed laws in 1907 and 1908 making it difficult for
Jews, even those who were Ottoman subjects, to buy land in Judea and the
Galilee. Hibbat Zion leader Menachem Ussishkin argued that this made
land purchase in Lebanon all the more important, especially since this
farm apparently lay within the limits of the autonomous Lebanese province, making Ottoman interference in Zionist programs less likely.[5] No
steps were ever taken toward purchasing the farm, probably due to the
meager resources of the organizations involved and their preference for
property more in the heart of Eretz Yisrael; but the proposal did serve to
raise the issue of the geographical vagueness of Zionist activity.

The Jews of Sidon did not dispute Ussishkin's description of Sidon as
the first colony in Eretz Yisrael. The Jewish community there received
aid from the Zionist Commission in Jerusalem commensurate with that
received by Jewish communities in the Holy Land, and Sidon's Jews voted
in the election for the first Jewish Elected Assembly in Eretz Yisrael. When
the community fell on hard times and lost its Hebrew school, its leaders
dispatched a passionate letter in which they identified themselves as "the
residents of Sidon, which is in Eretz Yisrael," and concluded their plea for
assistance from Jerusalem by asking why they should receive less than "the
rest of the Jewish communities of Eretz Yisrael."[6] Others used biblical
sources to establish southern Lebanon as part of Eretz Yisrael, or "biblical
Palestine." These scriptural geographers deduced that the Hebrew tribe
of Naphtali had dwelt along the Litani river, and that the tribe of Asher
had settled in the area of Sidon.[7] Sidon's claim to be within the divine
boundaries of Eretz Yisrael notwithstanding, mainstream Zionist interest
in southern Lebanon, based solely on security and economic imperatives,
stopped at the Litani river.

The Sykes-Picot Agreement of 1916, by which the British and French
divided the Levant into zones, constituted the first serious attempt at de-
marcating a Palestine-Lebanon border. As World War I drew to a close,
the two Allied powers created Occupied Enemy Territorial Administra-
tions (OETAs) for themselves on the eastern Mediterranean coast based
on Sykes-Picot, but with several significant modifications. British OETA
South was in essence "Palestine" (although no such formal entity yet existed), while Lebanon became French OETA North. Some Jewish settlements ended up in the French sphere of influence, as did the entire Litani
river. As a military boundary, the line between the two areas was not necessarily permanent, so technically, the question of the Palestine-Lebanon
border remained open. Worried lest the military line become permanent,

the Zionists launched a campaign to ensure the inclusion of the Litani's vital water resources in Palestine.

The Zionists appealed to the British, who had seemingly committed themselves to the creation of a viable Jewish homeland in Palestine with the Balfour Declaration. They contended that viability in the north depended on sufficient water resources and a defensible border and that the 1918 line of demarcation deprived Palestine of both. Zionists suggested that if God and man had been less than precise about where the border should be, mother nature offered the Litani river as a natural frontier. Aaron Aaronsohn, a Palestinian Jew and internationally respected agronomist, surveyed the northern reaches of Palestine and concluded that the Litani river was essential for the irrigation and cultivation of the Galilee. The independent engineering firm of Fox and Partners, commissioned by the Zionist Organization to survey the economic potential of Palestine, confirmed his analysis. Its report reiterated that the northern frontier of Palestine must include the Litani, adding that while "the Litani will in the future be of great benefit to Palestine, it is of no value to the territory to the north."[8] This permitted the Zionists to argue that giving the river to Palestine was only natural and would not deprive Lebanon of any resource.[9] In the proposals submitted to the Peace conference, however, the Zionist Organization was careful to note that with proper management, the waters in question could "be made to serve in the development of the Lebanon as well as of Palestine."[10] David Ben-Gurion expressed the same concern for the water resources of a future Jewish state and similarly concluded that its northern border should run along the Litani.[11]

Zionist claims foundered on the rocks of British-French rivalry. The French, who only grudgingly authorized modifications to the Sykes-Picot agreement, refused to cede southern Lebanon to the British primarily because they did not want to give in on anything else but also because their Maronite clients expressed an interest in an enlarged Lebanon. The British declined to force a showdown over the issue because the existing boundary did serve British aims, if not those of the Zionists. Palestine's economic viability was not terribly important to the British. They valued Palestine as a buffer thwarting French access to the Suez Canal. The security argument also fell on deaf ears since Palestine itself was the security belt guarding Suez, and a few miles north or south within the Galilee region was inconsequential to the defense of the canal.

The British also refused simply to let the French have their way, however. Arguing the Zionist position, Aaronsohn wrote that although the "historic and religious associations with Palestine centre round Jerusalem and Judea, . . . for its hopes of a great secular future Palestine must depend mainly on the country north."[12] But when the border issue arose at the Paris Peace Conference, British prime minister David Lloyd George adopted the biblical slogan "from Dan to Beersheba" as his boundary policy. Frederic Hof notes the irony in that while "the Zionists were writing thoughtful boundary proposals based on security and economic considerations for what they hoped would someday be a Jewish State, . . . British Protestant statesmen were thumping tables in favor of 'Dan to Beersheba.'"[13] Lloyd George's biblical diplomacy ultimately lost the Litani for Palestine. According to his biblical atlas, the Sykes-Picot line had been too generous to Palestine in the northwest, at Lebanon's expense. The ministers agreed that it was only fair to compensate by lowering the border in the northeast, consequently leaving the Litani totally in Lebanon. Subsequent minor adjustments, codified in 1923, brought the northernmost Jewish settlements into Palestine but made no allowance for Zionist access to Galilee water resources now permanently in Lebanon. Zionist planners were bitterly disappointed.

The final demarcation of a Palestine-Lebanon border, however, did not sever Zionist involvement in Lebanon. Despite the intense scrutiny placement of the frontier received, the final boundary line bisected private, communal, and religious property, as well as local trade routes. Inhabitants on both sides of the border responded by going about their business as if the new border did not exist. Jews from isolated settlements in northern Palestine continued to buy and sell goods and produce in Lebanon and found Beirut, throughout the 1920s, the closest destination when they needed a hospital. After several unsuccessful attempts to close the border, the mandatory powers contented themselves with regulating cross-border activities by signing a Good Neighborly Relations accord in 1926. This legalized commercial trafficking between the inhabitants of southern Lebanon and the Jews and Arabs of the Galilee, and permitted the Jews of Metulla to cross daily into French-controlled territory to work their land. Metulla's residents paid taxes on that property to the Lebanese government.[14] Local Christians, Shi'a, and Druze continued to approach Zionist representatives with offers to sell land in southern Lebanon; and one Druze leader reportedly urged the Zionists to aim for the Awali river, beyond Sidon, for the northern border of the Jewish national home.[15] French officials in Paris, Jerusalem, and Beirut worried throughout the early and mid-twenties about possible Zionist land purchases in southern Lebanon, fearing Zionist irredentism and a disruption of public order and security. Despite the assurances received from Col. Kisch, head of the Palestine Executive, the French consul general in Jerusalem recommended contacting Baron Edmond de Rothschild, the wealthy French Jew bankrolling much of Zionist land purchase activity, to "advise him of the French desire that Jews not acquire land in Syria and Lebanon on the border of the Jewish national home."[16] In practical terms, however, southern Lebanon continued to function economically as a virtual extension of northern Palestine, remaining familiar and accessible to Zionists.

In 1926, a most unlikely source, the French high commissioner in Lebanon, Henri de Jouvenel, next raised the possibility of extensive Zionist settlement in the French-mandated Levant. By his own admission "jealous" of the benefits that Zionist activity brought to British mandated Palestine, Jouvenel hoped to put Zionist capital, manpower, and expertise to work in the underdeveloped regions of Lebanon and Syria. Jouvenel noted enviously that while the French had to assist the Maronites in their endeavors, the Zionists supported themselves. Revealing a typically Western misunderstanding of Arab nationalist sentiment, he dismissed the threat of Muslim protest as a passing phase and insisted that "the people of this country are too well attached to their own interests not to reconcile themselves quickly enough with those who will enrich them."[17]

Jouvenel first revealed his plan for Jewish colonization in the French Levant to Weizmann and Kisch when they visited Beirut in April of 1926. He invited the two Zionists to a dinner party at his residence and then, according to Kisch, ignored the rest of his guests for the entire evening while he regaled Weizmann and Kisch with details of his proposal. He emphasized that he spoke only for himself but offered to raise the issue with Paris if they so desired.

Jouvenel envisioned Zionist settlements in northern Syria, beginning at the Euphrates around Aleppo and moving south through Homs toward Damascus. He also suggested that the Zionists resurrect the ancient city of Palmyra in the Syrian desert. Kisch recorded his excitement at hearing such a proposal come "spontaneously" from the French high commissioner. Weizmann asked about Zionist settlement in French-controlled territory in the south, along the Lebanese border with Palestine, which had the "advantage of greater proximity to our present centres of colonisation, and historically, apart from this convenience, would have a greater appeal to the deep sentiments of the Jewish people."[18] Jouvenel adamantly opposed any Zionist activity in southern Lebanon for fear of Jewish irredentism and a new battle over the Palestine-Lebanon boundary. If Zionists established settlements around Sidon and Tyre, worried Jouvenel, they would surely begin agitating for the inclusion of that region in the Jewish national home. He repeated his arguments in favor of Jewish colonization in the north and Weizmann agreed to consider the proposal.[19]

Jouvenel raised the possibility of Jewish settlement in French-mandated territory in a letter to the Foreign Ministry in Paris. Interestingly, he represented the idea as Weizmann's and claimed to have listened without expressing an opinion. He then repeated his arguments in favor of the proposal and advised his colleagues to encourage Weizmann if he came to discuss the matter.[20]

Weizmann conferred with his British acquaintances. Puzzled by Jouvenel's proposal, the British doubted that the Zionists would accept the offer or could prosper there if they did. They decided that the introduction of an element friendly to France into Lebanon and Syria was in keeping with the traditional French policy of encouraging divisions in Syria. They also suspected that France saw the Zionists as a potential source of wealth for the territories under its mandate.[21]

The prospect of diverting energy, funds, and manpower, then concentrated in Palestine, to distant projects in the north troubled Weizmann. Southern Lebanon appealed to him, but the chances of France's approving Zionist activity there were slim. Always sensitive to great power sentiment, Weizmann did not want the Zionist movement to refuse the French offer outright. He offered evidence of a recent warming in Zionist-French relations, citing a new French interest in Jewish matters and the Palestine problem, manifestations of goodwill by French representatives in Palestine and their readiness to mitigate Catholic anti-Semitism, the recent formation of a French Committee of the Friends of Zionism (whose membership list included an impressive array of statesmen and academicians), and of course the recent Zionist conversion of Jouvenel.[22] Weizmann considered positive relations with the French a valuable asset to the general Zionist program and hesitated to offend French sensibilities by abruptly brushing off a gesture of French "generosity." One can also attribute his reluctance to dismiss the offer to his personal affinity for the biblical notion of an Eretz Yisrael extending "from the river of Egypt to the Euphrates."[23] He quoted that passage several times in the context of the debate over Jouvenel's proposal and suggested that the practical question was whether to start at the Euphrates and work south or concentrate efforts in Palestine and hopefully work north at a later date. Concerning Arab resistance, Weizmann envisioned peaceful cooperation based on an exchange-of-services policy: "We could offer the Arabs what they have not got, that is to say, organization, means, etc. The Arabs could offer us what we have not got; they must accept the Balfour Declaration."[24] He recommended pursuing the idea tactfully and carefully.

Debate about the issue at the Jewish Agency Executive meetings of 24 June and 15 July 1926 proved that once again, Weizmann was out of step with mainstream Zionist thinking.[25] His Zionist colleagues permitted him to negotiate and counterpropose away; but when he presented them with his ideas for Zionist colonization in Lebanon and Syria, he found little support. The rest of the Zionist leadership believed that activity within Palestine took first priority and showed no interest in diverting attention and funds to far-flung Zionist outposts in the Syrian desert or along the Turkish border. The French archives document Weizmann's continued interest in Jouvenel's plan well into 1927, however, and a sustained lobbying campaign in 1930 by him and Victor Jacobson, then head of the Zionist office in Paris, in favor of Zionist colonization in French-mandated Lebanon.[26]

A flurry of proposals for Zionist activity in French-mandated territory by individual Jews was the only outcome of Jouvenel's plan. Encouraged by word of Jouvenel's willingness to admit Jewish colonists, Ussishkin revived his claim that part of biblical Palestine fell within Lebanon and Syria and turned to Israel Levy, Paris's chief rabbi, with a plan for French Jews, "with their considerable means," to fund the colonization of those parts of Eretz Yisrael under French mandate. The rabbi offered to consider the idea.[27] Kisch, sharing Weizmann's dual desire to concentrate funds on work in Palestine while retaining the option to colonize in Syria, wrote to Weizmann for advice when a group from Nahalal, led by Shmuel Dayan, approached him about settling lands in French territory owned by Baron de Rothschild. Dayan argued that Jouvenel's recent declarations dispelled all hesitations about proceeding with Zionist work under the French flag. Weizmann counseled that such action was premature as long as negotiations were underway and asked the Nahalal group to wait patiently.[28] When Rabbi Levy finally consulted with Rothschild, the baron declared himself absolutely opposed to Zionist settlement within French-mandated territory.[29] Although Weizmann's prominent French friends apparently put him off gently with vague promises to study the matter closely, French officials in Paris, Beirut, and Jerusalem expressed uniform concern and alarm at the prospect of Zionist settlement in Lebanon.[30] Fears of Zionist irredentism engendered an almost hysterically negative response to a request from the Jewish National Fund for permission for one Professor Brawer to enter Lebanon to complete research for a map including those parts of "historic Palestine" which lay within the area of the French mandate.[31]

All of Weizmann's negotiations came to naught, and the idea of Zionist activity north of the Palestine border dissipated. Responding to a query about Jewish settlement in southern Lebanon in 1930, French foreign minister Aristide Briand replied that he did not oppose Jewish immigration to those areas as long as the Jews understood that they would not be members of any Jewish state, but rather, French, Syrian, or Lebanese citizens.[32] This was certainly not what the Zionist movement envisioned as far as the recreation of a national Jewish presence in its ancient Middle Eastern homeland; and for the time being, the topic of Jewish immigration to the French Levant was dropped.

Because early Zionist interests in acquiring Lebanese territory were practical and not imbued with religious imperatives or underpinned by emotional attachments to the land, irredentist tendencies toward Lebanon remained mild. Despite the French rebuff of Professor Brawer, the Jewish

National Fund, in 1937, published a map depicting all of Palestine and part of Lebanon and Syria with the biblical verse "This is the Land which ye shall inherit," which aroused disapproval in the Political Department. Wrote Bernard Joseph,

> biblical quotations are no doubt spiritually refreshing but they may create untold difficulties when used without regard to political exigencies of the time. This one will no doubt want considerable explaining away if it falls into the hands of Syrian and Lebanese political leaders. I propose drawing the attention of the Executive to the map with a view to prohibiting its distribution.[33]

Although disappointed at losing a critical natural resource for the Jewish homeland, Zionist thinkers did not dwell on establishing a physical presence in Lebanon. If they could not possess the Litani, perhaps they could find a Lebanese partner with whom to exploit the river's resources for the mutual development of northern Palestine and Lebanon.

THE MARONITES

On numerous occasions, early Zionist representatives traveling throughout the Middle East reported pleasant encounters with Lebanese Maronite Catholics. A growing familiarity with this community and the warmth with which its members received them kindled Zionist expectations as to possible political or economic opportunities in Lebanon. The Maronite experience in Lebanon and the development of an extreme Maronite nationalism suggested that the community might be receptive to an alliance with the Zionists.

Maronites first appeared in northern Syria during the sixth century and fled to the Lebanese mountains during the Islamic expansion of the seventh century. The group takes its name from its patron saint, Maroun, an ascetic monk; but its founder and first leader was Yuhanna Maroun (d. 707 c.e.), "under whom the sect developed a distinct communal and political organization."[34] The Maronites developed their own Syriac liturgy and a monothelite theology. They drew closer to Catholic Europe during the Crusades and entered into full union with Rome in 1736. As Uniate Catholics, they accept the authority of the pope but retain for themselves some degree of autonomy and the right to practice rites of their own. Culturally and politically, the Maronites long enjoyed a special relationship with France.

Matti Moosa maintains that Maronite self-perception of being a separate and unique group within Lebanon crystallized during the early 1800s. According to Moosa, the church came to reflect the Maronite ethos and the patriarch represented both religious and secular authority.[35] Hourani argues that this condition occurred as early as the seventeenth century and characterizes it as the earliest phase in Maronite ideology, which he terms the "ideology of the mountain."[36] The original and permanent aspect of Maronite self-consciousness was "of a compact community, the Maronite church, living by itself under its own hierarchy, protecting itself from attack by the Muslim rulers of the cities and plains, and also against the more insidious attacks of Jacobites and other 'heretics.'"[37]

Entering its second stage in the nineteenth century, Maronite ideology espoused the concept of a Maronite nation living within a broader political system controlled by a hierarchy of leading Sunni, Maronite, and Druze families acting in concert. In the mid–1800s, French influence encouraged the Maronites to see themselves as both ethnically and religiously distinct. This attempt to "give historical depth to the idea of a separate and virtually independent [Maronite] political entity" led to what Hourani identifies as the third, "populist" strand in Maronite ideology, which aspired to a sovereign, autonomous Maronite state.[38] It is another coincidence of the convergence of Maronite and Zionist interests that political "Maronitism" and Zionism emerged in different corners of the world at roughly the same time.

Maronites and Druze comprised the principal communities of Mount Lebanon, a rugged area that offered refuge to minority sects from the ruling Sunni empire. Maronite-Druze coexistence fluctuated between genuine cooperation and bitter conflict, finally erupting in 1860 into a bloody civil war. It was that war which Itamar Rabinovich believes "brought to the surface and nourished a new ingredient in Lebanese politics of the nineteenth century—religious solidarity and religious hatred."[39] This same religious factionalism in twentieth-century Lebanese politics saw the Maronites casting about for a regional ally, one candidate being the Zionists.

The civil war of 1860 ended when French troops interceded on behalf of the Christians and the European powers negotiated with the sultan for the creation of an autonomous Lebanese province within the Ottoman Empire, the *Mutasarifiyya*. A non-Lebanese Christian governor appointed by the sultan with the approval of the Western powers administered the Mutasarifiyya. Autonomous Lebanon maintained its own police force and judiciary system, and while it had a clear Christian majority and character, all denominations enjoyed political representation and some degree of political power. According to Moosa, it was during this prosperous period that the Maronites, reveling in their newfound predominance, broadened their perspective and came to regard Lebanon as their exclusive homeland. For them, "Lebanon" became synonymous with "Maronite." In this sense, the Maronite church became the champion of a fledgling Lebanese nationalism.[40]

The Ottoman government abolished the Mutasarifiyya and placed Lebanon under direct military rule at the outbreak of World War I. That

conflict ended with French control over Lebanon and Syria. The Maronites sent a delegation to the Paris Peace Conference in an attempt to win
once and for all a Christian state in Lebanon.[41] The French favored the
creation of an autonomous Maronite state, but debate erupted about its
appropriate boundaries. At issue was the Maronite demand that the new
Lebanese state comprise a substantial enlargement of the territory of the
old Mutasarifiyya.

The creation of independent Greater Lebanon on 1 September 1920
involved the annexation of overwhelmingly Muslim areas to the Christian
core of Mount Lebanon. Even at the time, some understood that the unwilling inclusion of a large Muslim population in the new Christian state
threatened the state's survival. There is no simple answer as to why the
French and Maronites ignored the danger. Hof contends that in the context of their conflict with the British over the boundary between their respective mandates, the French eagerly accepted their traditional role as the
Maronite patron and lobbied on behalf of Maronite interests as a counterweight to British and Zionist claims. France received satisfaction merely
at having secured southern Lebanon for its Maronite client at the expense
of the British-backed Zionists. In satisfying Maronite expansionist dreams,
France tightened its bond with its one reliable ally against hostile Arab
nationalists, simultaneously serving French imperial interests by "extending the political sway of a narrow, largely Francophile Christian majority over the largest land area possible."[42] On the basis of recently declas-
sified documents in French archives, however, Meir Zamir contends that
prominent French politicians, including Prime Minister Clemenceau, considered making concessions to nationalist Muslims in Lebanon and Syria
at the expense of Maronite aspirations. An especially vocal opponent of
Greater Lebanon was Robert de Caix, secretary general of the French
High Commission. Unmoved by Maronite propaganda, de Caix warned
that the Christians' "megalomania" would sow the seeds of disintegration
for the state they were trying to create.[43] That conditions conspired to
force Clemenceau to surrender to Maronite demands are evident in his
letter of 10 November 1919 to the Maronite patriarch, Elias Butrus Hawayik, in which he promised to secure as much territory as possible for
Lebanon.[44]

Psychological, economic, historical, and political factors motivated the
Maronites in their demands. Although some Maronite clergy questioned
Lebanon's expansion on demographic grounds, the leader of the Maronite
delegation, Patriarch Hawayik, overrode their objections. Exercising both
temporal and spiritual authority, Hawayik played a key role in the establishment of Greater Lebanon, a role that some characterize as "more important than that of all the politicians of the area."[45] After years of Maronite religious autonomy, Hawayik was deeply humiliated at being the first

patriarch in generations forced to appeal to the Ottoman sultan for his investiture, an incident which fueled his desire for an independent Maronite state where the ritual of Christian life did not depend upon the good graces of a Muslim ruler. Tens of thousands of Mount Lebanon Christians starved during World War I, impressing upon the Maronites the importance of self-sufficiency for the new Lebanese state. Their land grab aimed at fertile plains and ports. The need for economic viability, a romantic yearning to recreate the historic boundaries of the *Imarah* (the pre-Mutasarifiyya Maronite-dominated Lebanese entity), and the successful Maronite experience during the Mutasarifiyya led many Maronites to disregard the Muslim threat and others to believe that by virtue of their superior Western education, initiative, and ties to France they could dominate the new state despite its expanded Muslim population.[46]

Only a few Maronites saw the contradiction between Christian Lebanon and Greater Lebanon. Among the more prominent was George Samne, an editor who advised his coreligionists to choose between a small, independent Christian state or an enlarged, heterogeneous Lebanon linked to Syria. To seek an enlarged Christian state, Samne wrote, was to attempt the impossible: "the squaring of a circle."[47] According to Amin Sa'id, Emile Eddé supported Jouvenel in 1926 when the high commissioner proposed reattaching Tripoli and Akkar to Syria. Sa'id reports that Eddé "pledged to convince his people to grant Tripoli to the Syrians and . . . placed his signature on the document concerning the union."[48] On several other occasions Eddé expressed support for the territorial reduction of Lebanon, arguing that only by amputating those overwhelmingly Muslim areas annexed in 1920 could the Maronites safeguard Christian control of Lebanon. This was an unpopular position within the Maronite community, however, and in the context of his campaign for the presidency, Eddé could only explain his position privately to the French authorities, hoping they would take appropriate action, which they did not.[49]

Common sense and current scholarship see the creation of Greater Lebanon at the root of the ongoing conflict in that state. The incorporation of large areas populated almost exclusively by Muslims into a Christian state resulted in a cataclysmic disruption of the demographic balance in Lebanon and the birth of Syrian irredentism. The establishment of an enlarged Lebanon proved to be of great importance for the Maronite-Zionist relationship. Hof explains that having satisfied their desire for extended territory, the Maronites in Beirut and the Mountain then found the southern area too poor, rural, and Muslim to be of interest. The resulting neglect of the south by Beirut initially permitted Zionists continued access to southern Lebanon but ultimately allowed enemies of both Zionism in Palestine and Maronite supremacy in Lebanon to overrun the region. In the course of the Arab rebellion in Palestine in the late 1930s, the use of southern Lebanon as a staging ground for Arab attacks against the Yishuv began to dictate Zionist policy toward Lebanon.[50]

Hourani contends that with the incorporation of Beirut and the city's rise to economic predominance, Lebanon began to be guided not so much by the "ideology of the mountain" as by the philosophy of a commercial city, where all types of people must be able to do business in peace, with open access to the outside world.[51] Zionists perceived an exaggerated mercantile ethos among the Lebanese and considered this one of the keys to a special Lebanese receptivity to Jewish Palestine and all it could offer in the way of trade, commerce, and technology. Of greatest consequence both for Lebanon and for Maronite-Zionist relations, however, was the demographic time bomb the Maronites planted in their midst when they insisted on extended borders for their country. The single most powerful force driving the Maronites toward an alliance with the Zionists was always their fear of being overwhelmed by the Muslims, whose birthrate—and eventually numbers—far exceeded their own.

The prospect of being a minority in their own national haven had a tremendous impact on the evolution of Maronite ideology after the establishment of Greater Lebanon. Hourani explains that in a country pieced together by the arbitrary amalgamation of highly factionalized sects, it was inevitable that varying conceptions arose of what Lebanon ought to be. Writing in the late 1940s, he identified several distinct views of Lebanon. Sunnis and Arab nationalists of Muslim or Christian extraction generally advocated Lebanon's absorption into a larger Syrian state. The older generation among the minorities asked only that Lebanon be a safe haven, regardless of its form of government. A small portion of the Maronites, wishing to be both fully Arab and fully Christian, argued for a Lebanon with a mission, namely to be a bridge between the Arab east and the Christian west. Most of the Maronite community, however, adopted the position that Lebanon was a Mediterranean Christian country: "not the western edge of the Arabic Muslim world but the eastern edge of Western Christendom."[52] Extremists espoused a philosophy of "Phoenicianism," which held that the Maronites were not even Arabs but, rather, direct descendants of the ancient Phoenicians, who inhabited the Lebanese coast long before the Arabs' arrival. Proponents of this unusual theory offered the Zionists yet another opportunity to commune with the Maronites on the basis of the cordial biblical Phoenician-Israelite relationship.

Tewfik Khalaf contends that while the Muslims eventually developed a sense of "Lebanonism" superseding other loyalties, Maronite Lebanonism remained grounded in its own defensive conception of Maronite identity, supremacy, and distinctiveness.[53] Modern Lebanese history challenges the conclusion that non-Maronite groups replaced loyalty to their group with loyalty to the Republic of Lebanon, but it is true that the Maronite vision of Lebanon remained narrow and sectarian. Two pillars supported the continued cohesion of the Maronite community: the pervasive influence of the patriarch and church, and a political philosophy emphasizing a Western orientation and an overriding fear of the Muslims.

Events conspired to reinforce this Maronite perspective. A curious sideshow to the 1925 Druze rebellion against the French in Syria is a case in point. The revolt spilled over into southern Lebanon, where it degenerated into a Druze-Maronite conflict. With only a skeletal force in the area, France took advantage of traditional Druze-Maronite antagonisms and armed the Christians.[54] This incident reinforced the Christian tendency to look at politics in terms of communal survival and to turn to non-Arabs for assistance in their battles with other Arabs. Hof credits the events of 1925 with confirming Maronite isolation and encouraging Maronite willingness to look upon the Zionists as plausible allies.[55]

Years of conflict with other Lebanese Arabs, an inclination to look to outsiders for assistance, and a sense of Western superiority characterized the Maronite experience in Lebanon. Maronite history thus laid the groundwork for a Zionist-Maronite relationship, in theory. Those optimistically inclined toward a special bond between the two groups insisted that the possibility for such a relationship existed in practical terms, as well.

EARLY ZIONIST-MARONITE INTERACTION

Zionist activists in the first decades of the twentieth century found cause for encouragement in their encounters with Maronites. The antecedents of a Zionist-Maronite friendship had emerged in 1860, during the Maronite-Druze civil war. The Druze had decidedly seized the upper hand and were methodically slaughtering the Christians, whom the Ottoman authorities declined to rescue. In desperation, the Maronites cried out for help to the European nations. Two of the first European personalities to respond to their appeal were Sir Moses Montefiore, a wealthy Jewish communal leader in London, and Adolphe Cremieux, a distinguished French Jewish statesman. Montefiore arranged for the Maronites' plight to receive prominent coverage in the London *Times* and set up a fund to assist the survivors, to which he gave generously of his own money. Cremieux proved instrumental in persuading the French to send troops to Lebanon to save the Christians. French intervention rescued the Christians and brought about the creation of the Maronite dominated Mutasarifiyya.[56] The circumstances of the Maronite-Druze civil war hinted at the future intertwining of Zionist and Maronite interests when some Christian proto-Zionists in France, appalled by the apparent vulnerability of the Lebanese Christians, suggested that a Jewish buffer state in Palestine might help advance the position of France and Christians in the Middle East.[57]

Montefiore devoted much of his philanthropy to establishing Jewish settlements, schools, and commercial interests in Palestine. Cremieux founded the Alliance Israelite Universelle, a Jewish educational organization that established the first Jewish agricultural school in Palestine. But in supporting the beleaguered Lebanese Maronites, Montefiore and Cremieux acted as humanitarians and not as Jews per se—certainly not as "Zionists." This episode's relevance to Zionist-Maronite relations lies in its prominence in the collective Maronite memory. Eliahu Epstein first learned of Cremieux's role in support of the Lebanese Christians when he met Antoine Arida, the Maronite patriarch. Over the years he observed that the patriarch mentioned Cremieux's efforts on behalf of Lebanon's Maronites every time he received Jewish visitors at the patriarchal seat in Bkerke and whenever he addressed Lebanon's Jewish community.[58] Arida saw the Montefiore/Cremieux incident as the historical precedent for Zionist-Maronite friendship. His fond feelings for these two Jewish humanitarians gave him a sense of familiarity with twentieth-century Zionists and contributed to his eagerness to join forces with them, reviving, as it were, a bond forged almost three-quarters of a century earlier.

That sentimental and practical forces combined to create a pro-Zionist attitude on the part of many leading Maronites surprised early Zionist emissaries. In 1913, Arabs looking to harness Jewish influence and means to their struggle against the Ottomans approached Sami Hochberg, the Jewish editor of *Le Jeune Turc* and a Zionist activist resident in Istanbul. The Zionist Executive authorized Hochberg to travel to Cairo, where he met with the Cairo and Beirut committees of the Arab Nationalist movement. He came away from the meetings generally encouraged as to the prospects for an Arab-Jewish entente and surprised at the Lebanese committee members' enthusiastic support for Zionism. Maronites meeting with Hochberg insisted that the best guarantee for an autonomous Christian Lebanon was an autonomous Jewish Palestine.[59] Aharon Cohen summarized the Christian position as explained to, and reported by, Hochberg as follows:

> Not only did they want Jews to come to Palestine and Syria, but they hoped that this influx of settlers would be large and quick, because it matched their own political and economic interests as Christian Arabs. The Arab Christians were a minority and so were the Jews. If both these minorities increased in numbers, they could form a bloc that would counterbalance the overwhelming numerical superiority of the Moslems, which the Christians feared. The intellectual superiority of the Jews and Christians could balance the Moslems' numerical supremacy. . . . From an economic standpoint, the Arab Christians knew full well that the Jewish immigrants would bring with them valuable skills that would help develop these areas. The Christians were first and foremost men of trade and commerce and, as such, they realized that capital, mod-

ern industrial plants, and up-to-date production methods would create a climate of prosperity, not only for those who introduced them to the Middle East, but also for the indigenous population.[60]

Hochberg's account of the Christian position is worth quoting at length because it embodies all the primary sentiments of the later Zionist thesis advocating close cooperation with the Maronites. That the Christians initiated the concept of a Zionist-Christian bloc was already one point in its favor, as was the fact that the Maronites were the only group to express a desire to undertake such a far-reaching commitment. The belief in a natural harmony of political and economic interests between Jews and Christians is evident, as is the perception of an inherent superiority of Western, sophisticated, civilized, and educated Jews and Christians vis-à-vis Muslims. Duly reported to the Zionist Executive in full, the unexpected pro-Zionist position of the Lebanese Maronites in 1913 introduced into Zionist thinking the seeds that later blossomed into full-blown minority alliance proposals in the 1930s and 40s.

Reports concerning the positive attitude of the Lebanese Christians toward Zionism came from other quarters, as well. In 1919, Abraham Elmaleh, then head of the press office of the Zionist Commission, traveled to Lebanon and Syria to coach local Jewish community leaders on their testimony about the Palestine question before the King-Crane Commission. A journalist by profession, Elmaleh investigated the political situation in the Levant and the positions of the various factions there toward Zionism. Elmaleh concluded that all Syrian Arabs opposed Zionism. He noted, however, that "all the Lebanon together with the parties which support France in the coastal cities of Syria favor Jewish immigration and do not place obstacles in its way."[61] Elmaleh was referring to the Maronites, who once again had impressed a Zionist observer with their readiness to accept the Zionist endeavor in Palestine.

Individuals whose experiences in Lebanon led them independently to the same conclusion nurtured the concept of a joint Zionist-Maronite front throughout the teens and twenties. One such person, Pinchas Na'aman, a young Russian Jewish immigrant to Palestine, worked for the Zionist Commission in the Jewish communities of Lebanon and Syria. From 1920 to 1922, Na'aman directed the Jewish school in Sidon and served as spokesman for the Jewish community there.[62]

In the wake of World War I, old hostilities flared between Shi'a and Maronites in southern Lebanon, resulting in a rout of the Christians. Most of the inhabitants of the hardest hit Christian villages fled, many ending up in Sidon hungry and penniless. Na'aman cabled the Zionist Commission requesting special funds with which to assist the Christian refugees, and the Zionist Commission promptly complied. The response of the grateful

Christians toward this unexpected humanitarian assistance encouraged Na'aman to urge upon the Zionist Commission a pro-Christian policy that he felt would also serve Zionist political interests. Na'aman theorized that by investing a relatively small amount of money in relief for Christian refugees, the Zionist organization would garner support among the Christians, who would eventually return to their villages and spread the good word about Zionism. After disbursing yet another contribution from Jerusalem among the unfortunate Maronites, Na'aman reported enthusiastically that "the number of our friends among the Christians is growing daily" and requested additional funds for clothing for Christian orphans, noting that it would be a shame to miss this opportunity to bring the hearts of the Christians ever closer to the Zionists.[63]

Na'aman asked the Christian leaders and local authorities to draw up a list of needy persons among whom to divide the latest Zionist monies. He assured Jerusalem that the poor knew that "the Zionists in Palestine" were their benefactors. Na'aman reported to the commission that the money ran out just as he reached the end of the list of 400, but that many people remained in line. Despite instructions not to exceed his budget, Na'aman decided not to refuse the latecomers so as "not to ruin the good impression dividing up the money had made on all the Christians" and the few Muslim recipients. He apologized for going over his budget but asked to be reimbursed for the money he borrowed to assist the additional refugees, insisting that

> the results of what we did were invaluable. There is now not a single Christian who will not remember the name of the Zionists favorably. . . . Don't forget that these people will return to their homes which, according to rumor, will be on the border of our country, and the community heads will talk and wield great influence and it is very important to us that they be indebted to us.[64]

He forwarded to Jerusalem thank-you notes from Christian leaders as proof that the good deed showed palpable results. The letters ranged from the perfunctory thank-you to sweeping expressions of heartfelt gratitude; and Na'aman must have been particularly pleased by the letter from the villagers of Deir Mimus, vowing "We will immortalize your memory on the pages of our hearts all the days of our lives" and expressing hope that God would reward the Jewish benefactors with the success of the Zionist mission.[65]

Some Christians apparently asked Na'aman to enlarge the Jewish school to accommodate their children; and Na'aman willingly relayed the request to Jerusalem, along with his opinion that "as much as we will spend on them now we will gain politically much more."[66] He seemed to delight in having stumbled upon a course of action that was both morally correct and politically beneficial and used both arguments in his appeal that the Zionist Commission continue to fund Christian relief efforts.

The commission was torn between the prospect of creating a political ally among Lebanon's Christians and the many more direct Zionist projects demanding its meager resources. Enlarging the Sidon Hebrew School was out of the question, but Na'aman received instructions to admit Christian children to all classes except the religious ones. The commission treasurer acknowledged the extraordinary situation caused by the refugees in Sidon and the political value of Na'aman's work but warned, nonetheless, that he should not exceed his budget.[67] While the concept of gaining friends among the Maronite community interested Jerusalem, the commission did not buy Na'aman's bold plan to spare no expense in winning the hearts, souls, and political support of Christian refugees. Nevertheless, Na'aman expressed the opinion several years later that the Zionists' speedy aid enhanced their reputation among the Christians and the Lebanese authorities.[68] While there is no empirical evidence one way or the other, it is probable that Na'aman's pro-Christian campaign contributed to the Maronite propensity to see the Zionists as potential benefactors, as well as to the growing inclination among some Zionists to look upon the Maronites as possible allies.

The Shi'a-Maronite violence that inspired Na'aman led to an even more direct call for a Zionist policy of cooperation with the Lebanese Christians from a pro-Zionist journalist in Beirut. Writing directly to Weizmann, J. J. Caleb offered his unsolicited assessment of the situation's relevance to the Zionist cause. Caleb recited a litany of horrors allegedly perpetrated by Muslims against Christians, noting that Jews recently suffered a similar outrage at Muslim hands in Jerusalem. He described Christian bitterness toward the Muslims and claimed that many Christians approached him to confide

> that they want to unite with the Zionists to form a close force that will be able, if needed, to resist the Muslims; that they understand now that we are two minorities with the same interests and they are ready to act in this sense among the Christians in Palestine.[69]

Caleb maintained that with Christian Lebanese assistance the Zionists could splinter the Muslim-Christian bloc in Palestine.

Caleb proposed that the Zionists send a permanent representative to Beirut to create Jewish-Christian organizations to combat anti-Zionism. He approached Ussishkin for the means with which to found a Zionist-Christian front and expressed to Weizmann his impatience at having to wait until after the special conference of Zionist leaders in London the next month. "The present minute," he warned, "is the psychological minute for action."[70]

Caleb's argument touched upon the points familiar to the pro-Maronite school. He saw Christians and Jews as suffering similar fates in the face of a common Muslim enemy. He perceived their shared destiny to be a function of their status as religious minorities and foresaw security for both communities emerging from a close alliance between them. He believed that Christians had something tangible to offer, namely, a pro-Zionist influence among Palestinian Christians. It is easy to explain the fact that the Zionist leadership did not pursue Caleb's suggestions. The Zionist Commission, to which he addressed a copy of his letter, knew of the situation presented by the Muslim-Christian rift in Lebanon but concluded that it could not do more than send what money it did to Na'aman for relief work among the Christian refugees. Preparations for the upcoming conference, a milestone in Zionist history that saw the election of Weizmann as president of the Zionist Organization, preoccupied those Zionists who received copies of Caleb's letter.

That the unconventional ideas of one individual far removed from the Zionist mainstream went unheeded is not striking. Caleb's letter is of note, however, in that it provides yet another example of how familiarity with the Maronites and with circumstances prevailing in Lebanon at the time led one Zionist after another to the independent conclusion that the Maronites were friendly to Zionism and potential political allies.

A ZIONIST-MARONITE TREATY, 1920

On 26 March 1920, a Zionist land-purchasing agent interested in Jewish-Arab relations and three Maronite activists signed a treaty, apparently confirming the pro-Christian intuitions of Na'aman and Caleb.[71] Orchestrated by the intrepid Maronite Nejib Sfeir, the pact was negotiated between Yehoshua Hankin, who professed to represent the "Zionist Organization in Palestine," and the "Nationalist Group in Syria and Lebanon," led by Sfeir. In this far-reaching accord, the Maronites recognized the Jews' right to create a national home in the Land of Israel and endorsed unlimited Jewish immigration to that home. In return, the Zionists recognized an independent Christian Lebanon separate from Muslim Syria and pledged to assist both governments in developing their countries with money and expertise.[72]

Hankin, however, never presented the terms of the accord for discussion among the Zionist leadership; and, while technically a Zionist representative, he was empowered to purchase land, not negotiate political treaties. The Arab participants were totally devoid of authority. According to Neil Caplan, "The entente was, in fact, never discussed publicly or revealed. It remained an inoperative piece of paper, largely because of the lack of authority of the Arab signatories, who would surely have been denounced by the advocates of a 'Greater Syria' in Damascus."[73] Nejib Sfeir's prominent role in facilitating the treaty is significant. Both Maronite nationalism and the prospect of self-gain motivated Sfeir to pursue a relationship with the Zionist movement. Soon after signing the treaty, Sfeir began badgering Weizmann for funds with which to establish a newspaper. Upon learning of Sfeir's request, Weizmann's friend and executive member David Eder sent Weizmann a strongly worded objection, indicating that he had been alerted about Sfeir, who seemed to be "nothing but a crook," and advised against sinking money into the enterprise "even if you have it."[74] Although high-ranking Zionists repeatedly sought to keep the relentless Sfeir at bay, French intelligence in Beirut worried that he had been "purchased by the Zionists to make propaganda for them, particularly within Lebanese clerical circles."[75]

No doubt encouraged by his success in reaching an agreement (albeit inoperative) with a Zionist official, Sfeir reappeared regularly throughout the pre-state period. Twice Shertok noted in his diary that Sfeir turned up every few years like a "meteor," invariably leaving disappointed but sure to return with some new and ambitious plan.[76] His basic premise remained, however: Lebanon for the Christians, Syria for the Muslims, and Palestine for the Jews. Sfeir's early interests in using the Zionists to advance both personal and political aims evolved into a passionate call for a narrow Maronite-Zionist alliance.

The 1920 treaty reflects the basic principles of the minority alliance idea. Zionists and Maronites traded recognition of sovereign Jewish and Christian states in Palestine and Lebanon, respectively. The emphasis on development with Zionist assistance indicates the exchange-of-services approach to Jewish-Arab relations. That development should proceed along the lines of Zionist activity in Palestine signals the Maronite preference for European mores and greater ties with the West. This treaty is also important because it exemplifies the positive and negative aspects of doing business in Lebanon: it was certainly possible to find people prepared to accommodate and facilitate the Zionist operation in Palestine, but their questionable ability to make good on their end of the bargain challenged the usefulness of these alliances.

CONCLUSION

Ambiguity concerning the geographical boundaries for Zionist settlement found Zionists investigating property for sale in Lebanon on several occasions. It was easy to speak stirringly about a Zionist homeland in Palestine or Eretz Yisrael but difficult to determine the location of those entities on a map.

The demarcation of the Palestine-Lebanon border did not sever Zionist activity or interest in Lebanon. Jewish settlers in the Galilee continued to buy and sell goods in southern Lebanon, cultivated both business and

social relationships across the border, and (in the case of Metulla) continued to own and farm property there. Arab landowners approached the Zionists with attractive land sale proposals. Despite their having officially
lost southern Lebanon at the Paris Peace conference, the region remained
open to the Zionists. Even the French, in the case of Jouvenel, did not rule
out the possibility of Zionist settlement in Lebanon. That Zionist organizations did not actually effect land purchases or settlement in Lebanon at
this time was due to a decision in principle to concentrate their limited
financial and human resources in the heart of Palestine and in the politically more secure territory of the British mandate.

Although Maronite and Zionist interests coincided over time, the
Zionists' bid for the inclusion of northern Galilee/southern Lebanon in
the Jewish national home actually put them in competition with the Maronites. Neither realized the immense political implications of incorporating
into their projected national entities the region's large Shi'a population.
In a dubious triumph, the Maronites succeeded in having south Lebanon
attached to their new state, an act of enormous consequence for both Lebanon and Zionist-Maronite relations. In an immediate sense, Maronite neglect of the region allowed southern Lebanon to persist as an economic
extension of northern Palestine and encouraged continued Zionist interest
there. Anti-Zionist Arab activists later filled the political vacuum in southern Lebanon, and security issues came to dominate Zionist thinking about
Lebanon. Of greatest significance to Zionist-Maronite relations, however,
was the desperate demographic danger in which the Maronites put themselves.

Generations of Maronite national aspirations culminated in the creation of Greater Lebanon in 1920. Maronite ideology developed a narrow
perspective which distinguished the Maronites from the rest of the peoples
in Lebanon by their allegedly superior Western orientation and their Catholicism. They saw themselves as the indigenous population of the country; and for them, "Lebanon" became synonymous with "Maronite."
Conflicts with non-Maronite sects imbued Maronite ideology with a defensive, anti-Muslim, even anti-Arab thrust. As it became clear that Christians would one day become a minority in Lebanon, Muslims increasingly
opposed continued Christian domination of the state. Some Maronites argued for power sharing with the Muslims within and a reconciliation with
the Muslim Arab nations without as the best way to protect the Maronite
position, but most refused any relinquishment of Christian privilege. The
threat of being overwhelmed by a Muslim majority sharpened their sense
of isolation. This overarching fear of their Muslim compatriots revived the
Maronite tradition of looking for a Western, non-Arab, non-Muslim ally
and set the stage for Maronite interest in a relationship with the new Zionist neighbors next door.

The teens and twenties were a period of adjustment and exploration for the Zionists. Palestinian Arab hostility encountered by Jewish settlers in Palestine tempered their euphoria over the Balfour Declaration and the reality of a Jewish national home. With the Zionist administrative apparatus in Palestine in flux, serious activity among the Arab countries had to wait until the expanded Jewish Agency emerged in 1929. Even then, hampered in its activities by a shortage of funds and British control over Palestine, the Zionist organization could only test the diplomatic waters of the region. Received hospitably by leading Arabs throughout the Middle East, Zionists nevertheless met only resistance and rejection of their claims to a homeland in Eretz Yisrael. They eagerly sought a friend in the region to relieve their isolation. No master plan to seek out other national minorities existed. It was, rather, the cumulative effect of a series of chance encounters with Lebanese Maronites that introduced into Zionist thinking the notion that there existed a particular receptivity toward Zionism among the Maronites and an unusual potential for cooperation. Maronites encouraged the perception that they would respond enthusiastically to a pro-Christian policy and that a Zionist-Maronite alliance would well serve Zionist interests.

The various proposals for a Zionist policy favoring Lebanon's Christians embodied similar assumptions. They all perceived a superior, Western orientation on the part of Christians and Jews and postulated that this common ground was fertile for cooperation. Fear of Arab nationalism and recognition of a common Muslim enemy figured prominently, as well. The treaty of 1920 reflected these sentiments. Despite the insignificance of the pact in practical terms, it certainly indicated that the Zionists had something to talk about with the Lebanese and someone with whom to talk. Optimists could take comfort from a start's having been made and speculate that perhaps the next attempt would be more meaningful.

One can characterize these early proponents of a pro-Christian policy as small-time Zionist activists. Involved in their own immediate projects or charged with a limited, specific mission, they were not part of the intimate circle of major decision makers responsible for large-scale Zionist policy. This explains why their recommendations did not become policy. It is possible that the concept of a special relationship with the Christians appealed to them precisely *because* they were minor players. Moving among the Maronites in the field, these Zionists got caught up in the daily rhythm of Lebanese life; and their scope of vision was narrower. In the little world of Sidon or even in the political and press offices of Beirut, the Maronites certainly seemed like a force to be reckoned with and an influential group to have on one's side. The perspective of the Zionist Executive in Jerusalem or London, however, focused on the broad thrust of Zionist policy and progress; and in the big picture, Christians played only a tiny role.

If the first reports of Maronite receptiveness did not persuade the Zionist organization to adopt a pro-Christian or pro-minority policy, they did introduce into the lexicon of Zionist foreign policy the concept of a minority alliance based on a Zionist-Maronite bond. Coupled with opportunities suggested by early Zionist experiences in southern Lebanon, this first phase in Zionist attention to Lebanon ended on a pleasant note. Legitimate interests had been identified, as well as friendly people with whom to discuss them. From the Zionist perspective, Lebanon appeared promising, even inviting. The foundation had been laid for the next, active stage of Zionist involvement in Lebanon, and for the blossoming of the relationship with the Maronites.

– 3 –

ZIONIST EXPERIENCES IN LEBANON

MUCH OF ZIONIST thinking about Lebanon centered around Lebanon's supposed receptivity toward a friendly relationship with Jewish Palestine. Proponents of a minority alliance made a strong case, in theory, for a natural community of interests between Maronites and Zionists. Actual Zionist experiences in Lebanon would put this perspective to the test.

Jewish Agency involvement in Lebanon began in earnest in the early 1930s, especially once Eliahu Epstein established himself in Beirut. Largely due to his efforts, the Agency created a web of pro-Zionist contacts running through religious and political circles in Lebanon. The question remained, however, whether those Lebanese most amenable to Zionism carried enough weight to constitute potential partners in an alliance with the Yishuv. With Lebanese society divided along clan lines and each clan torn by rival factions, the Agency's choice of companions affected its range of activity in Lebanon.

PRO-ZIONIST MARONITES IN LEBANON

The Zionist vision of a minority alliance relied upon the cooperation of a certain type of Maronite nationalist. From a Zionist perspective, the ideal Maronite envisioned Lebanon as a Christian country; saw himself as a Christian and a Westerner, rather than an Arab; and feared a Muslim threat to Christian privilege. For him, Jewish Palestine constituted the logical ally in the Maronite-Muslim struggle over Lebanon.

The Jewish Agency counted Antoine Arida, patriarch of the Maronite church, among the Zionists' staunchest supporters in Lebanon. For generations, patriarchs wielded enormous influence in all spheres of Maronite life and in the larger Lebanese political arena, as well. In this tradition, Arida brought to the patriarchate sharply defined political beliefs and a willingness to exercise on their behalf the considerable power, spiritual and temporal, that his office commanded.[1] Arida stood in a tradition that saw Lebanon as a unique Christian entity distinct from the Arab world. He based his call for an independent Christian Lebanon on his fear of a Muslim threat to Christian well-being in the East. He often expressed the conviction that Jews and Christians would share a similarly unhappy fate under Muslim domination.

Arida became patriarch in 1932, and Epstein met him at the patriarchal seat at Bkerke shortly thereafter. Epstein found Arida "much more aggressive" toward the Muslims than even his predecessor Hawayik and heard for the first of many times the story of the assistance rendered by Cremieux and Montefiore to the Maronites in 1860.[2] At this initial meeting, Arida demonstrated the little bit of Hebrew he remembered from his studies at the Vatican; and Epstein, harkening back to his childhood Talmud study, managed to follow the patriarch's Aramaic, as well.

Although he subscribed to the cultural and spiritual legacy of the West and conducted his affairs in French, Arida's insistence on absolute Lebanese independence put him in conflict with France. During the period of the Ottoman Mutasarafiyya, the political predominance of the patriarch increased dramatically, only to be curtailed by the mandate and the constitution of Greater Lebanon, which granted exclusive power to the president.[3] This fact, as well as his unwillingness to choose sides in intra-Maronite conflicts, frustrated the Agency when he could not, or would not, speak out in its behalf. The Zionists considered him a genuine friend of their movement, nonetheless. Epstein and the rest of the Zionist leadership in Jerusalem cultivated the relationship with Arida, and most of them visited him at the patriarchal seat. As early as 1934, he corresponded with Weizmann, expressing sympathy for the "brave Israelites" suffering tribulations in Palestine and placing at the service of the Zionist movement two Maronite attorneys in Beirut, should the Jews need legal assistance in French-mandated Lebanon.[4] The Zionists were emboldened by their friendship with this important man and by the warmth with which the bishops in his court received them.

Ignatius Mubarak, the outspoken Maronite archbishop of Beirut, proved an even more vocal champion of Zionism. He also viewed Lebanon as Christian, separate from the Arab world, and superior to it. Mubarak consistently called for the creation of a Jewish state, making the now-familiar argument that the civilized, Westernized Jews and Christians shared a similarly precarious position in the Middle East and that the best defense for a Christian Lebanon lay in a Jewish Palestine. He weathered repeated attacks from most Lebanese circles for his public pro-Zionist position. He responded with bitter assaults of his own against the Muslims, whom he saw as intent upon destroying the Christians, and the local French and Lebanese authorities (including the Maronite president and parliament members) whom he characterized as incompetent and corrupt. At the height of his political opposition, Mubarak called for a civil insurrection against the Lebanese government. For generations, the church had guided Lebanon spiritually, socially, economically, and politically, declared Mubarak; and he refused to relinquish those responsibilities to politicians.[5]

As archbishop of the Beirut diocese and the most prominent clergyman outside of the patriarch's court, Mubarak used his position unabashedly in pursuit of his political goals. William Haddad writes that Mubarak did not view the Jewish state, whose creation he supported, in a theological framework. Haddad contends that had the demographic features of the Middle East been reversed, Mubarak would have adopted a pro-Muslim, anti-Jewish position. His interest lay in the creation of any non-Muslim state that would bolster Christian Lebanon and not in the fate of the Jews per se.[6] Be that as it may, Zionists delighted in finding such an ardent supporter.

The Agency's closest friend in Lebanese political circles, Emile Eddé, was a member of parliament when Epstein first met him in 1931. Born to a Maronite Francophile family and educated in Catholic schools in Beirut and France, Eddé preferred the European aspect of his heritage to the Eastern. He received no formal instruction in Arabic and never achieved more than a superficial knowledge of that language. As president of Lebanon from 1936 to 1941, Eddé conducted state affairs in French and often required assistance in dealing with Arabic-speaking constituents and other Arab leaders. Removed from the reality of a pluralistic Lebanon, Eddé only saw and reacted to what he perceived as the Muslim threat to the Christians.

Eddé saw pan-Arabism and the Greater Syria program as excuses for Muslim domination and believed that Lebanon's future lay in closer ties to the West and the preservation of the country's Christian character. He confided in Epstein that he dreamed of an in-gathering of Maronite expatriates whose numbers, wealth, professional skills, and sophistication would once and for all guarantee the prosperity of Christian Lebanon.[7] Eddé saw Zionism as a natural ally in the Christian-Muslim struggle. Elath writes that Eddé supported every proposal for enhancing ties with the Zionists ever presented to him and credits Eddé with encouraging Arida and Mubarak in their pro-Zionism.[8] Eddé's role as a politician, rather than a religious figure, however, necessitated a greater sensitivity to non-Maronite and Muslim sensibilities. Zionists never doubted the authenticity of his friendship but despaired of his professed inability to speak publicly in favor of a Jewish Palestine or a formal Lebanese-Zionist accord, both of which he fervently supported. Nevertheless, his pro-Zionist inclinations were something of an open secret; and when the Lebanese Jewish community sent a delegate to him to express its desire for a Jewish representative in parliament, Eddé "replied jokingly: 'You are already well represented in the Lebanon. I am [said to be] a Jew!'"[9]

Albert Naccache, a member of one of the wealthiest and most influential Maronite families in Lebanon, met and married a young Jewish woman active in Zionist circles during his studies in Switzerland prior to World War I. Through her, he became an ardent supporter of the Zionist movement. The couple returned to Lebanon, where the Naccache family's lofty public standing quickly propelled him to prominent positions in both Maronite and Lebanese affairs. Naccache served in one of Lebanon's early governments, acted as Patriarch Arida's economic advisor, and prospered as an engineer and industrialist in the private sector. When Epstein first arrived in Beirut, he carried a letter of introduction from an acquaintance of Naccache's wife in Jerusalem. From their first conversation, he found Naccache knowledgeable about the Zionist program in Palestine and eager to use his resources to further friendly relations between Lebanon and the Yishuv.[10]

A close friend and confidant of the patriarch, Naccache shared Arida's fear of the Muslims and concern for the preservation of Christian Lebanon. Naccache told Epstein that the June 1930 treaty, by which Britain granted Iraq independence, had inspired Arab nationalists in Lebanon and Syria to press for independence from France. He worried that the Christians would not be able to hold their own if the French followed the British example and withdrew from an independent Syria.[11] Naccache saw the Zionists as logical allies in the Maronite-Muslim struggle.

The Zionists found Naccache an important contact because of his own prestige and because he opened doors to other important personalities. It was Naccache who introduced Epstein to the patriarch; to Alfred Naccache, a judge and later president of Lebanon (1941–43); and to George Naccache, editor of the French-language newspaper *L'Orient*. In a report to Jerusalem, Epstein characterized the family as

> the elite of the local aristocracy. . . . One of the assimilated Arab families who only speak French in their home and loathe anything that is of Arab origin (except local money and posts!). . . . The children . . . go to Paris to study and return 101 percent French, full of hate for the Moslems and imbued with French patriotism. [The Naccache family is] not an isolated case in Beirut. The vast majority of the Maronites belong to this category.[12]

Albert Naccache also introduced Epstein to the poet Charles Corm, a friend with whom Naccache founded the Society of Young Phoenicians. This small circle of intellectuals gave formal expression to the view that the Maronites did not descend from the Arabs but, rather, from the ancient Phoenicians, whose civilization preceded the Arab invasion and whose heirs constituted the indigenous population of Lebanon. The group devoted itself to restoring Lebanon to its Phoenician origins and ridding it of influences absorbed from the Arab Muslim conquerors: "The sand of the desert disturbs the clarity of the sea."[13] The Young Phoenicians aimed to persuade the Maronites to look upon themselves as the true Lebanese and upon Phoenicia as their ancient homeland and spiritual center. Inspired by archaeological discoveries, including an abundance of literary material in Ugaritic, Corm and his followers challenged their fellow Maronites to revive their national consciousness and language, much as the Jews were doing in their ancient homeland and with their ancient tongue. Corm further compared the Maronites to the Jews, praising the way the two peoples maintained their distinct characteristics despite the influence of conquering nations.[14] Some dubbed the ideology of the Young Phoenicians "Lebanese Zionism," and the society did advocate close relations between Lebanon and the Yishuv.[15] Epstein suspected that Arida was really a Young Phoenician at heart.[16]

During his 1933 trip to Lebanon on behalf of the Jewish Agency, Victor Jacobson addressed a meeting of the Young Phoenicians and drew sustained applause when he cited the biblical relationship between King Solomon and Phoenician King Hiram as the basis for a renewed friendship between their descendants.[17] Young Phoenicians drew on the legacy of the Solomon-Hiram alliance in advocating that the Middle East minorities create, in Corm's words,

> A common front against their principal enemy, and that is the Muslim Arab proclaiming pan-Arabism. [The Muslim danger forced] Christian Lebanon to find "partners in fate" and among them is the Jewish community in Palestine and Zionism in general. . . . The Jews and the Lebanese must find a way to mutual understanding and regular relations and we are ready for this.[18]

Hindsight discounts the Young Phoenicians as effective allies; but in the early 1930s, Epstein and others in the Political Department could not quickly dismiss a group that actively sought close ties with the Yishuv, whose ideology dovetailed with Zionist needs, and that claimed as members fairly influential persons.

In the non-Maronite camp, the Agency maintained regular contact with Druze leaders like Nejib Shukeir, Sultan al-Atrash, and Sitt Nazirah—a woman, leader for a time of the Jumblatt clan.[19] Although the Druze often expressed an enthusiasm for cooperation with the Zionists, the uncertainty of their position within Lebanon and Druze-French animosity suggested that the Druze had neither the autonomy nor the resources required of an effective ally beyond the local level.[20]

More promising were Agency relations with Riad al-Sulh, a Lebanese Sunni active in pan-Arab circles in both Lebanon and Syria, future co-author (with Maronite Bishara al-Khoury) of the 1943 National Pact, and a future prime minister of Lebanon (1943–45, 1947–51). In 1921, al-Sulh began conversations with Weizmann and other Zionist leaders.[21] In discussions with Zionist delegations throughout the 1920s and early 1930s, al-Sulh consistently evinced interest in an "exchange-of-services" Arab-Zionist agreement whereby the Arabs would accept a Jewish national home in Palestine (perhaps in federation with a larger regional pan-Arab entity) and the Zionists, in return, would put their money, influence, and skills at the service of the Arabs. A Jewish journalist (and great admirer of al-Sulh) reported to Weizmann al-Sulh's conviction that

> The Arabs of Palestine are rich in property, of which they may give away a certain amount. The Jews—so the Arabs still believe at least, are rich in gold. . . . This happy parallelism ought to remain . . . the basis for the natural entente between the Jewish and the Arab worlds.[22]

In this early period, al-Sulh portrayed himself as enjoying considerable influence within the Arab nationalist movement. He suggested that if the Zionists threw their financial and political influence behind the Arab cause in Greater Syria, he could produce an "Arab Balfour Declaration" and persuade the Palestinian Arabs to accept it. He made these promises to the highest Zionist leadership, namely Ben-Gurion and Shertok in 1934 and Weizmann in 1936.[23] As the thirties wore into the forties, however, and the situation in Palestine deteriorated, al-Sulh publicly adopted an anti-Zionist stance, privately explaining that only after a general Zionist-Arab reconciliation could he carry out his plan to concede Palestine to the Jews and strike a political bargain with them. Although the Agency suspected that at times al-Sulh accepted money from the mufti in exchange for adopting an appropriately belligerent tone, he did take money from the Zionists, as well, which could account for some of the favorable discussions he conducted with them.[24]

Because of al-Sulh's political prominence, the Zionists maintained contact with him; but the relationship lacked that sense of genuine affection which many Zionists thought motivated their Maronite friends. As its ties with the latter progressed, the Agency came to believe that it shared a wide range of interests with at least certain important Maronite factions.

What practical benefit would come of these shared concerns, however, remained to be seen.

PRACTICAL ZIONIST-LEBANESE INTERCOURSE

It did not hurt that the Maronites (or at least an important segment of the Maronite elite) stood to profit from a relationship with the Zionists. After his 1933 trip to Lebanon, Jacobson reported that some of the Maronites, especially Arida and Naccache, expressed great interest in undertaking joint projects with the Jews. Naccache had already established several factories and electrical power stations in partnership with Arida, a wealthy man in his own right. Now the two men desired the partnership of Jewish capital, which, they pointed out to Jacobson, was not finding much of an outlet in the region. They argued that together Maronite Lebanon and Jewish Palestine could become a giant industrial center, with the Middle East for a hinterland dependent upon their products. They proposed the establishment of a Jewish-Maronite bank in Beirut to manage joint economic ventures, an idea that Naccache brought up again with Epstein after Jacobson's departure.[25] Despite his burgeoning friendships with both men, Epstein relayed Naccache's proposal to Jerusalem with the warning that

> his interest in these joint ventures includes self-gain. He is a big industrialist and will take into his own hands part of the control of the activity of this capital. That is also the intention of the Patriarch Arida, as a man of means and economic initiative.[26]

As a rule, the Jewish Agency hesitated to commit itself to economic concerns beyond the borders of the British mandate but encouraged the success of private Jewish ventures in Lebanon.[27] When the Political Department perceived special benefit in a particular project, it often facilitated matters for the Jewish businessman by putting him in touch with its contacts there, thus expediting the deal without officially involving the Agency. Sometimes, the Maronites sought out Jewish businessmen directly. Arida and Naccache maintained active ties with Zionists in this way. In 1933, the Jewish Nur match company opened a factory in Damur, a Maronite village in Lebanon that had fallen on hard times. Epstein learned that the Maronite clergy gave the company an old monastery in which to house the factory and that Arida guaranteed in writing that should any dispute arise either locally or with the government in Beirut, he would personally see to it that the matter was settled to the company's advantage.[28] Shortly thereafter, Arida referred to Weizmann a Maronite hotelier interested in selling his hotel to Jewish investors. Weizmann reported that he could not find any takers but asked that the man convey his respects to the patriarch.[29] Arida likewise requested that Weizmann intercede on behalf of a young Lebanese Maronite who applied for a job with the Shell Oil Company in Palestine but had not been informed as to whether the position was his or not. In a direct appeal to Weizmann, the young man wrote that Arida assured him that due to Weizmann's great influence and "the mutual friendship existing between himself and your Honor you will, no doubt, obtain the sanction of my engagement from the Head Office in London."[30]

At the same time, Weizmann was being courted by the patriarch's executive secretary, Monsignor Joseph Rahme, who informed Weizmann of an opportunity for the Zionist Organization to take over the majority of shares in northern Lebanon's sole electric company, La Kadisha. Rahme claimed that the board of directors specifically wanted Jewish investors from Palestine to invest in the company and urged, "As a friend I recommend you to make this purchase."[31] When Weizmann delayed in replying, Rahme had a Maronite colleague repeat the offer, reiterating Rahme's vague promise that a controlling Zionist interest in La Kadisha would no doubt lead to future Jewish immigration to Lebanon.[32] These and similar incidents created a steady intercourse between the Jewish Agency and the Maronite church, which devoted equal attention to issues of financial, as well as spiritual, well-being.

Naccache similarly maintained a regular exchange with the Agency, offering his services to Jewish entrepreneurs interested in business opportunities in Lebanon. Epstein responded with a promise to take him up on his offer and furnish interested persons with letters of introduction to him. He also extended a reciprocal offer to lend assistance to Naccache or anyone referred to the Agency by him.[33] The Jewish Agency took Naccache at his word, as demonstrated by the case of a private Jewish investor trying to resurrect the Phoenicia glassworks and develop business contacts in Lebanon. Shertok suggested that he invite "some suitable Maronite gentleman to serve on the board," and directed him to Naccache.[34] He also instructed Epstein to meet with the man and give him some tips on how to approach the Lebanese. This episode is indicative of the policy of assisting private Jewish interests in Lebanon without directly involving the Agency.

Naccache's most promising proposal concerned joint Lebanese-Zionist exploitation of the Litani river for the purposes of irrigation and hydroelectric power.[35] He told Epstein that he believed the project would bring immediate agricultural, industrial, and economic benefits, as well as play an important role in political relations between Lebanon and the future Jewish state. The Jewish Agency Executive discussed Naccache's plan and decided, characteristically, to pursue the matter through a Zionist institution not directly connected to the Agency. It turned the proposal over to the Palestine Economic Corporation in New York, an organization funded and run by American Jews interested in the development of Jewish industry in the Yishuv. In Naccache's opinion, French authorities were less likely to object to his procuring the official documents he needed to complete his plan if the Jewish Agency were not involved; and both sides agreed that when the new Jewish state came into being, it would assume responsibility for following through on the Zionist side of the Litani plan.

The Palestine Economic Corporation sent an engineer to meet with Naccache and on the basis of his highly favorable report authorized Naccache to proceed with the project in greater detail. The French mandatory authorities objected vehemently to the plan, however, and Naccache shelved the entire endeavor. The last French troops had hardly fled the south in the face of the British invasion of 1941, however, when Naccache dusted off his proposal and re-presented it. In the summer of 1942, Epstein accompanied Naccache and the Palestine Economic Corporation's engineer on a tour of the proposed dam site. Free French Intelligence followed the enterprise and, despite Naccache's precautions, understood that his silent partners were American and Palestinian Jews.[36] Since World War II prevented Naccache from engaging the necessary Swedish and French experts, he and Epstein optimistically agreed to resume the project as soon as the war ended.[37]

Non-Maronite Lebanese also attempted to profit from a relationship with the Zionists. This Lebanese willingness to open commercial relations with the Yishuv suggested that the Agency could look forward to accomplishing one of its primary goals with respect to Lebanon, namely, binding the Yishuv and Lebanon together so tightly that the profits of peace outweighed any incentive for enmity. Shortly after Jacobson's trip, Shertok noted that "there has been no scarcity . . . of offers of friendship and cooperation" from Lebanon, most of an economic nature but some with a certain political advantage.[38] Already a group of wealthy Muslim merchants in Beirut had offered to assist the Zionists in their land-purchasing campaign by buying property in Palestine from Arabs unwilling to sell to Jews. The Beirut group would then sell the land to Jews, making a nice profit for itself in the process.[39]

By the mid-thirties, imports and exports between Palestine and Lebanon/Syria far exceeded those between Palestine and any other Arab country.[40] Large and small concerns alike carried on a brisk trade across the northern border, and Jewish and Lebanese merchants made regular business trips to each other's cities. Consistent with its policy of distanced involvement, the Jewish Agency cooperated with several Zionist financial institutions to create the Foundation for Foreign Commerce in Palestine. The foundation encouraged the distribution of the Yishuv's manufactured goods in the Arab countries, and the Agency directed foundation representatives to its friends in the Arab world.[41] As late as 1940, a group of Zionist economic experts assembled by the Jewish Agency met a warm reception when it arrived in Beirut to explore means of enhancing the still-steady commerce between the two countries. The Lebanese were all business, their report concluded; and they encountered no extremist rhetoric and no sense of Palestinian Jews being undesirable business partners.[42] Even in 1944, a jointly owned Christian and Muslim travel agency in Beirut contacted the Jewish Agency to inquire about opening a branch office in Palestine. The Lebanese maintained that strong commercial ties between Lebanon and the Yishuv would accelerate the economic development of their own country. Responding for the Agency, Epstein followed the familiar policy of excusing the Agency from involvement in the plan but wished the Lebanese success in their venture, especially to the extent that it advanced relations between the two sides.[43]

The development of strong economic relations with Lebanon and Syria especially interested Eliahu Sasson, both for the immediate economic benefit and as a prelude to political cooperation. World War II cut short his call for a commission of joint economic activity among the Yishuv and its Arab neighbors, so he proposed instead setting up a similar economic consortium along private lines with the Agency's friends in Lebanon and Syria. This project reflected Sasson's conviction that regional peace required the integration of the Jewish national home into the Arab world. The initial Lebanese response encouraged Sasson, as did the happy coincidence that just at this time, a group of Jewish merchants in Tel Aviv approached him about setting up a Jewish-Arab company in Beirut. The proposed firm would distribute Yishuv and Lebanese products in these two countries and eventually in the markets of the neighboring Arab countries.[44] Much to Sasson's disappointment, the worsening political climate—locally, regionally, and globally—impeded efforts by interested parties on all sides to bring plans such as these to fruition.

Jewish tourism to Lebanon served as the most direct economic connection between the Jewish national home and Lebanon and affected the greatest number of people. An old joke held that Eretz Yisrael was the perfect place to live: one could winter in Egypt and summer in Lebanon. For the owners and employees of the many resorts in the cool Lebanese mountains, the most tangible evidence of their common interests with the Yishuv lay in the thousands of Jews who fled the Palestinian heat each summer. In 1930, a geography teacher in Palestine published a comprehensive travelogue for Lebanon in Hebrew with precise information about the physical layout of the country, the climate in different areas, and modes of transportation from one place to another.[45] Even more remarkable is a tourists' guide to Lebanon published in Hebrew in 1935 by the Economic Department of the government of Lebanon. An error in the Hebrew print on the cover notwithstanding, the book gave a detailed account of thirty-four Lebanese cities and resorts, covering such topics as historical and rec-

reational sites, climate, public transportation and directions for private vehicles, hotels, postal services, banks, restaurants, and a list of those diseases
for which the climate and waters of each resort were reportedly therapeu-
tic. The preface concluded with the exhortation that

> anyone who wants to lengthen his days, taste paradise, and feel the world to
> come should spend some time in Lebanon beneath the shade of its splendid
> cedars, breathing its healthy air, drinking its good waters, and pampering him-
> self with its glorious visions of nature.[46]

Lebanon obviously welcomed Jewish tourists!

Because of the great influx of Jewish vacationers each summer, Lebanese hoteliers went to great lengths to increase accommodations and services. Many hired kosher cooks and subscribed to Hebrew newspapers.[47]
Taxis traveled regularly between Jerusalem, Tel Aviv, Haifa, and major
Lebanese resorts. Arida and Mubarak occasionally visited the Palestinian
Jews at the hotels; and according to a French report, on one occasion, a
bishop in the patriarch's entourage fell into conversation with a Jewish
guest and offered to sell him the hotel in which they were chatting.[48] The
wide array of Arab ministers, journalists, and businessmen he met at the
resorts so impressed one Jewish tourist that he contacted the Jewish
Agency with a proposal that the Agency "plant" staff members in each resort to meet and befriend these influential Arabs, creating relationships
that could serve as the foundation for an amiable agreement over the Palestine question.[49] Epstein hesitated to commit the Agency to a specific propaganda program among the resort guests but suggested in an internal department memo that perhaps the Agency should brief individuals, like the
tourist Turgman, so they could undertake effective propaganda activity.
Sasson disagreed, worrying that some of these well-meaning free-lancers,
yearning for peace with the Arabs at any price, might offer concessions
that the Agency could not endorse. This could complicate official Zionist
dealings with the Arabs and lead to charges that the Zionists spoke with
many voices. Sasson's view prevailed and Epstein met with Turgman to
persuade him that his grand plan could backfire and actually damage the
Zionist cause.[50] The department concluded that the sheer number of Jewish holidaymakers and the money they spent during their stay in Lebanon
constituted effective propaganda enough. Convinced that the Lebanese
knew Jewish tourism and Jewish business from the Yishuv to be a corner-
stone of Lebanese economic well-being, many Zionists remained confident that the political struggle in Palestine could not harm the economic
ties binding Lebanon and the Yishuv.

The Agency permitted Epstein more leeway in his efforts to establish cultural bonds between Lebanon and the Yishuv. He monitored

discussions between the Hebrew University of Jerusalem and the American University of Beirut concerning possible cooperation between the two institutions. The deliberations resulted in a tentative agreement in favor of mutual scholarly exchanges and copublication of scholarly research.[51] Occasionally communication between scientists and scholars in Lebanon and the Yishuv did occur. Among the quainter examples is a rainfall map prepared by the Hebrew University for President Eddé ,and assistance from Yishuv experts to Lebanese scientists examining agricultural problems in Lebanon, in return for which the Zionists requested cuttings of a very old cedar tree that they wanted to study.[52] Epstein also involved himself in the arrangements for a group of Jewish doctors to attend a medical conference in Beirut. He directed the delegation to contact the presidents of various universities in Beirut with an eye toward establishing regular ties between the Hebrew medical institutions in Eretz Yisrael and the medical institutions of the Lebanese universities and arranged for the French language newspaper *La Syrie* to publish an interview with one of the physicians. He also instructed the delegation to meet with high-ranking Lebanese and French mandatory officials. Seeing an opportunity to turn the doctors' visit to a political advantage, Epstein directed the group to stress that as much as Jewish doctors liked to send their patients to Lebanese sanatoriums, anti-Zionism in the Lebanese press caused many to reconsider. He hoped that this thinly veiled threat would prompt the prevailing powers to take appropriate action to curb the unfriendly press. The physicians submitted a report to the Agency upon their return, as well as a memo concerning friendly conversations with Arida. Epstein thanked them for their assistance, writing, "We appreciate and value the important activity undertaken by our delegates to the medical congress in Beirut and hope that your propaganda in influential circles in Lebanon and in the newspapers in Beirut will be to our benefit."[53]

Epstein likewise tried to wring economic and political benefits from the Tel Aviv Levant Fair of 1936. Meeting with local businessmen, journalists, and travel agents in Beirut, he argued that if they wished continued business from Palestinian Jews they should reciprocate in kind, recommending a strong Lebanese showing at the fair.[54] He reported that his offer to dedicate one night of the fair to Lebanon, complete with films and lectures about their country, greatly pleased them. President Eddé responded enthusiastically to an invitation to attend, although the eruption of disturbances in Palestine in the days immediately preceding the fair prevented him from doing so. Eddé sent personal greetings, however; and the Lebanese pavilion impressed Palestinian Jewry, although the president's absence disappointed Epstein. Full Lebanese participation in the fair was, he believed, "a matter of the utmost political importance in connection with the question of the development of our relations with the country that is near-est to us in many senses."[55]

The connection with Corm and the Young Phoenicians also offered potential for joint Zionist-Maronite cultural activity. In 1935, Corm pro-posed the establishment of a Palestine-Lebanon Club to draw Jews and Maronites closer together through the interaction of literary, scholarly, and artistic circles in Lebanon and the Yishuv.[56] Epstein seized upon the idea enthusiastically, securing the consent of Jewish artists and scholars whom he thought suitable participants and welcoming prominent Leba-nese to Palestine.[57] This was not necessarily a new approach on the Agency's part. Already, in 1930, French Intelligence in Beirut reported that Zionist agents in Beirut had sent a Christian Lebanese writer, Marie Ajami, to lecture in Jerusalem on the topic of a Christian-Jewish alliance. The French speculated that the Zionist objective was to divide the Palestinian Arab opposition along religious lines.[58] Despite Jewish Agency interest in the Palestine-Lebanon Club, Corm delayed so long in preparing a final charter that he lost the influence necessary to establish such a society. Al-though no formal Phoenician-Zionist association emerged, Corm invited individual Jewish speakers to address the Young Phoenicians and Epstein did his best to ensure that they accepted the invitations, which he believed "in addition to the importance of opening cultural relations between us and the Lebanon . . . could have . . . a political benefit."[59]

Non-political intercourse occurred between Palestinian Jews and Leb-anese in a variety of ways. More often than not, however, political exigen-cies disrupted, constricted, or canceled even the most benign exchanges. Growing support throughout the Arab world for the Palestinian Arabs in-creased anti-Zionist sentiment, and some Lebanese hesitated to involve themselves with their counterparts in the Yishuv. Accordingly, the Agency tried to use its connections with Lebanese journalists and editors to mini-mize anti-Zionist rhetoric in the Lebanese media. The Political Depart-ment struggled to devise an effective policy for influencing the Arab press. It opposed the method adopted by the Jewish community of Beirut, which paid the local papers to print denials of previously published false informa-tion. Department officials suspected that this custom actually encouraged the papers to print increasingly damaging reports for the express purpose of collecting Jewish money for retractions.[60]

As an alternative, Epstein and Sasson suggested that the Agency con-tract with papers in Lebanon and Syria for a certain number of pro-Zionist articles each month. The Agency discovered that Syrian papers adhered to fairly strict standards concerning the content of articles and often refused to publish pro-Zionist pieces, even for a high price. But the Beirut papers' print-for-pay policy reinforced the Zionist image of Lebanon as a place where everyone and everything were for sale.[61] From the Zionist perspective, the wider circulation of the Lebanese papers in Palestine and the other Arab countries made them more useful, anyway.

Sasson suggested that department members share the task of choosing subjects and writing articles for the Arab press. He also proposed translating and submitting for publication appropriate articles from the Hebrew, American, and European papers. Topics could be political, economic, or cultural, as long as they served the primary purpose of detracting attention from the unrest in Palestine, emphasized a conciliatory tone, and highlighted the Zionist success in bringing prosperity to Palestine. In the late thirties, the department increasingly directed its Arabic press campaign against the mufti, and then against the White Paper. Some articles appeared under fictitious Arab names and others as commentary by the papers' editorial staffs. By 1939, the department claimed to have placed over 280 articles in both the Muslim and Christian press, primarily in Lebanon.[62]

The Agency maintained a special relationship with two French-language papers. George Naccache, the Maronite editor of *L'Orient*, adopted a pro-minority, pro-Zionist orientation, which Epstein hoped might win over the French officials who read the paper regularly. George Vayssie, editor of *La Syrie*, was on the Agency's payroll; and Epstein characterized his paper as "one of the most loyal and devoted to Zionism." The connections with these papers paid off in that by 1938, when the rest of the Lebanese press presented a uniformly anti-Zionist perspective, the only friendly voices were those of Naccache and Vayssie.[63]

The Political Department extended its propaganda efforts beyond the press to distribute its own bulletins and booklets in Arabic.[64] Sometimes published under Arab names and sometimes in the name of the Jewish Agency, these writings stressed the economic blessings brought by Zionism to the Palestinian Arabs and the advantages of a peaceable Jewish-Arab settlement. It is unlikely that they impressed many Arabs, but they apparently succeeded in preaching to the converted. Sasson reported that the Zionists' friends in Lebanon loved the material and often reproduced it.[65] Due to its limited resources, the Agency struggled with the decision of whether to keep allocating funds for the never-ending propaganda battle. According to Shertok, experience proved that if the department only had the means, it could orchestrate "comprehensive activity" in the Arab press.[66] But the papers demanded more and more money for printing pro-Zionist material as Zionism became more and more unpopular. On several occasions, journalists attempted to extort money from the Agency by threatening to print wildly inflammatory pieces if it withheld funds. One Agency official recommended terminating all business with the Lebanese press, swearing that

> Once these swinish Lebanese journalists have been made to realize that they
> cannot indulge in their blackmailing tactics they will be grateful for even small
> crumbs from our table.[67]

At worst, he reasoned, they would write unfavorable articles, which most of them did anyway.

It is doubtful that either the few friendly articles in the Arabic press or the Zionists' own Arabic propaganda accomplished anything in terms of swaying public opinion. The effort served primarily as a steady drain on the department's limited budget. Arab anti-Zionism proved too much for the Agency's press-and-propaganda campaign as the British mandate drew to a close and the threat of Jewish sovereignty in Palestine appeared increasingly real. Although ultimately unsuccessful in any practical way, Zionist involvement in the Lebanese press meant continuous contact with leading members of Lebanon's journalistic circles in this period. To the extent that they succeeded in selling articles to the press, the Zionists were encouraged in their perception of a Lebanon where money spoke louder than political ideology. That the friendliest papers were Maronite encouraged the Zionists in their perception that coordination with this group was possible.

Like Lebanese editors, Lebanese property owners proved equally interested in taking Zionist money. The high prices Zionists paid, often in European currency, made many landholders more than eager to sell their property to the Jews. In the early 1930s, Zionist officials recorded an abundance of offers finding their way to the Agency from all directions. "We have more than enough offers" of land for sale in Syria and Lebanon, read a report from the Palestine Land Development Company; "Arab landowners and ordinary Maronites continue to worry our people with various proposals," reported Epstein; and Weizmann marveled that the Zionist Organization was "being inundated with the most attractive offers from landowners in Syria and the Lebanon."[68] Jacobson returned from his Lebanon tour with the paradoxical message that despite public opposition to Jewish settlement in Lebanon, many Arabs had privately expressed to him interest in selling their land to Jews.[69] Some Lebanese emigrants in America contacted the Agency through American Zionist organizations, offering to sell the family homestead in the old country, whereas others with property to sell in Lebanon either found their way to the Agency directly or prevailed upon Jewish intermediaries to present their offers.[70]

An agent for the Palestine Land Development Company contacted the Agency for instructions on how to handle the offers pouring in, noting that

> in Lebanon the attitude of the inhabitants, especially the Maronites and the
> Orthodox, is very pleasant toward the Jews, and if we realize only a part of the

guarantees of the owners and the agents (among whom are men of important political standing) concerning the attitude of the inhabitants to Jewish settlement there, it could be like paradise.[71]

But without a clear decision by the Agency in favor of land purchases beyond the borders of the British mandate, he added, the company had no intention of pursuing any of the offers.

The Political Department politely declined the offers it received, informing landowners that Zionists had no intention of settling anywhere but within the borders of the Jewish national home. Negotiations over the Palestine-Lebanon border in the 1920s had clearly put Lebanon beyond the scope of any future Jewish state, and the Zionist leadership decided then that settling Jews in far-flung corners of the Levant did not satisfy the basic Zionist aims of acquiring and populating the territory of the national home. It seemed that the Agency had adopted a decisive position against Zionist settlement activity across the Palestine border.

From Berlin to Beirut: The Proposal to Bring German Jewish Refugees to Lebanon

But events in Germany conspired to reopen the issue of Jewish settlement in Lebanon within the Jewish Agency. Hitler's rise to power in 1933 and the immediate worsening of conditions for Germany's Jews sent thousands of them in search of refuge. The Zionist Organization wanted to bring these people to Palestine, believing that the Jewish national home badly needed their numbers, skills, and capital. As Nazism consolidated its hold in Germany the situation of the Jews became more desperate. Zionists heralded Palestine as the exclusive Jewish haven but quickly realized that Britain would admit only a tiny fraction of the Jewish refugees.

Weizmann entered into extensive negotiations with French and British authorities concerning the acquisition of lands in Lebanon for the absorption of German Jews. The Agency greeted Weizmann's efforts with skepticism but when word of his plan leaked out many Lebanese, Maronites in particular, responded enthusiastically. Weizmann himself understood some of the difficulties such a plan posed, even if well received by the indigenous population, as he believed it would be:

> The Arab population, particularly in the Lebanon, is most anxious for the coming of the Jews to their country. Rather naively they seem to expect a cure for all their economic evils in the coming of the Jews, apparently thinking that our coming will bring with it a sort of gold rain over the whole of Syria and the Lebanon! These exaggerated hopes naturally do not make things any easier for us. The Arabs are quick-tempered; their hopes are easily raised, and their disappointment, when their hopes are deceived, is very acute. If the gold

rain should be delayed, then public opinion would soon swing round in the opposite direction and people who are now very friendly may turn into violent opponents.[72]

Other problems included French disinclination to upset the status quo by admitting large numbers of German Jews into the area of the French mandate, the real possibility of sustained opposition by Arab nationalists (despite Weizmann's dismissal of that factor), the fact that German Jews might be uninterested in relocating to Lebanon, and the question of how they could make a living there. Nevertheless, as the crisis for German Jewry deepened, Weizmann and the Agency began to explore more seriously the prospect of bringing refugees to Lebanon.[73]

Continuing reports of Lebanese enthusiasm for the settlement of German Jews in their country encouraged the Zionists. Many Lebanese seemed anxious to receive wealthy German Jews who could invest in new industries and whose "brains, energy, and money" could inspire the economic development of the country.[74] Even the director of the Bank of Syria and Greater Lebanon assured Weizmann that Lebanon welcomed Jewish settlement and capital and advised him that the entire coastal area from the Palestine border up to Beirut was available for sale and badly in need of development, which, in his opinion, would never come about without the German Jews.[75] Weizmann believed that the intellectual, industrious, and mercantile German Jews would quickly find themselves at home among the business-minded Lebanese. Despite his misgivings about disappointing Arab hopes for a Jewish-powered Lebanese renaissance, Weizmann became an avid supporter of the plan. In the autumn of 1935, he wrote to an interested French industrialist, "We have decided to make a preliminary attempt [at Jewish settlement], however modest, on the coast between Beirut and the Palestinian frontier," pending the "permission and goodwill of the French Government and of the Lebanese."[76] There is no evidence, however, indicating that the Jewish Agency had debated and decided in favor of Jewish settlement in Lebanon, as Weizmann's "we" seemed to imply.

Nevertheless Weizmann, often accompanied by Victor Jacobson, repeatedly made the rounds in Paris, pressing for the admission of German Jews to Lebanon. Private Jewish defense organizations that sprung up in the wake of Nazism's success in Germany also petitioned the French to allow a Levant haven for Germany's persecuted Jews. All similarly appealed to French economic sensibilities by describing the huge influx of capital, technology, and financial acumen which would supposedly accompany a vast German migration.[77] Tempted by the economic incentive but terrified of unleashing an anti-French backlash, the French waffled and tried to devise a plan whereby Lebanon could enjoy maximum Jewish resources while admitting a minimum number of Jews. Suggestions ranged from an outright prohibition against agriculturists and colonists ("creeping Zionists"), as well as doctors, lawyers, and practitioners of the "liberal professions" (unwelcome competition), to a case-by-case review of the financial assets of would-be immigrants, primarily industrialists and big businessmen, who would be required to renounce Zionism.[78]

Immediately after Hitler's rise to power in 1933 and again after Kristallnacht in 1938, rumors swept through Lebanon that Zionists wanted to purchase large tracts of land for German Jews. These rumors prompted a flurry of land sale offers and proposals from firms and individuals ready to construct housing and provide services to the refugees.[79] Many Muslim Lebanese looked to profit from the influx of German Jews; but, as usual, the keenest interest in the idea came from the Maronite community. Economic, political, and demographic factors can explain the Maronite position.

With considerable land holdings and comprising the majority of Lebanese industrialists, the Maronite elite stood to benefit both from land sales for Jewish settlement and the economic revival they expected the wealthy German Jews to orchestrate. To safeguard Lebanon's future from economic competition from Palestine, many argued, Lebanon needed an active economic force of the same scope and initiative as that which "turned the economic wheels of Palestine."[80] A related argument held that a united economic front of Jews and Maronites would strengthen the political standing of the Maronites in Lebanon. Recognizing that the growing Muslim majority threatened their political predominance, the Maronites nonetheless refused to cede those predominantly Muslim territories annexed in 1920. As an alternative, they eagerly supported the introduction into Lebanon's demographic equation of a Jewish factor that could reclaim numerical supremacy for the non-Muslim communities.[81] Eddé proposed that 100,000 Jews be settled in the overwhelmingly Muslim regions of Tyre and Sidon, specifically.[82]

The Zionists' other friends among the Maronite elite similarly involved themselves in the proposal to bring German Jews to Lebanon. Cesar Eddé, a relative of the president, offered to sell land in Lebanon's Bekaa valley, where he was sure Jewish colonists would find a great future in agriculture and industry.[83] Charles Corm informed the Agency of villas for rent at surprisingly low prices all along the Lebanese coast and offered to act as the Zionists' intermediary.[84] Nejib Sfeir reappeared, meteor-like, with a proposal to settle the refugees around Tyre and Sidon and in the swamps of northern Syria.[85] In Beirut's synagogue, congregants listened to an open letter from Patriarch Arida, in which he cited Cremieux's 1860 assistance, condemned Hitler's persecution of the Jews, and proposed that all Maronite churches hold special services to pray for the Jews in Germany.[86] Privately, Arida offered to sell patriarchal property near Beirut to the Zionist Organization for the settlement of German Jews.[87] Arida personally addressed the congregation in Beirut's synagogue in 1937, again offering his sympathy for the plight of Europe's Jews. Archbishop Mubarak, who accompanied the patriarch to the synagogue, proclaimed in his usual grandiose way that Lebanon had plenty of room for those Jews

> expelled from Germany and not friendly received by the Arabs of Palestine. . . . We, his Beatitude and myself, want to say to you: Be welcome, Jews. If I have said once that His Beatitude was the patriarch of the Jews, I now declare myself as the archbishop of the Jews.[88]

In mid-1936, Ben-Gurion called a meeting to discuss the possibility of land purchase in Lebanon. Deliberations with a prospective Lebanese partner ended in a preliminary deal for the resettlement of 15,000 Jewish families in Lebanon over a ten-year period.[89] Final negotiations faltered, however, when the outbreak of disturbances in Palestine caused some Zionists involved to worry that the plan would further enrage Arab public opinion and leave them open to the charge that the Jews, not content with Palestine, intended a hostile takeover of Arab land everywhere. Ben-Gurion and Weizmann agreed to postpone action until further soundings could be taken in Paris.[90] Less than a year later, a priest from Jounieh, a Maronite stronghold in northern Lebanon, came to Sasson with the message that his coreligionists had designated him to conduct negotiations for selling hundreds of thousands of dunams of land in the city's environs to Jews. Sasson reported to Ben-Gurion that he had duly informed the man that until Jewish immigration to Lebanon had been appropriately sanctioned, the Jewish Agency would not be purchasing any property in the Lebanese interior.[91]

The Jewish Agency did not attempt to bring Jews from Berlin to Beirut primarily because of the objections of the French mandatory authorities to the settlement of Jewish refugees in Lebanon. Although Weizmann eventually received the tentative approval of the government in Paris, the French High Commission in Beirut remained steadfastly opposed. Better acquainted with Muslim sensibilities and local politics, then high commissioner Damien de Martel feared, correctly, that large-scale Jewish immigration to Lebanon would result in protests by the masses, who, unlike the wealthy Lebanese elite, saw little benefit in a creeping Jewish foothold in their country. Although Epstein had blithely opined that "with the help of the French it would not be very difficult" to manage the widespread opposition that was sure to greet a large German Jewish influx into Lebanon, the commission did not share his easy confidence in its ability to squelch popular protest.[92] Traditional French suspicions that Britain used Jews as agents and fears that Jewish settlement near the border with Palestine would encourage Zionist irredentism toward southern Lebanon no doubt influenced the commissioner, as well. Weizmann appealed to Arida— whom he overestimated as "a great power in the Lebanon"—for help in changing de Martel's mind.[93] Nevertheless, the high commissioner concluded that Zionist colonization would require a substantial protective force and that the mandatory power had no obligation to facilitate the settlement of foreign colonists in the country.[94] His colleagues in Rome and Jerusalem added their concerns that the plan would elicit anti-French repercussions in French North Africa and Palestine, respectively.[95]

French opposition effectively ended speculation about bringing German Jewish refugees to Lebanon. The failure to attempt such a large-scale, visible program had serious consequences for the Zionist-Maronite relationship and the minority alliance idea, not to mention the potential refugees. The prominent Maronite role in encouraging the plan and making available property for Jewish settlement reinforced the Zionists' image of the Maronites as allies. Mubarak assured the Jews that he and the patriarch tried to influence the French authorities to allow the entry of German Jews, and the deluge of offers and expressions of encouragement gave the Zionists reason to believe that many Maronites worked toward this end.[96] In fact, however, none of the many French officials documenting the proposal reported having been lobbied by ranking Maronites on behalf of the refugee plan. Instead, an archival review reveals French awareness of Zionist sympathies on the part of the Maronite elite and an understanding of Maronite interests in bringing wealthy German Jews to Lebanon but complete ignorance of the Maronite role in encouraging the Agency with detailed offers to sell land and provide services to the newcomers.

Similarly, a comment in one of Epstein's reports that the patriarch, unlike Mubarak, declined to announce *publicly* Lebanon's readiness to receive German Jewish refugees suggests that perhaps factors other than French opposition helped impede the settlement of Jews in Lebanon.[97] As the Agency learned, public denials and private assurances constituted standard operating procedure for its skittish Maronite friends. A Zionist attempt to implement the plan surely would have provoked Muslim opposition and caused the patriarch and other leading Maronites to back away from their privately supportive positions. Although the many expressions of interest in the proposal attracted Zionist attention, rumors of a mass influx of German Jews to Lebanon certainly produced widespread expressions of opposition, as well. In 1934, France attempted to allay Arab agitation over rumored Jewish settlement in Lebanon by decreeing that the Lebanese or Syrian governments would have prior authorization of large land sales and long leasing arrangements.[98] Mubarak's 1937 sympathetic pronouncement in Beirut's synagogue produced a deluge of hostile press reports and public demonstrations in favor of the Palestinian Arabs. The archbishop and the mandatory authorities were both inundated with angry missives from Lebanon and beyond, denouncing both Mubarak and Zionism and, in one instance, questioning the archbishop's mental state.[99]

An attempt to realize the refugee plan would have constituted the first true test of Maronite friendship under fire. Maronite willingness to persist in a cooperative venture with the Zionists despite the outrage of their Muslim countrymen was a crucial factor in the dispute between Zionists who advocated a minority alliance policy and those who rejected it. Would the Maronites have made good on their offer to help settle German Jews, in the face of Muslim opposition, had the French not stood in the way? Maronite disavowal of the plan would have vindicated those who discounted an alliance-of-minorities policy. Had the Maronites facilitated a German Jewish immigration, the Political Department might have considered a formal minority alliance policy more seriously. In effect, French opposition permitted the Maronites to advance their friendly posture with the Zionists without actually going out on a political limb for them. It is likely that French rejection of the plan did not entirely disappoint Arida and the others. The lack of a test case for the Maronite-Zionist alliance allowed the prospect of such a union to persist as a policy option in Zionist foreign policy thinking.

LEBANESE JEWRY AND THE PHALANGE: IMPLICATIONS FOR ZIONIST ACTIVITY IN LEBANON

In response to Hitler's rise to power in Germany in 1933, Beirut's Jewish leaders established a local branch of the International League Against Anti-Semitism. French Intelligence sanctioned their actions as long as they did not provoke the ire of the German consulate in the city.[100] Two years later, Lebanon's Jewish community upped the ante by petitioning the high commissioner to permit German Jewish immigration to Lebanon, thereby adding a local Jewish factor into the Zionist-Lebanese equation.[101] Zionist thinking about Lebanon's receptivity toward Jews and Zionism would suggest that the indigenous Jewish community must have enjoyed a particularly secure position. Zionist theories about a natural Jewish-Maronite bond should have applied, as well, to the Jewish and Maronite communities within Lebanon. Levels of enthusiasm for Zionism varied among Jewish communities in the Diaspora, so it is necessary to consider what relationship existed between the Jews of Lebanon and the Jewish Agency, before addressing the question as to whether the indigenous Jewish population worked with the Agency to further Zionist goals.

By the late 1930s, Lebanon's Jewish population numbered about 6,000, the vast majority of whom resided in Beirut.[102] Lebanese Jews did not predominate in any one field; and although they enjoyed disproportionate representation in commerce, they were not among the wealthiest merchants and played no significant role in the politically powerful merchants' association. As a whole, the community was fairly well off and possessed sufficient resources to look after its religious needs, the education of its young, and the care of its elderly. Although they refrained from active engagement in Lebanon's domestic politics, Jews participated in elections, and Muslim and Christian parties courted their votes. Jewish merchants maintained extensive business relationships with both their Muslim and Christian counterparts. As a rule, the community tried to keep a low profile, avoid politics, and enjoy its quiet prosperity.

Jewish youths enrolled in the schools of the anti-Zionist Alliance Israelite Universelle emerged educated but largely disinterested in Jewish activities in Palestine. Those active in Beirut's Jewish youth movements learned Hebrew, and many adopted a Zionist orientation. Youth group leaders received guidance from their chapters in Palestine and sometimes traveled to the Yishuv for training. Almost all Lebanese Jewish families had relatives in Palestine and exchanged visits between Beirut and Jerusalem regularly.

J. David Farhi, head of the Beirut Jewish community, maintained close contact with the Political Department. A capable leader often frustrated by what he perceived as local Jewish apathy, Farhi supported Zionist aspirations in Palestine. Nevertheless, he believed that Jewish well-being in Lebanon depended largely upon the apolitical nature of the community and repeatedly emphasized to the Zionist leadership that Lebanon's Jews simply could not adopt an active pro-Zionist position.[103]

The Jewish community of Beirut did what it thought it safely could to assist the Zionist program. Lebanese Jews raised money to combat the hostility of the local press. The community hid or employed within the Jewish quarter illegal Jewish immigrants trying to reach Palestine via Lebanon and raised more money to feed and clothe them. Although most Lebanese Jews had no desire to emigrate, individuals set up an underground railroad to smuggle Jewish refugees, and later, arms, across the border into Palestine.[104] Special Agency departments and the Haganah dealt with immigration and the acquisition of arms, so these activities did not figure prominently in the operations of the Political Department.

The Political Department accepted information from the Lebanese Jewish community; and Agency representatives usually visited the Jewish quarter of Beirut, attended synagogue, and often shopped and stayed there while in Beirut. The Agency adopted a policy of not getting embroiled in intra-communal affairs, however, and, as a rule, did not use local Jews as spies or operatives.[105] The Agency based this policy on the assumption that political activity by Lebanese Jews on behalf of Zionism would raise charges of treason and seriously jeopardize the physical and material security of the community. The Agency quickly developed sufficient contacts in Lebanon such that it did not need to rely on the Jewish community for assistance, anyway. As relationships progressed with such highly placed figures as Arida and Eddé, there was no reason to make local Jews privy to extremely sensitive proceedings. Although leading Lebanese Jews repeatedly espoused this same line, some felt this indicated a lack of confidence in their community.[106] Despite Farhi's connections, many Lebanese Jews eschewed the Jewish Agency and maintained contact with Eretz Yisrael through the Council of the Sephardi Community in Jerusalem, a Zionist organization that opposed the Jewish Agency on the grounds that its European-born leaders discriminated against Middle Eastern Jews.[107]

That Lebanon's Jews enjoyed a close relationship with the Maronites independent of the Agency's ties to the Maronite community lent credence to the thesis that a natural bond between Jews and Maronites existed. Although the Jewish community contributed to Maronite church charities and maintained a cordial relationship with Arida and Mubarak, its primary connections were with Pierre Gemayel and the Lebanese Phalange. Gemayel founded the Phalange in 1936 as a vigilante youth movement motivated by Maronite nationalism and dedicated to the preservation of an independent and Christian Lebanon. Italian and German fascism originally inspired the Phalange; but due to Gemayel's political pragmatism, other concerns soon overtook the fascist component. Nothing indicated that the fascist origins of the Phalange had anything to do with anti-Semitism.[108]

The Jews of Lebanon found their closest friends among the Phalange. Although the community paid the police to ensure its security, it was unwilling to rely on official protection alone and also came to a financial arrangement with the Phalange, whose militia assumed responsibility for defending the Jewish quarter whenever pro-Palestinian demonstrations threatened to turn against the local Jews.[109] As the end of the British mandate in Palestine neared and war there seemed imminent, the community also undertook to prepare its own youths to defend their homes and businesses. Jewish boys enrolled in Phalange sporting clubs and scouts, where they trained in the use of firearms. The Phalange also sold weapons to the Jews for their self-defense. During the 1948 war, the Phalange made good on its promise to protect the Jewish quarter.[110]

Beirut Jewry's reliance on Gemayel, as opposed to Eddé, highlighted the factionalized nature of the Maronite community, which was not without consequence for the Jewish Agency's activities in Lebanon. Although both men were Maronite nationalists and separatists, Gemayel was one of Eddé's chief political rivals. This meant that the Jewish Agency, on the one hand, and the Lebanese Jews, on the other, had allied themselves with competing Maronite cliques. Eddé repeatedly warned Epstein against Gemayel, describing the latter as an Italian agent and a fascist; but Epstein

reported to Jerusalem that he could find no proof of a political connection
between the Phalange and either the Italians or the Germans.[111] Nevertheless, Gemayel and his organization did not share the clear pro-Zionist orientation of Eddé, Arida, and Mubarak, although one Phalangist suggested
that this reflected practical reservations about the Jews as serious economic
rivals and not political anti-Zionism.[112] On at least one occasion in the late
thirties, Gemayel evinced admiration for Jewish aspirations and industry
in Palestine and hinted at a readiness to draw closer to the Zionists. Aware
of the close relationship between the Agency and his rival Eddé, however,
he apparently assumed that Eddé was its man in Maronite political circles
and hesitated to make a play for Zionist affections himself. It seems that at
one time, the Political Department considered establishing closer ties with
Gemayel but felt constrained by its commitments to Eddé.[113] A similar
reservation characterized the department's contacts with yet another Maronite faction, headed by Bishara al-Khoury, although the al-Khoury group
advocated power sharing with the Lebanese Muslims and recognized a natural link between Christian Lebanon and the surrounding Arab world.

The Agency's close friendships with the Maronite church, led by Arida, and with the political faction led by Eddé, guided deepening Zionist
involvement in Lebanon. Zionist reliance on these particular cliques affected the course of Zionist policy in Lebanon. The fact that those Maronites with whom the Political Department had the closest relations were
all proponents of an extreme form of Maronite nationalism influenced
Zionist perceptions of Lebanon. These hard-line Maronite nationalists
saw Lebanon as Christian, Maronite, and Western: separate from, superior
to, and threatened by the Muslim Arab world. Anti-Muslim, pro-Western
positions drew these Maronites to the Zionists. Although aware of the divisions within the Maronite community, the Agency, confident that with the
patriarch and the president it had thrown in its lot with the most influential
and representative Maronite circles, underestimated the importance of
other Maronite factions that were not interested in an alliance with the
Zionists.

Although the department did not doubt the sincerity of the friendship
offered by Arida and Eddé, it often registered frustration with their professed inability to speak publicly the pro-Zionist sentiments they readily
expressed privately. This should have been, to those who championed a
minority alliance policy, a clear warning light that the Maronites were not
capable of shouldering their end of the bargain. To a large extent, Zionist
policy objectives in Lebanon, which a Zionist-Maronite alliance policy was
supposed to serve, turned on publicly demonstrating to the world that
some important Arab groups did accept Zionism. To that end, secret assurances of support served no practical political purpose. Eddé repeatedly
promised that as soon as he consolidated his position once and for all, he

would openly defend the Zionist cause. But Lebanon had resisted the domination of any one group for decades, and it was doubtful whether Eddé would ever have the chance to make good on his promises.

CONCLUSION

Although slow to deliver the political goods, the business-minded Maronites who befriended the Zionists quickly made economic opportunities available; and many non-Maronite Lebanese also sought to do business with the Jews of Palestine. The Agency encouraged many of the proposals it received but distanced itself from direct financial involvement in Lebanon, preferring, instead, to refer particularly promising projects to private Jewish entrepreneurs. This lively commercial exchange reinforced the Zionist perception that a mercantile ethos in Lebanon outweighed popular anti-Zionist sentiments prevailing throughout the Arab world. Pleased with the increasingly strong economic ties between the two countries, many Zionists believed that the Lebanese would not let the Zionist-Palestinian conflict interfere with the economic links binding Lebanon and the Yishuv together.

With Lebanese encouragement, the Jewish Agency supported efforts to create cultural relations between Jews and Lebanese. The Political Department tried to wring political benefit from these activities with an exchange-of-services approach. It encouraged positive relations between individual Jews and Lebanese, winning favorable exposure for Zionist medical, cultural, technological, industrial, and agricultural accomplishments in Palestine and threatening to halt mutually beneficial ties if the Lebanese press did not control its anti-Zionist content.

The campaign to break the anti-Zionist thrust of the Lebanese media consumed much of the department's attention, energy, and resources. It is unlikely that any of its efforts actually served to soothe Arab concerns or mitigate Arab opposition to the Jewish national home. But success in planting pro-Zionist articles in the Lebanese press contributed to the perception that the key to relations with Lebanon was finances, not politics. An especially obliging attitude on the part of the Maronite papers only added to the image of the Maronites as allies. The minority alliance school should have paid more attention to the fact that they and their Maronite friends lost the propaganda war.

Despite the Zionist leadership's decision that concentrating settlement activity in Palestine best served the movement's goals of creating, populating, and defending the Jewish national home, the plight of German Jewry forced a reconsideration of the proposal to bring Jews to Lebanon. Reports that many Lebanese, both Muslims and Christians, favored the immigration of wealthy industrialist German Jews and an inundation of offers for land and services encouraged both the proponents of the resettlement plan and those who perceived a substantial receptivity toward Jews and Zionism on the part of the Lebanese. De Martel's veto of the refugee resettlement plan highlights the peculiar nature of relations between the Jewish Agency (a non-state entity) and mandate-era Lebanon (a not-quite-independent state). Although Zionists and Maronites enjoyed some influence in Paris, the French high commissioner generally prevailed on local issues and in this way stymied the most ambitious Zionist-Lebanese proposals, as in the cases of the Litani dam and the German Jews.

The refugee plan aimed to save Jewish lives, not build a Jewish state. As such, it reflected Jewish, not Zionist, concerns. It would have benefited Zionist interests, however, by serving as a litmus test of the Maronite ability to stick with a pro-Jewish, pro-Zionist program in the face of widespread condemnation. This issue could have been the deciding factor for or against the alliance-of-minorities concept. It would have behooved the Agency to test the feasibility of a Maronite-Zionist alliance at this early date. If unworkable, the department could have discarded the idea and concentrated policy in a more realistic direction. In light of serious Arab/Muslim opposition, Eddé, Arida, and their supporters would have probably retreated from their openly supportive postures, while assuring the Agency privately that they welcomed German Jewish immigration to Lebanon. As it was, the exercise served only to enhance the image of the Maronites as allies without putting them to the test, permitting the concept of a Maronite-Zionist alliance to persist as an option in Zionist foreign policy thinking.

It was indicative of the Agency's uneasy relationship with the Lebanese Jewish community that the latter pursued its own connection with Gemayel independent of the Agency's links with Eddé and Arida. Although tempted at times to explore relations with other Maronite factions, concern that consorting with Eddé's rivals would spoil the existing relationship evidently persuaded the Jewish Agency that it had to choose among the different Maronite cliques. If the Agency had played by the rules of traditional Lebanese politics, characterized by rapidly changing alliances and unlikely marriages of convenience, it would have tried to simultaneously develop ties with several Maronite groups. Unwilling to get involved in intra-Maronite disputes or jeopardize the relationship it already enjoyed, the Agency chose one Maronite faction with which to pursue relations. It left Beirut's Jews and the Phalange to their own devices, by and large, and committed itself to Arida and Eddé.

By restricting its intimate connections to that one extremist Maronite school, the Agency formed its perceptions of Lebanon and planned its policy based on skewed and limited input. Sharp divisions among the Maronites would seem to have seriously handicapped any minority alliance proposal. Astute observers like Sasson realized that the Maronites did not represent all Lebanese or even all Christians and that Arida and Eddé did not even represent all Maronites. Underestimating the seriousness of intra-Maronite rifts and miscalculating the relative strength of the different factions, the Jewish Agency bet on the influential church and the sitting president, confident that it had the two most powerful figures in Maronite Lebanese politics in its corner. The two sides enjoyed close relations, dreamt up grand schemes, and watched the activity between them grow increasingly brisk and profitable. It seemed that the foundation had been laid for serious political cooperation.

Chaim Weizmann. (Zionist Archives and Library, New York.)

David Ben-Gurion. (Zionist Archives and Library, New York.)

Moshe Shertok [Sharett]. (Central Zionist Archives.)

Eliahu Sasson. (Zionist Archives and Library, New York.)

Eliahu Epstein [Elath]. (Zionist Archives and Library, New York.)

Ya'akov Shimoni. (Zionist Archives and Library, New York.)

Patriarch Antoine Arida. (Middle East Research & Studies, Ltd.)

Monsignor Ignatius Mubarak. (Middle East Research & Studies, Ltd.)

Emile Eddé. (Middle East Research & Studies, Ltd.)

Charles Corm. (Middle East Research & Studies, Ltd.)

Alfred Naccache. (al-Hayat.)

Bishara al-Khoury. (al-Hayat.)

Henri de Jouvenel. (French Ministry of Foreign Affairs.)

Damien de Martel. (Middle East Research & Studies, Ltd.)

Chaim Weizmann and Moshe Shertok visit Hanita, 1938.
(Haganah Archives; donated by Joseph Busthenai.)

Tegart's Wall, Palestine-Lebanon border, 1939.
(Haganah Archives; donated by Izik Eshel.)

~ 4 ~

ZIONIST POLITICAL ACTIVITY
IN LEBANON

THE PROSPECT OF political advantage haunted the close commercial and cultural relationships developing throughout the thirties between the Yishuv and Lebanon. According to one school of Zionist thinking, the rapid growth of business connections reflected a natural Lebanese receptivity toward Zionism. Confident that economics spoke louder in Lebanon than ideology, these Zionists pronounced the foundation of Yishuv-Lebanese relations sturdy. The temptation existed for both sides to build upon that foundation and enhance their shared political aspirations with an equally close political relationship.

Zionist-Lebanese relations did not take place in a political vacuum. The Arab Revolt of 1936–39 dominated events in Palestine and influenced the Agency's goals with respect to activity in Lebanon once the mufti and his supporters established themselves there. An examination of local Jewish-Lebanese relations along the Palestine-Lebanon frontier is a useful corollary to the study of high-level Zionist-Lebanese relations under the stressful conditions created by the disturbances in Palestine. Did the local border experience confirm the perception of Lebanese receptivity to Zionism and the thesis that Zionists would find a natural ally among the Christians? Mainstream Zionist policy toward Lebanon rested on those two assumptions. Its Maronite contacts encouraged the Jewish Agency in the belief that a relationship between the two sides could produce political, as well as economic, benefits for the Yishuv.

ATTEMPTS AT CONCLUDING A ZIONIST-LEBANESE AGREEMENT

In the mid-to-late thirties, Maronites and Zionists made several attempts to give concrete political expression to the affection and shared interests between them. Proposals from both sides reflected common concerns, as well as different expectations as to what each could offer and what was feasible given prevailing political conditions in the region.

The earliest hint of a possible formal alliance between Christian Lebanon and Jewish Palestine came during Victor Jacobson's initial fact-finding mission to Lebanon in the spring of 1933. Jacobson reported that Albert Naccache and the patriarch Arida had made a case for an economic partnership, insinuating that a political partnership could follow, "But about that," wrote Jacobson, "they don't have any but foggy ideas."[1] But Emile Eddé and George Naccache spoke in more definitive political terms. According to Jacobson, they perceived a Syrian threat to an independent Lebanon and acknowledged Lebanon's continuing dependence upon the protection of the mandatory power. At the same time, however, they argued that Lebanon should strengthen its position by allying with Jewish Palestine, which was in a similar situation. The two countries could enjoy a secure future, they assured Jacobson, on the basis of a close union between them. And if circumstances forced the mandatory powers to withdraw their support, a coordinated Jewish-Lebanese effort could defend their shared coastline against an attack from the Muslim hinterland. Expressing hope for friendly relations among all countries in the region, the Maronites insisted, nonetheless, that prevailing geographic, economic, and political considerations compelled the two minorities to seek protection in a close political and military union. Although surprised by the far-reaching nature of these proposals, Jacobson advised the Political Department to take them under consideration.

Two years later, Shertok entered into discussions with Arida and his senior clerics concerning the creation of a Lebanon-Palestine Society, as proposed by Young Phoenician poet Charles Corm, in order to build upon existing bonds between Lebanese Maronites and Palestinian Jews and serve as a basis for future cooperative activity. Despite professed interest on both sides, the idea languished until Corm revived it in 1937.[2] The Peel Commission recommended the partition of Palestine in that year; and with the prospect of an independent Jewish Palestine in mind, Corm and Naccache wanted to lay the groundwork for friendly relations between Lebanon and the new Jewish state immediately. Thus, they revived the idea of a cultural "friendship society." To enhance the prestige of the association, the Maronites offered to secure the patronage of the patriarch and suggested that Epstein obtain the endorsement of some prominent Palestinian Jews. By keeping the society's name neutral and the stated goals apolitical (i.e., the development of mutually beneficial social, economic, and cultural relations between Lebanon and Palestine), the Maronites hoped eventually to attract Druze and Muslim members, particularly from among the merchant class.

The Jewish Agency liked the proposal and asked Corm to author a constitution for the organization, suggest Lebanese members, and offer a specific plan of action. After a long delay Corm returned to the Jewish Agency with articles of association for a Lebanon-Palestine Society for which he had obtained the patronage of the patriarch.[3] Shertok went over the document personally, suggesting simple revisions but in no way altering the fundamental principles of the proposal as drafted by Corm.

Ostensibly non-political in nature, the constitution of the Lebanon-Palestine Society was, in fact, a skeletal blueprint for subsequent attempts at a political alliance. The call for the development of social, cultural, and economic relations constituted, in effect, a *bon voisinage* treaty; and the stated goal of facilitating comprehensive peaceful relations throughout the region clearly necessitated political activity. An attempt to realize the plan would have served as an excellent test case for the feasibility of a Maronite-Zionist alliance, but external circumstances again intervened to prevent the experiment from taking place. The outbreak of World War II produced more pressing priorities for both sides, and the British occupation of Lebanon threw that country and the Maronite community in particular into turmoil. Formerly prominent individuals such as Naccache and Corm lost a large measure of their influence; and within the already-fractured Maronite community even Corm's Phoenician circle split into rival factions. According to Epstein, the plan for a Lebanon-Palestine Society died a natural death before having been born.[4]

As with the plan to bring German Jewish refugees to Lebanon, one can only wonder whether the creation of a Lebanon-Palestine Society would have confirmed or negated the practicality of a Maronite-Zionist alliance. Despite the self-declared apolitical character of the organization, Lebanese Muslims and supporters of the Palestinian Arab cause surely would have objected to the actualization of such a close union between Lebanon and the Yishuv. The Maronites' ability to weather the political squall would have been a telling point and could have influenced the Jewish Agency to discard or pursue the minority alliance option. Once again, however, the Maronites earned points with the Agency for their apparent eagerness to cooperate without having to prove that they could make good on their offers.

As a private citizen, Corm could push the political efficacy of his Lebanon-Palestine Society only so far. While exploring Corm's idea, the Jewish Agency made even more serious attempts to reach an explicit political agreement with the government of Lebanon. No sooner had Eddé been elected president of Lebanon in 1936 than the Jewish Agency Executive contacted him to congratulate him on his new position and remind him of the proposals he had made to Jacobson, expressing the hope that "in your present position you will have the opportunity of developing the friendly relations between your country and Palestine for the welfare of both of them."[5] Eddé had spoken often of his intention to conclude a formal Zionist-Lebanese accord; and in the first autumn of his presidency, it suddenly appeared as if the time might be propitious for such an agreement.

In September of 1936, the French and Lebanese governments entered into negotiations for a Franco-Lebanese treaty; and the French premier Léon Blum recommended to Weizmann that the Zionists set about formalizing their relations with Lebanon. Blum had already told Weizmann that he understood the Lebanese (i.e., Eddé and his Maronite faction) to be "anxious to cooperate intimately with the Jewish national home, with which they share a number of problems and difficulties."[6] Now Weizmann relayed to Shertok Blum's suggestion that

> if we have some definite proposals by the time the treaty is ready, it might not be impossible to incorporate such proposals in some form or another into the Treaty, and so obtain for them not only the agreement of the Lebanese but also the sanction of the French Republic.[7]

Shertok recalled that when Epstein met with Eddé in August, the president had spoken "not only of his desire for friendly relations with us in Palestine" but also of his intention, "when the new status of Lebanon was settled, to come out with a public statement in favour of a Jewish-Maronite alliance."[8] Shertok promptly sent Epstein back to Beirut to suggest to Eddé that it was not necessary to wait for a Franco-Lebanese Treaty to go into effect but, rather, that the process of negotiating that treaty could itself provide the means for giving concrete shape to the Maronite-Zionist alliance. The timing was perfect, suggested Epstein, what with their mutual friend Blum in office in Paris and prepared to endorse a Lebanese-Zionist accord.

The agreement that Epstein described for Eddé called for close Lebanese-Zionist cooperation in economic, political, military, and cultural spheres.[9] Epstein reported that Eddé received his remarks enthusiastically and replied at length, repeating his familiar convictions that Zionism constituted a positive force in Palestine; that their superior cultures and common Muslim enemy made Jews and Maronites natural allies; and that a formal, public pact between them was certainly necessary. If it were up to him, he insisted, he would open negotiations at once. He was convinced, however, that despite Blum's blessings, only the approval of the French high commissioner in Lebanon, Damien de Martel, who adamantly opposed such an undertaking, could make a Lebanese-Zionist treaty possible. Eddé made it clear that he would take no steps in that direction without prior authorization from the mandatory authorities in Beirut.[10] From Epstein's report, Shertok understood that "if we were interested in seeing progress made with the Jewish-Maronite accord, it was up to us to get our friends in Paris to send to Beirut a suitable instruction."[11] He immediately cabled the executive in London to get word to Weizmann that Eddé favored the Agency's proposals but would not act unless the French high commissioner received appropriate instructions from Paris. He suggested that Weizmann do his best to persuade Blum to take care of the matter. A cryptic message from Epstein to an Agency contact in Beirut a week later suggested that after meeting with Weizmann, Blum had sent the appropriate instructions to the high commissioner.[12]

De Martel refused to sanction the Zionist bid, however, and Eddé refused to defy him. Frustrated, Shertok shelved, at least temporarily, the idea of a formal Yishuv-Lebanese accord. Unbeknownst to the Political Department, however, in his capacity as president of the World Zionist Organization, Chaim Weizmann mounted a new campaign to press Eddé for a separate Lebanese-Zionist pact. In this venture, he relied upon French Zionist Isaac Kadmi-Cohen as his personal emissary. In the boldest step yet toward formalizing the Lebanese-Zionist relationship, Kadmi-Cohen presented Eddé with a detailed and polished draft Treaty of Friendship on 23 December 1936.[13] This accord recognized the territorial integrity of independent Lebanon and the future Jewish state in Palestine, foresaw a political and military alliance between the two, and provided for extensive economic cooperation. In the spirit of the "natural harmony of interests" school, the pact stated that destiny decreed that the two sides and their respective homelands draw closer together and pronounced this reconciliation a historical mission.

Not surprisingly, Kadmi-Cohen reported that Eddé reviewed the agreement with enthusiasm and voiced complete approval.[14] As usual, however, he expressed concern that the French high commissioner would disallow the pact. Aware that de Martel exercised a veto over Eddé's participation in a Lebanese-Zionist partnership and had prevented the actualization of any such alliance to date, Weizmann made every attempt, with this proposal, to placate the high commissioner. The accord made repeated reference to French privileges in the region and specifically stipulated that before formal ratification, the parties would submit the pact to France, in the person of the French high commissioner, for comment and approval.

The attempt to pacify de Martel failed utterly. The high commissioner received a draft of the accord from Eddé and categorically rejected it.[15] Despite his self-proclaimed anti-Zionism and an unfriendly acquaintance with Weizmann, de Martel's objections were not unreasonable and reflected an accurate reading of prevailing political currents. De Martel correctly estimated that open encouragement of Zionist aspirations in Palestine and Zionist activities in Lebanon was anathema to all Muslims, most non-Maronite Christians, and many of those Maronites opposed to Eddé. Only that Maronite clique represented by Eddé and Arida truly welcomed a Zionist presence in the region, and it was merely one of Lebanon's many political oddities that the leader of this minority was also the president and claimed to speak for the republic. Most of the Lebanese population opposed such an accord. Keenly aware of what he termed the "considerable, perhaps insurmountable problems" confronting the Zionists in Palestine, the high commissioner saw no reason to import trouble to Lebanon. The provision for a concentrated zone of Zionist activity in Lebanon, which he perceived as the first step toward an eventual annexation of southern Lebanon by Jewish Palestine, especially disturbed him. An attempt to expand into Lebanon would make Zionism the centerpiece of every local party's platform, he claimed, "and I will have to mediate the conflicts. No, France will not permit the extension of Zionism here."[16]

Although events finally proceeded to the point where an explicit Lebanese-Zionist alliance existed on paper, de Martel's opposition killed the plan before the would-be signatories ever unsheathed their pens. Instead of confirming or refuting the alliance-with-Lebanon option, this latest in a series of aborted partnership proposals only served to tease, bringing the two sides a little closer together but never consummating the relationship.

Weizmann's renegade maneuver in sending Kadmi-Cohen to Eddé reflects upon the policymaking mechanics of the Jewish Agency and testifies as to Weizmann's own sense of estrangement from colleagues who rarely heeded his counsel. With Lebanon in mind, he brought Kadmi-Cohen on board as his personal political advisor in June of 1936, when Blum raised the possibility of a Zionist-Lebanese accord.[17] Apparently wanting to infiltrate the Political Department with one of his own, Weizmann recommended Kadmi-Cohen to Shertok four months prior to the presentation of the draft treaty; but Shertok responded with alarm.[18] Kadmi-Cohen was an old classmate of his, he informed Weizmann, a talented man but ignorant of the realities of the situation in Palestine and one whose "bonnet is full of bees which are sure to do positive harm if let loose on any field of Zionist activity to which he would come as a complete stranger. In my submission, this analysis rules him out for any independent political work."[19] Shertok advised assigning Kadmi-Cohen to an "apprenticeship" in the department, suggesting a stint in Paris and then a trip to Lebanon and Syria with Epstein as his tutor and guide. In Shertok's opinion, "only time and experience" would show whether the department could rely upon Kadmi-Cohen to undertake operations on his own, which Shertok clearly doubted.

A mere thirteen weeks later, Weizmann entrusted Kadmi-Cohen with the daunting and delicate task of selling the Lebanese-Yishuv agreement to de Martel. The high commissioner's report of the meeting bears out Shertok's misgivings about Kadmi-Cohen.[20] De Martel found Weizmann's envoy nervous, ill at ease, and prone to long and confused explanations when confronted. The high commissioner reprimanded him sharply for trying to "play a double game" by at first posing as a French investor interested in Lebanese public works projects and then trying to minimize the scope of his political mission in Lebanon, with which de Martel was fully familiar. De Martel dismissed a discouraged Kadmi-Cohen, who made no secret of his intention to override de Martel by winning approval for the treaty from higher political echelons in Paris.

During the same week in which Kadmi-Cohen met with Eddé, Weizmann appeared before the Peel Commission and testified that the Zionists were currently "negotiating some sort of open Treaty of Friendship . . . with the present Government of Lebanon."[21] Three weeks after de Martel's rejection of the proposed pact, Weizmann met with Blum in Paris and informed him that de Martel stood in the way of a Zionist-Lebanese treaty. Weizmann argued that such an alliance served France's interests and tried to persuade Blum to overrule de Martel and permit Eddé to commit Lebanon to an agreement with the Zionists. Although Blum "expressed the view that a Judeo-Lebanese alliance might be a useful counterpoise" to German economic and political activity in the Levant and again expressed his personal support for a Zionist-Lebanese accord, he declined to confront the high commissioner.[22]

As so often happened, even in pursuing this much-sought-after accord with Lebanon, Weizmann fell out of step with mainstream policy in the department. After failing to include a Lebanese-Zionist pact in the Franco-Lebanese Treaty, the department retreated from its campaign for an official accord with Lebanon. Although the Jewish Agency rapidly reached agreement with Eddé and Maronites like him on a wide range of cooperative political, economic, cultural, and military ventures, it could not persuade the Lebanese to transform their kind words into deeds. Inhibited by the realistic fear of Muslim outrage and the high commissioner's refusal to condone a Lebanese-Zionist accord, the Maronites refused to budge. Leaving Weizmann on the outside, the Political Department changed course and shifted its efforts from achieving a formal agreement to winning practical political benefits from its informal relations with high-ranking Lebanese.

THE ARAB REVOLT AND GENERAL STRIKE, 1936–1939

Threatened by rapidly growing Jewish immigration to Palestine and jealous of the progress other Arab countries were making toward independence, the Palestinian Arabs grew increasingly resentful. In April of 1936, the first violent wave of Arab rebellion swept through Palestine. Hajj Amin al-Husseini, the mufti of Jerusalem and Palestinian Arab nationalist leader, saw an opportunity to transform the spontaneous outburst of anti-Jewish violence into a concerted attack on Zionist aspirations in Palestine. He orchestrated the establishment of an Arab Higher Committee, with himself as president, and called for a nationwide strike of Arab workers and businesses. The rebellion presented serious security, economic, and political problems for the Jewish Agency and demanded its full attention. Lebanon watchers within the Political Department monitored the disturbances for a possible impact on Yishuv-Lebanon relations and on Lebanon's place in the broad scope of Zionist policy toward the Arab countries. Arab calls to boycott Zionist goods and markets tested the theory that brisk economic relations between Lebanon and the Yishuv made Lebanon immune to political pressures stemming from the conflict in Palestine.

Although punitive to the Palestinian Arab community, the strike actually stimulated the Jewish economy in Palestine. Jewish workers supplanted Arab laborers and Jewish farmers' fruits and vegetables replaced Arab produce in the markets. The closure of the port in Arab Jaffa prompted the development of a larger Jewish port at Tel Qasila near Tel Aviv and increased business at the port in Haifa. The Yishuv's economy adapted to the new conditions posed by the rebellion, but the economic ties long considered a foundation of friendly Zionist-Lebanese relations showed signs of wear under the strain.

The uprising and the call for neighboring Arab states to boycott Jewish markets and goods posed serious dilemmas for Lebanon. Palestinian Arab bands waylaid Lebanese trucks carrying produce and products across the border, destroying their loads and threatening reprisals if trade with the Yishuv continued.[23] The Agency received reports that Lebanese foodstuffs earmarked for sale in the Yishuv sat in warehouses and that fruit lay rotting for lack of alternative markets. Firms with branches in Palestine suffered, as did those which marketed Jewish manufactured goods in Lebanon.[24] Yishuv imports from Lebanon naturally rose along with rising Jewish immigration to Palestine, and the boycott hurt those Lebanese merchants who counted the growing Jewish population of Palestine among their best customers.

The Agency addressed the Lebanese government repeatedly, emphasizing the great damage the boycott could wreak on the economic connections between Palestine and Lebanon, connections from which Lebanon

itself derived great benefit.[25] Lebanese merchants and the Department's
highly placed friends readily agreed that Lebanon's economy was suffering
due to the boycott. The more tenacious managed to circumvent the boycott in ingenious, surreptitious ways. Nevertheless, the volume of trade
across the Palestine-Lebanon border decreased, suggesting that the strong
economic bonds upon which many Zionists counted for the continuance
of friendly relations between the Yishuv and Lebanon were fraying under
pressure.

The Agency found the fallout from the disturbances in Palestine on
Lebanese public opinion even more disconcerting. Palestinian Arabs active
in the uprising and forced to flee either the British or rival Palestinian
factions streamed into Beirut. Six months after the outbreak of the revolt,
David HaCohen visited Beirut and related encountering in that city a "Palestinian atmosphere," the likes of which were "not even to be found in
Palestine!"[26] A year later Sasson reported that the Lebanese public showed
more interest in the rebellion in Palestine than in Lebanon's coming elections.[27] The Department received similar information to the effect that

> the most abusive accusation which the rival parties can find to hurl at one
> another is to pretend that the other clique is the friend of the Jews. In short,
> for one and all we are the undesirables and we compromise those who have
> sympathy for us or who aid our cause.[28]

In the months immediately following the outbreak of the disturbances
in Palestine, many observers had speculated that the troubles in Palestine
would not greatly affect Lebanon. They based these predictions on the
conviction that Lebanese concerns vis-à-vis Palestine were commercial,
not political, and that most Lebanese recognized that their country's prosperity depended upon Jewish trade, tourism, capital, land purchases, and
assistance. In August of 1936, Britain's acting consul in Beirut, General
Furlonge, prepared a "Memorandum on the Repercussion in the Lebanon
of the Situation in Palestine," in which he asserted that "the vast mass of
the population are concerned wholly with matters of personal gain, and in
the matter of principle and policy their likes and dislikes are expressed in
big words which are seldom translated into corresponding action."[29] He
acknowledged an increasingly vocal anti-British (and anti-Zionist) sentiment but insisted that neither politics nor principles would deter the Lebanese in their headlong pursuit of material profit, which common wisdom
held depended on continuing economic relations with British-mandated
Palestine.

By 1938, the changes in Lebanese public opinion had become so striking as to require a revision of the 1936 memorandum. The new British
consul general in Beirut noted that the volume of trade between Lebanon

and Palestine had dropped and that the presence of many respectable Palestinians of moderate opinion among the refugees in Beirut had significantly influenced public opinion against both the British and the Jews. The revised memorandum acknowledged that public opinion was not monolithic and that Christians were still mostly troubled by the commercial hardships caused by the uprising, but added

> There is no doubt that a large and increasing proportion of them are shocked and deeply moved by what they hear and read relative to Palestine. . . . They have not the same religious and racial affinities with the Palestinian Arabs as have the Muslims, but they feel quite genuinely that a great wrong is being done to a neighboring people with whom they have much in common.[30]

Although the consul general described concrete action on behalf of the Palestinian Arabs as "negligible," he left no doubt as to where Lebanese sympathies, increasingly including those of the Christian population, lay. French officials in Beirut at the same time noted an increase in anti-Semitic propaganda, in both the Muslim and Christian communities.[31]

In September and October of 1938, Epstein's reports from Beirut similarly stressed the negative effect of the Palestinians "pouring in daily" on Lebanese public opinion. Lebanese sentiments, "including [those of] the Christians," now inclined toward Arabism.[32] Epstein attributed this pro-Palestinian shift to two factors, namely, the rebels' surprising success in thwarting the British and the effective anti-Zionist propaganda spread by the Palestinian Arabs. One must also include (although Epstein did not) the British consul general's observation that even Christians had begun to feel that the Palestinians were being wronged. Epstein lamented Palestinian-Arab advances in alienating Lebanon from the Yishuv and admitted that Palestinian claims, which never had found much of a serious audience in Lebanon, were "receiving much more echo these days, even in Christian quarters. . . . Now that the Palestinian refugees are mainly in the Lebanon they have very much furthered their case here, even among the Christians."[33]

Although commercial relations with Lebanon continued at a substantial pace, the not insignificant decline in trade suggested that if the disturbances in Palestine continued indefinitely, economic connections between Lebanon and the Yishuv would suffer. Of even more immediate concern was the impact of the uprising on Lebanese public opinion, particularly the increasing pro-Palestinian trend among Lebanese Christians. Even so, Zionist observers persisted in viewing Lebanon as fundamentally friendly and blamed rising anti-Zionism among the Lebanese on Palestinian propaganda and intimidation.

THE 1937 PEEL COMMISSION

Even while threatening to unleash British troops against Arab rebel bands, the British high commissioner promised the Palestinian Arabs that if they called off the fighting and the strike, His Majesty's government would dispatch an investigative commission to which the Arab Higher Committee could voice its grievances. The Royal Commission of Inquiry under the leadership of Lord Robert Peel arrived in Palestine on 11 November 1936 and spent the next several months hearing testimony from ranking Arabs and Zionists. Regarding Lebanon, the Political Department refocused its efforts on achieving practical Lebanese assistance in presenting the Zionist case before the Peel Commission, even in the absence of a formal Zionist-Lebanese agreement.

For the first time, the apparent irreconcilability of Arab and Jewish aims engendered a suggestion that Palestine be partitioned between the two groups; and in July of 1937 the commission recommended the division of Palestine into two self-governing communities as the only feasible solution to the problem. Zionist activity in London reached a fever pitch in the months immediately preceding and following the Peel report. The Agency lobbied for the creation of an independent Jewish state in Palestine within what it considered viable and secure boundaries. Specifically, it looked to Arida and Eddé to press actively for the contiguity of the border between Lebanon and the future Jewish state.

Jewish Agency members agreed unanimously that there should be no Muslim buffer wedged between southern Lebanon and the northern border of the Jewish state. This could have come about in two ways. During the Franco-Lebanese negotiations in 1936, the prospect always existed that France would decide to detach the heavily Muslim regions of southern Lebanon and cede them to Syria, creating a Syrian corridor between Lebanon and Palestine. The other possibility was that the Galilee would be included in the Arab portion of partitioned Palestine. Hof points out that even a common border between "Christian" Lebanon and "Jewish" Palestine was not necessarily trouble-free, since the population on both sides of the boundary was preponderantly Arab and Muslim.[34] Zionist policy aimed at enlarging the Jewish population in the Galilee so as to ensure that the Jews could hold the region in the event of war or a final partition plan, and the acquisition of land in the Upper Galilee along the Lebanese border became a Zionist priority. The Jewish National Fund entered into a flurry of negotiations, with one of the largest purchases being the land near the Lake Hulah basin, owned by Lebanese Christians.[35]

The Jewish Agency unleashed its big guns in the battle for the northern border. Weizmann declared that in the future, "the Lebanese Republic and the Jewish National Home in Palestine will have to 'hold hands,'" using the argument that "those two communities will look to the West as distinct from the surrounding Arab states."[36] Ben-Gurion proclaimed the "political need for a common frontier with Lebanon, a country with a large Christian community that could hold on only precariously in a Moslem ocean. The Lebanese Christians [are] in a similar situation to ours, and it [is] important for both that we should be neighbors."[37] Earlier he had confided to his son a more explicit political value in a contiguous Lebanon-Palestine border: "The Christians in Lebanon can barely survive without a Jewish state beside them, and we too are interested in an alliance with Christian Lebanon."[38] Two days later he elaborated:

> The Lebanon needs our friendship and support no less than we need its help. Not all of the Lebanon's inhabitants are Christian, and not all of the Christians are of one community; but the ruling community—the Maronites—are a minority, and without a Jewish neighbor [they] have no independent future. A Jewish state, by virtue of its strength and the possibilities it possesses, can ultimately win the friendship of all its Arab neighbors, although this friendship will not arise overnight. Being neighbors with Lebanon guarantees the Jewish state a faithful ally from the first day of its existence.[39]

The south of Lebanon limitrophe with the Jewish state, he enthused, would serve as the starting point from which understanding and goodwill between the Jewish state and its Arab neighbors would ensue.

Sir Author Wauchope, then high commissioner for Palestine, solicited Shertok's opinion of the partition proposal. Although he expressed deep reservations about the idea in principle, Shertok responded unequivocally that the viability of a future Jewish state required possession of the Galilee and a shared border with Lebanon. After making the case for allotting the Galilee to the Jews on military, agricultural, and hydrologic grounds, Shertok drew on the Agency's relationship with the Maronites for his most extensive argument:

> It is vitally important for the Jews that the area of their settlement should remain contiguous with the Lebanon. Ties of friendship have already sprung up between us and the Maronites and among the thinking people of both communities there is a strong hope that in the future this friendship will be cemented into a permanent economic and political alliance to the advantage of both communities and countries. Any wedge driven between us and the Lebanon will reduce the stability and prosperity for both countries and the Mediterranean littoral as a whole. . . . Thanks to the Jewish-Maronite friendship and to other factors at work there are fair prospects for Jewish agricultural settlement in the limitrophic regions of the Lebanon and Syria, which would be of great benefit both to the Jews and to those two countries. These prospects could only materialize if the contiguity to which I have referred . . . is maintained.[40]

Since the relationship with the Maronites figured so prominently in the Zionist demand for the Galilee and a common border with Lebanon, the Political Department sought to arrange for the Royal Commission to hear from ranking Maronites the expression of a desire to have Jews, not Muslims, as their southern neighbors. In appealing for Maronite support, the Zionists played on traditional Maronite fears of Muslim domination and pan-Arab irredentism. Epstein also suggested that a Muslim corridor separating Lebanon and the Jewish state would make tourism more difficult, burden the import-export trade with additional taxes and tariffs, and possibly give rise to a new port in competition with Haifa and Beirut.[41]

Although Eddé privately expressed "great satisfaction at the prospect of [Lebanon's] southern neighbor being the Jewish state and not the Arab state," he insisted that his delicate position in domestic Lebanese politics prohibited his involvement in the Peel affair.[42] In Epstein's estimation, Eddé refused to lobby for a Jewish state with a shared border with Lebanon because of the unprecedented degree of support he was then enjoying from the Lebanese Muslim community. The new treaty with France and the establishment of Lebanon as a parliamentary republic promised to diminish the political influence of the patriarch and enhance that of the president, which many Lebanese Muslims saw as a step in the right direction. A pro-Zionist stance would surely have estranged his new and unusual bedfellows.[43] Nevertheless, he delighted in the Peel Commission's recommendation for the partition of Palestine and the creation of a Jewish state. On the very day that the Peel Report was officially signed, Eddé met with Weizmann in Paris and declared, "Now that the Peel Report is an official document, I have the honor of congratulating the first President of the future Jewish state!"[44] He requested that the Jewish state's first *bon voisinage* treaty be with Lebanon. Neither his support for a Jewish state nor his refusal to work actively on behalf of it surprised his friends at the Agency. In outlining the Agency's plan to have the Royal Commission hear from Maronite witnesses in favor of a Jewish state contiguous with Lebanon, Shertok had written, "The president will not have the guts to say this, but the patriarch Arida might."[45]

In May 1937, Arida and his entourage set sail for Rome and then Paris. Epstein booked passage on the same ship, hoping to persuade the patriarch en route to advance joint Maronite-Zionist interests in a common border during his talks with the pope and the French. Epstein reported that the patriarch, looking old and very tired, received him warmly in his private cabin. Although he readily agreed that Maronite interests required a contiguous border between Lebanon and the Jewish state, Arida protested that "a massacre of the Christians of Lebanon at the hands of their Muslim neighbors" would result if "it becomes known, . . . God forbid, that the Maronites had a hand in establishing the borders between the Jewish and

Arab states in Palestine."[46] Epstein left the patriarch with the feeling that Arida would not speak out concerning the border issue. Weizmann met with Arida in Paris later that month. Despite the patriarch's assertion that he would be happy if partition resulted in a Jewish state contiguous with Lebanon, Weizmann, too, came away with the impression that "we shouldn't expect from the patriarch or any other Maronite leader any serious step on our behalf."[47] French files confirm this sentiment, revealing many letters from angry Arab quarters protesting the Peel plan but none from any Maronites arguing its merits.[48]

Reluctant to give up on the Maronite option, Epstein wrote to Shertok and suggested making use of Albert Naccache and Nejib Sfeir, who could perhaps arouse among the Maronites an outcry for a shared Lebanese-Jewish border by stressing the imminent danger of a Muslim corridor between Lebanon and Palestine.[49] Shertok responded with surprise that Epstein even considered using the volatile Sfeir.[50] Epstein persisted, however. Sfeir was well connected with that Maronite faction led by Bishop Abdullah Khoury. Khoury's group opposed Eddé, ostensibly on the grounds that he was too moderate in his opposition to Muslim and pan-Arab pressure but more importantly as part of the bishop's ongoing efforts to bring about the election to the presidency of his relative, and Eddé's main rival, Bishara al-Khoury. Sfeir told Shertok that if the Agency wanted public pro-Zionist support from Lebanon, it should help the Khoury group come to power.[51]

Epstein's slightly less ambitious plan entailed the bishop's presenting a letter to the French government demanding a contiguous Lebanese-Zionist border. Sfeir provided Shertok with a copy of the letter and asked him to forward it to Blum.[52] Despite Epstein's initial insistence that he saw no alternative to exploiting the Khoury group, he eventually came to agree with Shertok that the risk of Eddé's discovering that the Agency had cooperated with his Maronite opposition outweighed any possible benefit Khoury's letter might have.[53] Shertok pocketed the letter. Maronite silence notwithstanding, in the end, the Peel partition plan did provide for Jewish control of the Galilee and a common Jewish-Lebanese border.

Once again, the Agency had responded to the fractured nature of the Maronite community by choosing one group with which to ally itself exclusively. In this way, the relationship with Eddé's and Arida's narrow faction guided and constrained Zionist policy toward Lebanon. But Eddé's and Arida's refusal to assist the Agency on the border issue left the Zionists with no choice but to go it alone. One might think that the Peel episode finally constituted a test of the Maronite-Zionist relationship and that the Maronite failure to come through laid the Maronite alliance option to rest. Significant quarters within the Jewish Agency demonstrated a remarkable understanding of the Maronites' delicate circumstances, however, and an extraordinary optimism that when circumstances changed, the alliance could become a reality. Not long after his refusal to testify before the Peel Commission, Eddé met in Beirut with the department's legal advisor, Bernard Joseph, and agreed with Joseph's sentiment that "an agreement [between Lebanon and Jewish Palestine] already exists in our hearts." Joseph went on to add that he "hoped it would not be necessary for long to limit such agreement to private understandings expressed in personal interviews."[54] This persistent underestimation of the strength of Arab nationalism and Arab solidarity constituted a major political weakness in Zionist planning and contributed to the unrealistic expectation that a particular Maronite clique might be able to seize control of Lebanon and successfully commit that country to a pro-Zionist alliance.

THE MUFTI IN LEBANON

After the publication of the Peel report, the Arab uprising in Palestine flared anew. Longrigg writes that anti-Jewish outbursts in Palestine "excited great sympathy [in Lebanon], marked by demonstrations, . . . gun-running, and the departure of armed volunteers to Palestine."[55] Palestinians gathered in Beirut and in the south, promoting their cause and organizing raids against Jewish settlements in northern Palestine. The Agency shifted its focus in Lebanon accordingly, from its Maronite friends to its Palestinian enemies and the threat they posed from their new base of operations in Beirut. From its perspective, the most dangerous of all the Palestinian exiles in Lebanon was the former mufti of Jerusalem, Hajj Amin al-Husseini.

The British removed Hajj Amin from his post and abolished the Supreme Muslim Council and Arab Higher Committee on 30 September 1937, following a particularly bloody spate of violent attacks directed by the mufti against British targets in Palestine. Hajj Amin escaped the British authorities and fled to Lebanon, where the French grudgingly granted him sanctuary but confined him to a remote coastal village north of Beirut and extracted from him a promise that he would not engage in political activity.

Much to the consternation of both British and Zionists, the mufti persisted in exercising great influence in Palestinian politics and continued directing the rebellion in Palestine from his Lebanese haven. The Political Department regularly sent people to Lebanon to check on his activities.[56] In defiance of his pledge to the French, he received a steady stream of prominent Arab visitors and maintained daily contact with the rebels via his lieutenants, through whom he issued instructions. British and Zionist sources reported on the mufti's freedom of movement, his meetings with visiting Arab dignitaries, and his continued high profile in Palestinian politics.[57] Epstein recorded his impression that almost every Palestinian refugee who came to Beirut traveled to the village of al-Zoq to pay homage to the mufti.[58] Many of the Palestinian refugees in Lebanon worked diligently for the Palestinian cause under the direct guidance of the mufti, who also found supporters among the Lebanese Muslim population. With the substantial financial assistance he received from different sources, Hajj Amin purchased the services of a host of Lebanese journalists, government officials, and nondescript adventurers. Weizmann complained that the mufti had "made the Lebanon the centre of a far-flung net of political conspiracy against [Jewish] Palestine."[59] Beirut became the logistical base for Arab rebels operating against Jewish and British interests in Palestine and the center for Palestinian and pan-Arab propaganda.[60]

In response, Eliahu Sasson redoubled his efforts to dilute the anti-Zionist content of the Lebanese press, writing articles in Arabic and arranging for their publication in Beirut's papers.[61] It was a losing battle, particularly after the mufti's consolidation of power in Beirut. David Ha-Cohen's Lebanese business partner warned him soon after the uprising began that the "Arab newspapers are a disaster of the greatest order" and urged the Agency to pursue all steps toward halting their anti-Zionist incitement.[62] Despite the expenditure of much energy, effort, and money and the successful placement of several hundred pro-Zionist articles in the Lebanese press during the course of the rebellion, the Agency simply could not offset the support the mufti received from most of Lebanon's papers, including some Maronite publications. Many trumpeted the Palestinian cause out of conviction and the remainder responded favorably to being put on the mufti's payroll. In July 1938, Sasson informed Shertok that the Beirut weekly *al-Makshouf* had published a special sixteen-page booklet detailing the calamities that Jews had supposedly wrought upon Christian and Islamic countries in the past and the danger that they still posed. Sasson noted a strong ideological link to Hitler and fascism in some of the pieces and reported that most of the Beirut papers had alerted their readers to the publication of this booklet and urged them to study it.[63] Sasson persisted in his efforts to challenge the anti-Zionist thrust of the Lebanese media but reported gloomily after a meeting with the editor of *al-Ayaam* that

> in his opinion . . . there wouldn't even be a great advantage if we could buy all the Syrian and Lebanese newspapers. We should worry first and foremost about silencing the "Arab Propaganda Office" which puts out a daily special bulletin about Palestine and circulates 10,000 copies in all the Arab countries. It is not possible to silence it with money because it receives great sums every month from the mufti and from Arab sources and other foreigners.[64]

For their part, British mandatory officials in Palestine hounded their French counterparts in Lebanon to silence the anti-British campaign in the Lebanese press once and for all. The French high commission received a regular deluge of British communications charging that the Lebanese press was in the pay of the mufti, documenting examples of alleged distortions and untruths printed by the newspapers, and demanding that the high commissioner close down the most consistently offensive.[65] The French responded by periodically suspending various publications and with expressions of sympathy for the British position. Still, a particularly bitter complaint from the British consul general in Beirut provoked a piqued protestation from de Martel, who reminded him that in the past, British authorities were not very helpful when the Palestinian and Iraqi press had adopted anti-French positions. Wrote de Martel in his report of the unpleasant meeting,

> Just as the British told us then, I told him now that I cannot put a complete censure on the Arab press in Syria and Lebanon. But I use my authority in the fullest measure possible to moderate it.[66]

In a weak moment, some British officials seemed almost resigned to the unchecked rush of pro-Palestinian sentiment in the Lebanese press. As long as the Palestine problem continued to excite such strong anti-British and anti-Zionist feelings, suggested one, "Beirut must continue, to a greater or lesser extent, to serve as a fountain from which propaganda against our Palestine policy flows to all the other Arab countries."[67]

One tactic adopted by the Jewish Agency in its fight against growing anti-Zionism in Lebanon backfired and unwittingly provided more ammunition for Palestinian Arab propagandists. Working on the accepted assumption that the route to the heart of a Lebanese led through his wallet, the Agency let it be known that if the unfriendly environment in Lebanon persisted, Palestinian Jews were prepared to spend their holiday money elsewhere. During the first uncertain summer of the rebellion, many Jews chose not to travel, and the Agency learned that Lebanese resorts suffered as a result.[68] In May and April 1938, the Jewish press in Palestine picked up on this line of thinking and began issuing increasingly direct calls for a boycott of Lebanese resorts and of Lebanese products as long as the mufti set the tone for Lebanese-Yishuv relations. The *Palestine Post* stated bluntly that it was unlikely that "Jews, who have been in the past an important element among the summer tourists in the Lebanon, will visit that country while it harbors Hajj Amin"; and *Ha'aretz* declared that circumstances in Lebanon would soon force the Jews to "use the economic weapon at our disposal . . . if our neighbors in Syria and Lebanon do not understand that they cannot make war against us and profit from us at the same time."[69]

The Lebanese media seized upon these articles in the Jewish press, often reprinting them in translation in its own papers. The Jewish threat to boycott trade and tourism played into the hands of the Palestinian exiles, who appealed to Lebanese public opinion by claiming, among other things, that the Jews were hostile to Lebanon and intended to wreck the Lebanese economy and keep it subservient to their own. The proposed Jewish boycott especially dismayed the Maronite hoteliers. Nevertheless, Sasson recommended that the department press the threat to boycott the resorts at the highest Lebanese offices, arguing that the profits Lebanon derived from its relationship with Palestine's Jews logically dictated a neutral Lebanese stance vis-à-vis the conflict in Palestine.[70]

Both the threat to avoid the Lebanese resorts and the quasi boycott in the summer of 1938 backfired. The fall found Epstein reporting gloomily that an influx of tourists from Egypt and Iraq outweighed the absence of the Palestinian Jews. The hotels had been full; and in appreciation for increased Arab patronage, President Eddé threw banquets for prominent Egyptian and Iraqi guests, and the Ministry of Public Instructions and National Economy organized a lecture series for the new foreign visitors. The resorts enjoyed an excellent summer season; and Epstein estimated that despite the Jewish boycott, the number of tourists rose from 15,000 the previous year to 17,000. "This fact," concluded Epstein, "is appreciated by many people here as proof that Lebanon should not exasperate the Arabs by maintaining an attitude of benevolent neutrality toward the Jews."[71] The Palestinians and the press in Lebanon argued persuasively that the successful tourist season of 1938 challenged the government's plea that dependence on Jewish tourism prevented it from pursuing an active pro-Palestinian policy.

The Zionists' friends in top Lebanese circles claimed impotence as far as any ability to halt the swell of anti-Zionism was concerned. Weizmann acknowledged that with so many Lebanese either genuinely pro-Palestinian or on the mufti's payroll, no Lebanese government, however much it might detest Hajj Amin, could afford to pick a quarrel with him without exposing itself to internal trouble.[72] The Agency's Maronite friends secretly encouraged the Zionists in their efforts to muffle the mufti but could only propose that the Agency exert greater pressure on France to enforce its own ban against political activity by Hajj Amin. But France was clearly reluctant to move against the mufti. Torn between their Zionist friends and their French patrons, Eddé and his clique ultimately declined to confront the French, with whom they were then conducting delicate negotiations for Lebanese independence. Acknowledging, yet again, its Maronite ally's inability to take decisive action, the Jewish Agency directed its efforts toward pressuring the French to curb Palestinian activities in Lebanon.

Friction between the government in Paris and the French high commission in Beirut foiled the Jewish Agency in this approach. Premier Léon Blum agreed with Weizmann that Palestinian Arab agitation in Lebanon was dangerous and should be halted; but the high commissioner de Martel faulted Paris for being removed from the realities of the situation and worried that a French contribution to the British effort to put down the popular uprising in Palestine would touch off a rebellion in Lebanon. Many officials at the Quai d'Orsay agreed with the high commissioner's position, unwilling to risk upsetting the Muslims in the French colonies in North Africa by making a martyr of the mufti.[73] French Intelligence monitored the mufti's activities, phone calls, and visitors; but de Martel's unwavering refusal to move against him and the support he received in this position from important elements in the Quai d'Orsay convinced Weizmann that only explicit instructions from the prime minister in Paris could force the high commissioner to act. Shertok encouraged Weizmann to impress upon Blum the "vital necessity" of having the mufti ejected from Lebanon.[74] The ineffectiveness of Zionist lobbying in Paris, however, soon persuaded Weizmann that only the British could exert the kind of pressure on the Quai d'Orsay needed to bring about the removal of the mufti and his senior aides from the Levant.[75]

Weizmann implored the British to demand of the French that they evict Hajj Amin from the territory of the French Mandate on the grounds that he bore responsibility for the continued unrest in the territory of the British Mandate. Frustrated by his cool reception at the Quai d'Orsay, Weizmann wrote that "if the French get an urgent request from Downing Street it will be easier for Blum to overcome the sabotage of his anti-Semitic officials and of the high commissioner in Beirut."[76] In a calmer moment, he rephrased the sentiment, arguing that "Mr. Blum's hands will be greatly strengthened and actions will be taken by the French authorities if the matter is treated by the British Government as one of urgent concern, and pressed upon the French."[77] None too pleased with the anti-British propaganda and violence emanating from Beirut, however, the British were already, of their own accord, pressuring the French to crack down on the mufti and what they considered Palestinian Arab excesses in the press, with only marginal success. Brisk correspondence between the high commissioner and the Foreign Ministry indicates intense British lobbying in Paris. The new high commissioner, Gabriel Puaux, like de Martel before him, repeatedly assured the Foreign Ministry that he was doing all in his power to satisfy British complaints about Palestinian activism in Lebanon.[78] But as the numbers of Palestinian Arab refugees and rebels in Lebanon began to swell, de Martel had informed Epstein that, although aware of the dangers they posed, "we must nevertheless grant the political refugees the benefit of the rules of hospitality."[79] A French official in Jerusalem proposed resisting British pressure to act against the mufti, whom he characterized as "a personality against whom we have no apparent grievance."[80] Reiterations of joint Franco-British interests notwithstanding, the French view of Hajj Amin and the activities of his supporters was decidedly less hostile. No doubt secretly pleased by their British rivals' discomfiture, the French authorities took minimal action against the mufti.

With the mufti's men operating with relative impunity in Lebanon, the security situation along the Palestine-Lebanon border deteriorated and forced the Political Department to reconsider southern Lebanon's benign position on the Zionist foreign policy map. Far removed from the politics of Beirut and neglected by the government there, southern Lebanon persisted as an economic extension of northern Palestine, despite the official border demarcation. Many of the business opportunities in which Lebanese tried to interest Jews fell in southern Lebanon. People crossed the open border with minimum difficulty to farm land or conduct affairs on the other side. But the same absence of governmental interest and control that permitted southern Lebanon to maintain uninterrupted relations with the Yishuv also created a power vacuum quickly filled by Arab irregulars once the rebellion began in 1936.

Arab bands were recruited, based, armed, and trained in the region, from where they periodically crossed the border and struck southward against Jewish settlements. The Agency received information that even while still in Palestine, the mufti hired Lebanese government officials with familial links to the villages in the south to protect the gangs, organize the provision of arms to them, and facilitate their crossing the border, sometimes in government vehicles.[81] They smuggled large quantities of arms to the Arab rebels in Palestine, and fugitives fleeing the British crossed to safety in Lebanon. Local authorities on the Lebanese side were disinclined to try and halt Palestinian activities due to either support for, or fear of, the rebels and due to the fact that many of them profited from the trafficking in men and munitions across the border. To the extent that Eddé's government tried to prevent the movement of men and arms from Lebanon to Palestine, the media accused the president of acting in concert with the Zionists.[82]

French and British efforts to secure the border region met with only limited success. Under British pressure, the French reluctantly increased their troops along the border. French security, police, and mandatory authorities maintained regular contact with their British counterparts; and letters from British officials thanking the French for their cooperation in border operations aimed at Arab rebels attest to some degree of French responsiveness to British concerns.[83] But although French officials could point to the occasional interdiction of rebels and contraband, men and munitions continued to flow freely across the border. Smuggling continued unabated, especially on rainy nights when the patrols remained in their barracks. Zionist sources reported that some French soldiers who did arrest armed rebels quit the army after receiving death threats.[84] Keenly aware of the rising body count in Palestine and fearful of provoking an anti-French backlash in the Levant by appearing to help frustrate the popular Palestinian uprising, France's hesitancy in moving against the rebels and refugees can be attributed to prudence. Some scholars, however, assert that French authorities knowingly turned a blind eye to the activities of the Palestinian rebels based in southern Lebanon in revenge for alleged British support of Druze rebels confronting the French in 1925–26, a suspicion Epstein voiced in a meeting with de Martel.[85]

For their part, the British authorized a proposal by Sir Charles Tegart, security advisor to the Palestine government, for the construction of double and triple barbed-wire fences running the length of the Palestine-Lebanon border. Built in May and June of 1938, "Tegart's Wall" promptly incurred the wrath of local inhabitants on either side of the border, since it bisected pastures and private property. A barrier to the legal and illegal trade upon which much of the border region's population depended, the wall suffered continuous attack from both sides. Only with reluctant French assistance did the British manage to keep the fence more or less intact; and with the termination of the rebellion in 1939, the wall was rapidly dismantled.[86]

The basic Zionist goal of defending the Yishuv demanded a considerable measure of Jewish self-defense, especially when Zionist settlements found British protection from attacking Arab bands wanting. Initially, the Jewish military leadership responded to the violence of 1936 by advocating a purely defensive policy; but as the violence increased, the Haganah field commander, Yitzhak Sadeh, developed the concept of "active defense" characterized by mobile patrols and preemptive attacks. With the fighting intensifying, the British, lacking manpower, agreed to arm some 3,000 Jewish auxiliary police to protect isolated Jewish settlements. The British designated as the commander of the Jewish auxiliary police their own Captain Orde Wingate, who was, unbeknownst to them, an enthusiastic supporter of Zionism. Wingate organized his conscripts into "special night squads" and devised military operations much more aggressive than Sadeh's. In 1938, the special night squads expanded their field of activity to include forays into Lebanon to attack rebel bases and munition dumps there.[87] Jews who had previously crossed into Lebanon for social or business reasons now found themselves creeping across the same border in the dark with guns, looking for Arab rebel strongholds.

This constituted a new and unpleasant exchange between the Yishuv and Lebanon. The consequences of the final border placement in the early twenties finally confronted the Zionist leadership in the late thirties. Basing their claims to southern Lebanon primarily on economic and hydrologic considerations, the Zionists had delicately understated security concerns so as not to offend the great powers who would be assuming the mandates. The uprising appeared to justify Zionist worries about the military-geographic deficiencies of the border. Hof writes that the security of the Jewish settlements in northern Palestine had been based "on the unspoken assumption . . . that British sovereignty itself would be an adequate security guarantee. The real problem uncovered during 1936–1939, however, was that northern Palestine was penetrable almost everywhere."[88]

The experience along the border during the rebellion demonstrated for the first time that sleepy southern Lebanon could play a threatening role as a sanctuary and staging ground for the enemies of Jewish Palestine. Lebanon itself did not menace the Yishuv, but the inability of its government to control rebels operating in its territory permitted them to threaten Jewish positions in northern Palestine. The failure of Eddé's government to dominate events in Lebanon should have warned again of his weakness as an ally.

The same rebellion in Palestine that estranged much of the Lebanese Christian community from the Yishuv also reinforced the conviction of the Agency's Maronite friends that their fate was bound up with that of the Zionists. Shertok observed that the disturbances served as both political and economic "grist to our mill, as far as our relations with the Maronites are concerned. . . . They have driven home to the Maronites the menace of Moslem aggressiveness." Shertok also believed that the reduced tourist trade during the first summer of the revolt and the ruinous effect of the strike in Palestine on the Lebanese vegetable and fruit markets made it "abundantly clear to the Maronites how vitally interested they are in the safety and prosperity of the Jews in Palestine."[89] One should bear in mind, however (even though the Agency usually did not) that "Maronites" actually meant that Maronite faction loyal to Eddé or Arida.

Epstein traveled to Lebanon to confer with Eddé and Arida during the early months of the uprising and reported to Shertok that both men saw the disturbances in Palestine

> as proof of the meaning of Muslim majority rule. . . . They are terribly afraid lest the Arabs win this war. Such a victory would not augur well for the Maronites and all the Christian minorities. If the Christians in Palestine support the Muslims it is only because they are prisoners in their midst and they do not dare isolate themselves.[90]

Evidence suggests that some in the Jewish Agency proposed that the Lebanese Christians use their influence among the Palestinian Christians to splinter the uprising along religious lines and perhaps encourage a mutual Jewish-Christian entente.[91] But the Maronites again proved unable or unwilling to act on the Zionists' behalf, insisting that the time was not yet ripe for open pro-Jewish propaganda. Nevertheless, they continued privately to spur the Agency on in its efforts to dampen the disturbances.

At the height of the rebellion in 1938, Sasson reported that "the Maronites were very much concerned about the danger of Zionism suffering a setback and of the Muslim Arabs of Palestine becoming more powerful."[92] Epstein related a similar conversation with a Christian friend in southern Lebanon who maintained that his coreligionists followed the Jewish-Arab conflict in Palestine "with great alarm" and that most believed that an Arab victory would only incite further "Muslim fanaticism" in the region and lead to Muslim domination of the Christians.[93] Epstein's friend did not indicate, however, that the Christians were ready to join forces actively with the Zionists in this war in which they claimed to have great stakes; he could only suggest that the Zionists continue "cautious activity" among the Maronites in hopes of receiving some assistance. The Agency maintained regular contact with Eddé and Arida concerning the problems in Palestine, of course. But both men saw the mandatory powers as the only elements that could act effectively to halt the uprising and pressed the Agency to use its allegedly powerful influence in Europe to force the mandatory authorities to act. Zionists often noted that the Maronites (in fact, all the Arabs) overestimated the strength of Zionist influence in Paris, especially during the tenures (1936–37, 1946–47) of the Jewish premier, Léon Blum.[94] Eddé and Arida once again proved unable to offer the Zionists any assistance beyond secretly murmured encouragements.

In this context, the Agency's relationship with another of Lebanon's primary minority groups, the Druze, was slightly more useful. In response to Zionist appeals, leading Palestinian Druze leaders sent missives and emissaries across the border, urging their Lebanese brethren not to join or assist the Palestinian rebel bands.[95] Then aligned with the Maronites against a perceived pan-Arab threat to Lebanon's independence, the Druze proved less reticent than the department's Christian allies in openly supporting the Palestinian Jews and actively opposing the Palestinian Arab cause. Although pleased with Druze assistance at the local level in keeping Palestinian and Lebanese Druze from swelling the ranks of the rebels' forces, the Agency continued to look to British, French, and Lebanese government authorities (the latter being its Maronite contacts) to contain Palestinian Arab activities regionwide.

Ironically, the only offers of concrete political assistance in the war against the mufti came from the Lebanese prime minister, Khayr al-Din al-Ahdab, a Sunni Muslim, and a group of Palestinian Arabs apparently from the Nashashibi camp, the mufti's chief rivals. In early 1938, Ahdab visited Jerusalem and met with Shertok. In his report to the executive, Shertok related Ahdab's concern about the growing opposition to Eddé's administration in Lebanon and his own lack of funds necessary for strengthening his position. According to Shertok, the prime minister spoke at length about the chaos that the mufti and his followers were causing in Lebanon and worried that the mufti had turned Beirut into a center for pan-Arab propaganda and terrorism. Ahdab lauded the Agency's efforts to force the French to remove the mufti from Lebanon and went on to ask for financial support for his own anti-mufti plan. He proposed that the Jewish Agency fund a new newspaper in Lebanon to propagandize on behalf of the mufti's expulsion from Lebanon. Shertok expressed interest (although the sum requested was out of the question) but postponed a decision pending further investigation.[96] Within three months Ahdab was no longer in office. He remained in close contact with the Jewish Agency, however, and Epstein lamented that "he could probably have done more [for us] if the reigns of power in Lebanon had remained in his hands."[97]

The Jewish Agency received an even more detailed proposal for both stifling the mufti and creating peaceful relations between Lebanon and Palestine from a Lebanese Muslim delegation, apparently through the intermediary of one of the mufti's main Palestinian rivals, Fakhri al-Nashashibi.[98] The mufti's opponents promised to eliminate hostile acts against the Yishuv through the restriction of the mufti's activities in Lebanon or, if that failed, his expulsion. The Arab side also pledged to raise armed units to put down anti-Jewish demonstrations, create a political party in Lebanon that would advocate peaceful Lebanon-Palestine relations, undertake propaganda to that effect among the Lebanese public, and eradicate all anti-Jewish propaganda and activity emanating from Lebanon. In return, the Arabs expected the Zionists to fund the militia, the new party, a major Arabic newspaper to serve as its voice, and a campaign to win the other Lebanese papers over to a pro-Zionist perspective. The enormous amount of money required and overwhelming skepticism concerning the Arab side's ability to effect such a sweeping pro-Zionist program surely contributed to the Agency's unwillingness to agree to the proposal.[99]

The mufti's consolidation of power in Lebanon, Palestinian propaganda, and genuine sympathy for the Palestinian Arabs combined to encourage anti-Zionism in Lebanon. Finding its Arabic press campaign and pleas to the French equally unsuccessful in combating the mufti's influence, the Jewish Agency cast about for a Lebanese ally. It naturally looked first to its Maronite friends. Although never activated, the various proposals for thwarting the mufti offer interesting corroboration for some of the premises of Zionist thinking about Lebanon. Common interests based on a common enemy existed, as did people prepared to discuss seriously those interests and contemplate cooperative measures. Ironically, the most extensive proposal came not from Maronites but from Sunni Muslims locked in a power struggle with one of their own, Hajj Amin al-Husseini.

ZIONIST-LEBANESE RELATIONS ALONG THE BORDER

While Zionist and Maronite leaders struggled to wring political benefit from their relationship, Jews and Lebanese along the frontier carried
on with the concerns of daily life. Zionist policy aimed to increase the
Jewish population in strategic points within the Galilee in a bid to keep
the region in Jewish hands in the event of either war or a final partition
plan. Accordingly, Jewish settlements dotted the border with Lebanon.
Low-level activity among Zionist settlers and their Lebanese neighbors
provides a telling corollary to high-level political activity among ranking
Zionists and Lebanese in this period. Issues to consider are whether the
Agency attempted to correlate the local Jewish-Lebanese experience with
the plans for Zionist-Lebanese relations emanating from the Political Department, and whether the Jews' interactions with their Lebanese neighbors reflected the official Zionist bias in favor of the Lebanese Christians.

Three of the more prominent Jewish settlements on the Lebanese
border were Metulla and Kibbutz Kfar Giladi in the east and Kibbutz
Hanita in the west. Hanita was founded in March of 1938 in the midst of
the uprising in Palestine. Shertok assuaged British fears that the location
and timing of Hanita's establishment would exacerbate the already tense
situation along the frontier by producing an exchange of letters with his
friend, Lebanese prime minister Ahdab, guaranteeing the security of the
border region around Hanita.[100] The Agency heralded the successful establishment of Hanita as proof that the conflict in Palestine would not rupture
its friendly relations with Lebanon. Weizmann exulted, "Not only did no
rebellion follow the establishment of Hanita [but] it has already established
good relations with the neighboring Arab villages and we have even been
offered more land in the vicinity."[101]

Hanita's relations with its Lebanese neighbors are relevant to this
study as a test of the minority alliance thesis and as an indicator of the
lengths to which the Political Department was or was not prepared to go in
orchestrating Yishuv-Lebanon affairs. In this respect Hanita's experience
mirrored those of the other border settlements. Most of the Lebanese villages along the frontier were Shi'a; the remainder were Maronite. Jewish
settlers enjoyed uniformly good relations with both. Social relationships
developed; and the Jews received and reciprocated invitations to weddings,
parties, holiday feasts, and celebrations.[102] Jews who grew up along the
border spoke Arabic in addition to Hebrew and remember school field
trips to Beaufort Castle, soccer matches with their Lebanese counterparts,
and family outings to Beirut.[103] In general, Jewish settlers traveled easily
to such principal southern Lebanon cities as Tyre, Sidon, and Nabatiye;
and Lebanese crossed freely into Palestine, venturing as far south as Haifa
and Tel Aviv. The path from Lebanon to the Palestinian Arab market in
Bassa cut directly through Hanita.[104]

Jews who spent their young adulthood on the border cite four fields of Jewish-Lebanese activity beyond the purely social: (1) illegal Jewish immigrants paid Lebanese to escort them to the border of Palestine, where local villagers alerted the settlers to their presence and smuggled them across the border; (2) settlers bought guns from their Lebanese neighbors, who assisted in smuggling them into Palestine; (3) Jews used their neighborly contacts to find Lebanese landholders with property to sell in Palestine; and (4), the most thriving relationship, by which Jews and Lebanese bought and sold foodstuffs, livestock, produce, and manufactured goods across the border, both legally and illegally.[105]

Jews who lived along the border hasten to add that the region was not idyllic. One compared the period to that of the American wild West: there were a few murders, some horse thieves, and a general aura of lawlessness; but all frontier residents suffered equally.[106] During the disturbances in Palestine, Jewish settlements often came under attack; but their inhabitants uniformly insist that the assailants were always bands of Arab irregulars based in Lebanon and never their Lebanese neighbors themselves.[107] Former settlers contend that neither the riots in Palestine nor the Arab boycott curtailed activities with the Lebanese. They all share the impression that southern Lebanon existed as an entity unto itself, largely divorced from the politics of Beirut and unaffiliated with the Palestinian Arabs.[108]

Although one is hesitant to rely on people's memories, the almost identical recollections of the interviewees lend credence to their accounts, as do settlers' letters from the period.[109] One can combine their reports to paint a picture of the pre-state frontier. Three points of considerable importance to this study emerge from an analysis of local Jewish-Lebanese relations at the border. The first is that despite the Political Department's embrace of the concept of a natural bond between the Christian and Jewish minorities in the Middle East, on the local level, Jews showed absolutely no preference for Christian neighbors over Muslim. Former settlers are unanimous in their insistence that they enjoyed relations as warm and profitable with the Shi'a as with the Maronites. A related point is that each Jewish settlement made its own commercial arrangements, legal and contraband, with the nearby villages. The two salient factors that come to light are again that there existed no sense of a special community of interests with Christians as opposed to Muslims and that the Jewish Agency left the Jewish outposts to their own devices in their relations with the Lebanese.

The third point of interest focuses on this lack of communication between the Political Department and those Jews along the Lebanese border. One might think that as long as it was working toward an alliance with Lebanon, the department might have informed the settlers of its policy toward Lebanon and offered them some guidance in establishing relationships and advancing larger Zionist interests in Lebanon. One possible conduit between the department and the Jews on the frontier could have been the settlement *mukhtars* who served as security coordinators and liaison officers with the local authorities. At least one mukhtar voluntarily sent reports to the Political Department. Yosef Fein of Metulla (later mukhtar of Hanita) wrote regularly to Shertok, who found his reports valuable.[110] Settlers who accompanied Fein on trips through Lebanon marveled at his extensive contacts, ranging from border guards, effendis, merchants, and government officials to members of the high commission. Fein was an exception to the rule, however. He was already working in the service of the Jewish National Fund and Haganah Intelligence when he came to Hanita and was older than the other mukhtars, who were usually chosen from among the youthful settlers. Although the Haganah made full use of local Jews in intelligence operations, the Agency chose not to use settlers or the mukhtars to further its Lebanon policy.

One can imagine several sound reasons for the department's lack of interest in using Jews on the border as agents. Most of the settlers were barely out of their teens, and the department always worried that over-zealous or inexperienced assistants might misrepresent the Agency's goals or make commitments that the Agency could not endorse. The nature of Zionist-Lebanese relations (particularly secret relations with ranking Maronites) made most aspects of the Lebanon policy exceedingly confidential. It is also true that foreign ministries operate on the assumption that relations between states are created and consummated at the state level; and this applied even to the quasi ministry of the Jewish quasi state.

Nevertheless, by keeping its distance, the Political Department did not see that the daily reality of Jewish-Lebanese relations challenged the premise on which the minority alliance proposal and much of its policy toward Lebanon was based, namely, that Jews and Christians shared a natural affinity that favored the Maronites and precluded the Muslims as potential allies. On the other hand, the neighborly relations on the northern border, as opposed to the tension on all the others, reinforced the perception within the Yishuv that Lebanon differed from the other Arab states in its willingness to maintain friendly relations with Jewish Palestine.

CONCLUSION

Agency attempts in the mid and late thirties to turn friendly relations with Lebanon to a concrete political advantage produced a series of formal alliance proposals but no actual treaties. Continued Maronite willingness to discuss cooperative activity, despite repeated Maronite unwillingness to cooperate openly with the Agency, in the cases of the Peel Commission and the mufti, for instance, apparently did not sour the Zionists on the concept of a Maronite-Zionist alliance. The Agency expressed frustration but also understanding of Eddé's and Arida's delicate positions within Lebanese politics. The various alliance proposals offered or considered by these two men encouraged those Zionists inclined toward a minority policy in the expectation that an alliance could be forthcoming as soon as circumstances permitted. The campaign to achieve a formal Zionist-Lebanese accord foundered on the peculiarities of the Lebanese system. In dealing with the Lebanese president, the Agency had to contend with the French high commissioner's influence on Eddé, Eddé's need to placate his Muslims compatriots, and deep divisions within Eddé's own Maronite community. The French mandatory authorities controlled Lebanon so tightly that the president could not undertake negotiations or sign a treaty on behalf of his country without permission from the high commissioner. The split between French authorities in Paris and Beirut further complicated Zionist and Lebanese attempts to win French approval for their proposed pact. Meanwhile, the failure to implement any of these proposals amounted to a failure to test the feasibility of a Maronite-Zionist partnership, permitting the minority alliance policy to persist as a possible option. One should note that the assumption was always that if an alliance with the Maronites proved unworkable, it would be due to the Maronites' inability to hold up their end of the bargain. No one ever contemplated that the Agency would not be able to meet treaty obligations it might incur.

The factionalized nature of the Maronite community had tremendous significance for the pursuit of Zionist policy in Lebanon. The bitter rivalries among the different Maronite groups dissuaded the Agency from simultaneously developing ties with more than one faction. The decision to choose one Maronite basket in which to put all the Zionist eggs committed the Zionists to sticking with Eddé and Arida through thick and thin, regardless of whether the relationship was producing tangible results or whether a different Maronite group appeared to offer more practical assistance at any given moment. Intra-Maronite rivalries precluded a unified Maronite-Zionist alliance.

The Agency's friendship with Ahdab and the anti-mufti proposals submitted by Hajj Amin's opponents reinforced the Zionist perception that practical self-interest or national interests in Lebanon would overcome the ideological appeal of pan-Arabism and anti-Zionism. These feelers from outside the Christian community should also have indicated the myopic nature of the Agency's narrow focus on the Maronites. The local experience certainly indicated the possibility of a thriving, mutually beneficial connection between Zionists and Lebanese, Christian and Muslim alike. Left to their own devices by the Political Department, Jewish settlers along the Lebanese border showed no preference for Christian over Muslim neighbors and conducted equally satisfying relations with both. While enhancing the thesis of Lebanese receptivity to Zionism, this also challenged the pro-Maronite premise that Jews and Christians shared an organic harmony of interests.

Although the Maronites were unable to cooperate with the Agency on those occasions when the Zionists requested their assistance, the cumulative effect of the ongoing alliance proposals was to give the illusion of progress. Eddé made wild and sweeping suggestions for a Lebanese-Zionist pact to Jacobson, and Arida encouraged the Friendship Society proposal in the early thirties. By 1936, Eddé was prepared to negotiate an accord for inclusion in the Franco-Lebanese Treaty. By 1937, a draft treaty acceptable to both the Zionists and Eddé existed on paper. In 1938, a mutually acceptable charter for the Lebanon-Palestine Society also existed in writing. Those inclined toward a pro-Maronite position could easily blame external circumstances, primarily French domination of Lebanon, for the fact that none of these agreements became operative. The alternative was to admit that Eddé and Arida represented one small faction of one shrinking faction of Lebanese society, and simply would never be able to commit themselves publicly to a Zionist alliance unpopular with the bulk of their compatriots. Unfortunately for Zionist strategists, they failed to see that this constituted the most realistic evaluation of the situation.

The Agency and its Maronite contacts inched forward in their relationship; but in practical terms, were they really going anywhere? The pro-Maronite camp within the department predicted that a French withdrawal from Lebanon would both give Eddé the freedom he lacked to sign a treaty with the Agency and leave the Christian community feeling vulnerable enough to unite the different factions around such a pro-Zionist policy. The Agency's focus on Hajj Amin ended with the termination of the rebellion in Palestine in 1939 and the mufti's flight from Lebanon to Iraq and eventually to Berlin. But the British White Paper of the same year and the outbreak of World War II created trying new circumstances in the Middle East. In the context of the crises that would afflict both Lebanon and Palestine in the 1940s, there would be even more pressing attempts to finally make the Zionist-Maronite alliance work.

– 5 –

THE ZIONIST-MARONITE
ALLIANCE: PRESSURE TO
PRODUCE RESULTS

THE GLOBAL EMERGENCY created by World War II did not spare
Lebanon and Palestine. For the Zionists, the period brought pressing new
priorities, such as the conflicting battles against the 1939 British White
Paper and as British allies against the Nazis. When the world war ended,
the war over Palestine intensified. Locked in conflict with both the Palestinian Arabs and the British and torn by rival Zionist factions, the Yishuv
struggled to establish an independent state. By 1945, Ben-Gurion was focusing his attention almost exclusively on military preparedness, sure that
the birth of the new Jewish commonwealth would be bloody. Although
not necessarily in disagreement, the Political Department under Shertok
persisted in its diplomatic efforts to enhance the political position of the
Yishuv and secure the creation of a Jewish state.

Eliahu Epstein assumed the directorship of the Jewish Agency's political office in Washington, D.C., in 1945. Although Lebanon now took a
back seat to other Zionist concerns, Epstein, the department's primary
champion of a pro-Maronite policy, attempted to use his new post and
American connections to further the Zionist-Maronite relationship. The
Middle East tours of the 1946 Anglo-American Committee of Inquiry and
the 1947 United Nations Special Committee on Palestine presented opportunities for Zionist-Maronite cooperation. Now in the last stages of the
struggle for independence, the Jewish Agency was not averse to a final
attempt to importune practical assistance from its Maronite contacts, but
held no great expectations that the long-standing Zionist-Maronite

relationship would suddenly bear political fruit. With some alarm, however, the department observed events in Lebanon suggesting that "Christian Lebanon" was slipping away and into the Arab fold. The question was whether its Maronite connections were sufficiently troubled by the same perception finally to act decisively on behalf of joint Christian-Zionist interests.

The most significant outcome of wartime and post-war events in Lebanon for the Jewish Agency was the fall from power of its principal Lebanese friends. Demanding French withdrawal and a truly independent Lebanon, the country's competing factions battled for leadership of the new state. Lebanon's turbulent politics finally relegated those circles closest to the Jewish Agency to the political sidelines, while their rivals, under British tutelage, declared a more conciliatory policy toward the Lebanese Muslims and the Arab-Muslim world. Maronites such as Eddé and Arida found the combination of Muslim ascendancy and their own loss of influence intolerable. Were they finally desperate enough to consummate the relationship with the Jewish Agency in a last-ditch bid to use Zionist assistance to regain their own positions and that of their community? If so, was their remaining influence sufficient to uphold their commitments?

ZIONIST INFLUENCE IN LEBANON: A CASUALTY OF WAR

With the outbreak of World War II in September 1939, the new high commissioner in Lebanon, Gabriel Puaux, declared a state of emergency, dissolved the parliament, and suspended the constitution. Puaux retained Eddé as president but sharply restricted his authority. Having dedicated his entire political career to attaining the presidency, Eddé found the position greatly disappointing. "Overruled and often slighted by de Martel, Eddé's powers were further curtailed under Puaux," writes Kamal Salibi. If French interference were not trying enough,

> in his management of the government the president was faced at every step by obstruction from his old rival Bishara al-Khoury. Faced by all these difficulties, Eddé finally ceased to appear in his office at the Government headquarters. The little power that was left to him could easily be exercised from his private home.[1]

Four months after Puaux confirmed Eddé as head of state, Sasson reported that the mandatory authorities were running the country and that Eddé, a linchpin in Zionist relations with Lebanon, was "nothing but a symbol."[2] Desperate to strengthen his position, a panicky Eddé spoke again of allying with the Zionists and demanded weekly meetings with an Agency representative. Until Eddé was ready to present a plan for action, however, Sasson would only promise to visit whenever he came to Beirut.[3]

On 14 June 1940, German troops occupied France and brought a collaborationist regime to power in Vichy under Henri Pétain. At year's end, Puaux was replaced by a more enthusiastic Vichy loyalist, General Henri Dentz. When Eddé's tottering government failed to contain riots, Dentz seized the opportunity to force Eddé's resignation. The Zionists' staunchest political ally was no longer the president of the republic but, rather, a disillusioned member of the opposition. With Eddé's downfall, other Zionist supporters, such as Charles Corm and Albert Naccache, lost their principal source of official governmental support if not their own positions, as well.

Dentz appointed Alfred Naccache, a wealthy Maronite judge, as Eddé's successor in April of 1941. Alfred shared the pro-Zionist sympathies of his relative and the Agency's good friend, Albert Naccache. His appointment nonetheless constituted a blow to Agency influence in Lebanon. Naccache proved even more reserved than Eddé concerning decisive action on behalf of joint Maronite-Zionist interests. He was also further constrained in his presidential authority by the French. And unlike Eddé, Naccache maintained only a cold relationship with Arida. The deterioration of the ties between the new president and the patriarch over the next tumultuous months further weakened the Zionists' former bloc of Maronite support.

Lebanon assumed new importance to the Allied war effort in the spring of 1941 as German advances threatened British positions in the Middle East. British and Zionists alike observed with concern the successful infusion of German propaganda among the Lebanese and Syrians. Shertok initially worried that even the Christians might be inclined toward the Axis powers should a continuing weak French position prompt the Maronites to look to Italy, as the principal Catholic state and home of the Vatican, as their new patron.[4] Dentz's eagerness to collaborate with Nazi Germany clearly set the French Levant and British Palestine at odds, and Britain worried that the Nazis would soon walk en masse through the Lebanese door that Dentz so hospitably opened. Rumors reached the Jewish Agency that the Vichy government had signed an agreement with Berlin whereby Germany would release its French prisoners of war in exchange for a free hand throughout Lebanon and Syria and that hotel rooms had been reserved throughout the Lebanese resorts for an anticipated deluge of Germans.[5] The German threat became intolerable for the Allies when German armed forces began availing themselves of landing, refueling, and other facilities granted them by Dentz in Vichy-mandated Lebanon and Syria.[6]

Operation Exporter commenced on 8 June 1941 and lasted 34 days, during which time Allied forces captured Beirut and drove the Vichy regime and its troops from the Levant.[7] In proclamations issued as the first

Allied troops crossed into Lebanon, the British and Free French appealed for local support by promising that an Allied success would bring full independence for Lebanon and Syria.[8] In Beirut, Free French leaders General Charles de Gaulle and General Georges Catroux enjoyed a cordial welcome characterized by full Maronite support and cautious Muslim optimism.[9] Catroux replaced Dentz as the new "delegate general" in French-mandated Lebanon and Syria.

Sasson hurried to Beirut on the heels of the Allied invasion to assess the new situation. He discovered that continued British influence in Lebanon, even after the return of the Free French to power there, was provoking fears among the Maronites of Lebanon's inclusion in a British-orchestrated Arab union. Perhaps the Maronites and other Christians were now prepared for political cooperation with the Zionists, ventured the usually skeptical Sasson, precisely because they feared British success in forging an Arab union.[10] Even Bishara al-Khoury, champion of Maronite-Muslim coexistence, contributed to Sasson's estimation of Maronite concern by allegedly considering the use of Zionist assistance in securing the Maronite position.[11] As Sasson investigated the situation, it became clear that Eddé and his band had lost most of their leverage; but he also observed signs that Arida's political standing was slipping, as well. Two months after the invasion, Bishop Abdullah Khoury confided to Sasson that no British or French official had yet solicited the patriarch's opinions concerning Lebanon's political future.[12] The Agency's awareness of its Maronite contacts' deteriorating position throughout this period contributed to Lebanon's low ranking among Zionist priorities.

In November of 1941, Catroux proclaimed Lebanese independence and reconfirmed Alfred Naccache as president but reserved for France continuing special privileges.[13] His declaration aroused hostility throughout Lebanon and, of greatest consequence for Zionist influence in the country, instigated a full crisis in relations between the president and the patriarch. Arida objected to the incomplete independence that Catroux bestowed upon Lebanon and resented Catroux's blatant disregard for his own presidential candidate, Bishara al-Khoury. Despite Khoury's advocacy of cautious cooperation with the Muslims, Arida perceived Naccache's acquiescence in continuing French domination of Lebanon as the greater threat to Lebanon's independence. By Sasson's account, the patriarch stunned Lebanese society by refusing to send a representative to Naccache's inaugural, choosing, instead, to convene a special Christmas conference at Bkerke, at which he "attacked the new regime, the false independence, the members of government [and demanded] of the Lebanese people not to recognize the existing government and not to abide by any agreements signed by it."[14]

Epstein visited the beleaguered Naccache and conveyed to him the Agency's best wishes, noting with pleasure Naccache's interest in the Yishuv. According to Epstein, the president raised the issue of Maronite-Zionist cooperation by referring to "the special importance of tightening relations between us in order to defend our common interests in the coming peace conference, at which common enemies of Christian Lebanon and Jewish Palestine will surely be present."[15] Epstein assured him that the Agency was eager to meet with him again to discuss those common interests in greater detail.[16] Although Epstein found Naccache's pro-Zionist sentiments encouraging, in truth, the Agency's position in Lebanon was steadily worsening. In Naccache, a weak and unpopular president imposed upon the country by a foreign power, the Zionists had a friendly but ineffective ally. Furthermore, the conflict between Arida and Naccache splintered the pro-Zionist alliance of the religious and political establishments that the Agency had enjoyed during the Arida-Eddé years.

Tension between Britain and France over the issue of free elections in Lebanon and the outcome of those elections contributed to the further decline of Zionist influence there. The British liaison in Syria and Lebanon, General Edward Spears, repeatedly demanded that Catroux sanction free elections; fearing a nationalist victory, Catroux repeatedly refused. Lebanon's factions chose sides accordingly. Eddé led that Maronite group (including Alfred Naccache) which favored delaying elections and maintaining a special relationship with France; Khoury's Maronite group, joined by the Muslims and Arab nationalists, took the British side and demanded immediate elections and an independent Lebanon fully integrated into the Arab world.[17] Under relentless British pressure, France reluctantly agreed to permit Lebanese elections in the summer and fall of 1943. French fears were promptly realized with the election of Bishara al-Khoury to the presidency.

In his analysis of this latest turn of events, Sasson described Khoury's election as a victory for pan-Arabism. Despite the blow Khoury's election dealt to Zionist-Lebanese relations, Sasson could understand that in cooperating with the pan-Arabists, the new president, "a faithful Maronite and faithful Lebanese," had not betrayed the Maronite community.[18] Sasson credited Khoury with realizing that political and demographic currents were irrevocably eroding the Maronite position. While Eddé advocated relying on French support to sustain a Christian Lebanon isolated from the Muslim world, Khoury's strategy was to salvage what he could of Christian privilege through Lebanese collaboration with the Muslim world on Lebanese terms; that is, in exchange for accepting its natural place among the Arab nations, Lebanon demanded that its independence be uncurtailed by any Arab federation proposals and that the Muslim world recognize its unique Christian component.

Khoury's political savvy impressed France considerably less than it did

Sasson. Catroux's replacement, Jean Helleu, responded forcefully to the Khoury administration's declared intention to assume full governmental powers and reduce the status of the French delegation to that of a normal embassy. Despite Helleu's warning that France would not stand for unilateral Lebanese modifications of the constitution, the new Lebanese government persisted. At four o'clock in the morning of 11 November 1943, Helleu sent French troops to arrest Khoury and his ministers in their beds.[19]

In what was to be his final humiliation, Emile Eddé accepted reinstatement as the new chief of state. The Lebanese people responded with outrage; and Albert Hourani writes that for once, the "national cause took precedence over deep-seated sectarian conflicts and very few even among the Maronites dissociated themselves from the united front."[20] Two ministers who escaped capture directed the government from a secluded mountain village with the open support of the patriarch, all Christians, and nearly all of the population, while "Eddé, sitting almost alone in an empty building, failed to establish a government."[21] Sasson observed that by imprisoning Khoury and his government, the French made them heroes; and Catroux commented that "Helleu's act . . . had unified the entire Lebanese nation against France in a single night."[22] Hurewitz concludes that by moving against the Khoury government, the "Free French produced precisely the reverse effect of the one intended, for it sharpened the desire of the Christians and Muslims alike for proclaiming independence and their determination to prevent France from salvaging any privileged status in the land."[23] After twelve days, France relented and reinstated Khoury and his cabinet.

The Jewish Agency found post-election Lebanon decidedly less hospitable than before. Even the enthusiastically pro-Zionist Young Phoenicians split into pro-Eddé and pro-Khoury camps. With its heavy-handed treatment of the duly elected Khoury government, France made bitter enemies among most Lebanese and lost a considerable measure of Maronite support, as well. It took almost three more years of intermittent unrest before the last French official departed; and in this climate, the most unpopular Lebanese were those Maronites who remained loyal to France, namely, the Zionists' old friends like Eddé, Naccache, and Corm. Epstein wrote that the department found the halls of political power in Lebanon even less inviting as Khoury drafted into service those non-Maronite Christians (many of whom were pan-Arabists) whose strained ties with France had previously barred them from positions of political influence.[24] Of greatest significance for the Zionists, however, was the marked difference between Eddé's perspective on the Arab world and that of the new president.

Salibi compares the two men, describing Eddé as "thoroughly French in culture . . . arrogant [and] short-tempered," never gaining support beyond the confines of the Christian population and obsessed with the perception of a Muslim threat to his country and community.[25] Khoury, in contrast, emerges as man of quiet reserve, fluent in Arabic, steeped in Arabic culture, and politically well connected to important Muslim and Druze circles. Although kinder to his good friend Eddé, Epstein's description of Khoury corresponds to Salibi's portrait of a man at home among Arab intellectuals and accepted by both Christians and Muslims.[26] Whereas Eddé's pro-Zionism was an open secret, Khoury earned his pro-Palestinian credentials during the disturbances of 1936 with a bitter parliamentary speech attacking Eddé and Lebanese participation in the Tel Aviv fair of that year.

As Sasson observed, Khoury was no less a Maronite than Eddé, no less concerned for Christian influence in Lebanon, and certainly not unaware of the potential danger facing the Christians as a minority in the Middle East and possibly in Lebanon itself. Khoury proved less the ideologue, however, and more the practical politician. He believed that a Christian "mini-Lebanon" could not survive and that Greater Lebanon could do so only in the context of a Christian-Muslim partnership. Khoury accepted that Lebanon was inseparable from the surrounding Arabic-speaking countries, a point on which Christian and Muslim Arab nationalists agreed. Unlike Eddé, Khoury saw France not as the guarantor of Lebanese independence but, rather, as an obstacle to that Christian-Muslim cooperation which alone could ensure it. Khoury argued that Christians should take the lead in removing the French and recognizing Lebanon's bonds with the Arab world, thereby earning Muslim trust and ensuring their own security. Whereas Eddé saw the Muslims as Christian Lebanon's enemies, Khoury saw them as allies in the struggle against French colonialism.[27]

Too closely connected to Eddé, Epstein and others inclined toward a minority alliance paid insufficient attention to those factors which led many Maronites to espouse a cautious policy of Christian-Muslim accommodation. Sasson and other like-minded analysts understood that for these Maronites, a pro-Zionist position could serve no purpose but to inhibit the reconciliation they were trying to affect with their Muslim compatriots.

This philosophy of Christian-Muslim cooperation and the need to paint himself as Eddé's opposite in the context of the two men's rivalry led Khoury to espouse the nationalist, pan-Arab line (with a caveat reiterating Lebanon's independence), and there was no greater proof of one's Arabism than anti-Zionism.[28] Although the Jewish Agency maintained polite, irregular contact with the new president, Khoury was clearly no friend. Under his administration, Lebanon officially assumed an anti-Zionist posture and anti-Zionist Maronites came to the fore. The Agency learned that Khoury expressly instructed his new minister to London, Camille Chamoun, "to take an extremist, uncompromising stand against the Jewish development of Palestine."[29] Another report reached the department of the establishment in Beirut of an "anti-Zionist office" directed by a committee comprised primarily of Christians.[30] A Jewish businessman in Lebanon wrote directly to Ben-Gurion to inform him of increased anti-Zionist activities by Maronite youth.[31] In the fall of 1944, Epstein traveled to Beirut to protest attacks on Zionism by leading Maronites in the Lebanese Chamber of Deputies. But one of Epstein's informants reported that in light of British-Zionist antagonisms, Khoury had warned that "the Christians of Lebanon should be careful with contacts with the Jews of Palestine, since no good will come to them from this relationship but rather they will ruin themselves in the eyes of [both] the Muslims and the British."[32]

Officially endorsed by the Khoury administration, anti-Zionist sentiment within Lebanon expanded unhindered. Popular anti-Zionism reflected opposition to Jewish gains in Palestine, as well as fears of Zionist intentions vis-a-vis Lebanon itself.[33] Charges that Zionists were purchasing large tracts of Lebanese land and buying out Lebanese concerns prompted the promulgation of new laws severely restricting the penetration of foreign capital and land purchase by foreigners.[34] French security monitored the movements of Zionist officials traveling in Lebanon and suspected of trying to purchase property for the post-war settlement of European Jewish refugees, while the high commissioner came under great pressure to enforce the land sales restrictions.[35] Despite the new Lebanese laws, Arida's representative in Palestine secretly approached the Jewish National Fund several times with offers, allegedly from the patriarch, to sell property in Lebanon to Palestinian Jews or Zionist institutions.[36] Shertok publicly and explicitly repudiated claims of Zionist designs on Lebanon; but the Lebanese press, unconvinced, continued to publish reports that Jewish firms operating in Lebanon and certain Lebanese companies were actually Zionist fronts working to exploit Lebanon to the Zionist advantage.[37]

Much to the Zionists' dismay, Khoury made good on his calls for Muslim-Christian cooperation within Lebanon and for closer Lebanese cooperation with the rest of the Arab world. During his presidential campaign, Khoury allied with Riad al-Sulh, who joined in the call for an Arab but independent Lebanon. As president and prime minister, the two men formalized this Christian-Muslim compromise in an oral agreement known as the National Pact of 1943.[38] In essence, the Christians renounced their reliance on France in exchange for a Muslim renunciation of the demand for Lebanon's inclusion in an Arab union. The National Pact also introduced the unusual description of Lebanon as a nation with an "Arab face," which Walid Khalidi explains as "a compromise formulation between the outright description of Lebanon as an 'Arab country' and the denuding of Lebanon of any Arab characteristics."[39] The pact provided for a fixed six-to-five ratio in favor of the Christians in the distribution of parliamentary seats and, in distributing posts on a sectarian basis, formalized the tradition of a Maronite president. For Lebanon, this compromise permitted the emergence of a unified, independent republic and preserved Maronite preeminence for another three decades.

For the Zionists, the National Pact constituted yet another blow to the possibility of any large-scale Maronite-Zionist collaboration. Accepted by the overwhelming majority of Maronites, the pact established Christian-Muslim power-sharing as the foundation for Christian security and influence in Lebanon. Having confirmed their commitment to cooperation with the Muslims, there was no incentive for mainstream Maronites to pursue an active relationship with the Zionists and risk shattering the delicate power-sharing system whereby the Muslims agreed to continuing Maronite predominance. Voices from the Yishuv pleaded for Lebanon to throw off "the artificial mask of pan-Arabism which was bound to it from without," but Lebanon persisted in its newfound tilt toward the Arab world.[40]

Consistent with its program of integrating Lebanon into the Arab world, the Khoury government signed the Alexandria Protocol of 1944 and became a founding member of the League of Arab States in 1945. Khalidi contends that Lebanese participation in the league did not reflect Maronite acceptance of Lebanon's Arab character or of pan-Arab principles so much as "a ceremonial bow in the direction of Pan-Arab Lebanese Moslem sentiment."[41] Longrigg notes that although "an important section [of Lebanon's population] was known to be opposed to Pan-Arabism and tepid toward the Muslim world," Lebanon behaved as a loyal member of the Arab League.[42] In fact, a British official in Beirut reported to London that Khoury sought to persuade him that the Arab League, not Zionism, was a "vital British interest" and pushed for the British to adopt a clear pro-Arab policy in Palestine.[43] Similarly, Lebanon joined the rest of the Arab states in the spring of 1945 in sending letters to the American secretary of state outlining Arab fears of a Jewish-dominated Palestine. The Lebanese letter emphasized that "Lebanon, being limitrophe with Palestine, is particularly apprehensive of the possibility of a Jewish . . . state since Zionism is so dynamic as to be liable always to overflow its frontier."[44] Whereas Eddé and his prime minister Ahdab boycotted the pan-Arab Bludan conference of 1937, Khoury co-chaired the 1946 Arab conference at Bludan devoted to coordinating the pan-Arab campaign against Zionism.[45] "Christian" Lebanon, the notion of which guided the Jewish Agency's foreign policy toward Lebanon, was acting very much like an "Arab" country.

In joining the Arab League, Lebanon formally committed itself to participating in the boycott against the Yishuv, declared on 1 January 1946.

The Hebrew press seized upon the idea that due to the economic hard-ships suffered by Lebanon's farmers, businesses, and tourist resorts, practi-cal self-interest would compel Lebanon to resume quietly its friendly and mutually rewarding relations with Jewish Palestine. But despite prominent coverage of alleged Christian discontent with the prohibition on doing business with the Zionists and general Lebanese disinterest in the politics of Palestine, the papers could report no indication of Lebanon's with-drawal from its official pro-boycott position.[46]

In Lebanon's changing political constellation, the pro-Zionist star plummeted. Mainstream Christian and Muslim sentiment seemed pre-pared to give their newfound cooperation a chance. The most significant of those groups observing this Lebanese experiment skeptically was Pierre Gemayel's Phalange. By 1945, Agency Intelligence indicated that "the [Phalange] party has greater power and more adherents than any other organization in Lebanon."[47] The Phalange assailed both those Maronites who argued for continued French protection at the expense of Lebanese independence and those Muslims who would see the Lebanese Christians submerged in a vast pan-Arab sea. As the organization grew more power-ful, the possible consequences of the Agency's loyalty to Eddé over the years became more apparent. The paths of Agency and Phalange represen-tatives occasionally crossed; but, as with many Maronites, Phalange oppo-sition to the Khoury government did not translate into a pro-Zionist posi-tion, and the "Manifesto of the Association of anti-Zionist Lebanese Parties" of November 1945 listed the Phalange as a member in good standing.[48] Zionists anxiously following the ebb and flow of Lebanese poli-tics watched as the tide turned against their friends. Al-Khoury was in, Gemayel was holding his own, and Eddé was definitely out.

DESPERATION AS THE MOTIVATION FOR COOPERATION

Suddenly finding themselves on the political sidelines and apparently powerless to halt the deterioration of their position, the Francophile, pro-Zionist Maronites chose not to bow out gracefully. Desperate to regain control of Lebanon's future, were they desperate enough to turn to the Jewish Agency with concrete proposals for joint action? Lebanon's mem-bership in the Arab League so frightened this group with the vision of Lebanon's absorption into an enlarged Arab state, despite Arab assurances to the contrary, that they attempted to undermine the Khoury govern-ment. Archbishop Mubarak condemned Khoury for abandoning Christian interests and repeatedly denounced his administration. Although he ini-tially supported Khoury's election, Arida could not accept Lebanon's new-found "Arab face" and joined the opposition. Apparently putting their bit-ter feud behind them in the face of this emergency, former president Naccache let the Hebrew press know that he and Arida had met with Eddé

to plan a strategy for protecting Lebanon's "special [Christian] character."[49] In this context, these Maronites continued to believe in the utility
of Zionist assistance.

Eddé tried several times to persuade the Jewish Agency that with
Zionist financial support he could reclaim the presidency in the 1947 elections and promised that under his new administration Lebanon would finally sign an open treaty of friendship with the Yishuv.[50] Barry Rubin
writes of a letter delivered by Weizmann, presumably from the Eddé-
Arida-Naccache committee, to President Roosevelt and of another from
Arida conveyed to the American Maronite community by the Jewish
Agency's Tuvia Arazi. Both letters disparaged the Arab League and warned
of expansionist Arab designs toward Lebanon.[51] Arida publicly declared his
distrust of the Arab League in an interview with the Egyptian newspaper
Akhbar al-Yom, in which he brushed aside Arab guarantees for his country's
sovereignty and emphasized his fear that the Arab League was only the
first step toward a larger pan-Arab entity.[52]

Eliahu Epstein, always partial to the Maronites, adopted Arida's line
in an article tellingly entitled "The Rise of the Lebanon: Christian Refuge,
Maronites' National Home." Referring to the Arab League, Epstein concluded that "the bulk of Lebanese opinion regards with misgivings and
anxiety the beginnings of an Arab imperialism" that threatened Lebanon's
territorial integrity.[53] By 1945, the youth who had freelanced for the
Agency during his studies in Beirut had become something of an authority
on Lebanon within the department; but his writings indicate that a personal fondness for Arida, Eddé, and Naccache caused him to attribute far
more weight to their views than their actual influence within Lebanon af-
forded. His claim that "the bulk" of the population rejected Lebanese
membership in the Arab League was unfounded, even if he were referring
only to the Christian population. His reports show that the impressions he
recorded in his article are those he shared with the Political Department,
as well, thereby encouraging the department to overestimate the opposition to Khoury's government and the potential for a Maronite-Zionist alliance directed against Lebanon's "Arabization." The patriarch reinforced
this perception with his repeated denunciations of the Arab League and
his insistence that Lebanon had the right to maintain friendly relations
with all neighboring nations.[54] Agency observers never failed to note that
the patriarch specifically used neutral expressions like "neighboring nations," implicitly including Jewish Palestine.

Despite the bravado on the part of Mubarak and Arida, the tradition
of Maronite predominance was clearly slipping. Khoury had openly acknowledged as much by declaring that the Maronite position could only
endure in cooperation with the Muslims, not in opposition to them. The
Political Department was acutely aware that its previously influential

Maronite contacts no longer commanded positions of power, and that by agreeing to the National Pact and Lebanon's membership in the Arab League, the Maronite community had lost a large measure of its preeminence. The Hebrew press reported upon the patriarch's dispatch of emissaries overseas to plead for outside assistance in protecting the Christians. Yishuv readers learned of the panic allegedly gripping the Christians, whose hegemony was reportedly doomed by the rapid Muslim birthrate and Lebanon's continuing integration into the Arab world. *Haboker* lamented the "tragedy of a group witnessing its own decline from greatness."[55] The apparent deterioration of Maronite influence greatly distressed those Zionists who counted on the Christian factor to keep Lebanon distinct from the Arab world and inclined toward Jewish Palestine. Maronites of Arida's and Eddé's persuasion could not tolerate the situation. During this period, they and some of their Zionist supporters proposed increasingly wild plans that could only have been born out of desperation.

With the Christians' slim majority threatened by the higher Muslim birthrate, some Maronites sought to inflate the Christian population by other means. When Lebanese Maronites abroad did not respond to the call for their mass repatriation, some suggested that the émigrés should be counted among the Lebanese population nonetheless. Ayoub Thabit, Naccache's replacement in the months preceding the 1943 elections, lost his position due to the outcry that ensued when he tried to fix the distribution of parliamentary deputies between Muslims and Christians according to their proportions within the population based on estimates including the Maronite émigrés.[56] Arida demanded that all Lebanese expatriates, the overwhelming majority of whom were Maronite, simply be permitted to vote in abstentia in Lebanese national elections.[57]

After years of refusing to consider ceding those overwhelmingly Muslim areas tacked onto Lebanon in the 1920s, the more extreme Maronite separatists "were now willing, if necessary, to accept a reduction in the size of Lebanon which would give it once more a large Christian majority."[58] "Avi," a Jewish Agency operative in Beirut, reported that Archbishop Mubarak allegedly supported the idea. Relating information that his informant claimed to have heard directly from Mubarak, his report read in part,

> A plan which may reflect the actual state of mind of leading Maronite personalities is that of the partition of Lebanon (reminding [one] in a way [of] the Palestine partition plan). . . . If the present political situation of the Maronites [sh]ould become worse they will suggest the creation of a small state composed of Mt. Lebanon only, where the population would be purely Maronite, and that South Lebanon would be annexed to Syria. This miniature state, ac-

cording to my informant, would be protected by a French Garrison and will have "nothing to fear from the rapid natural growth of the Moslem elements in the South and in Beirut."[59]

Avi found the partition proposal significant primarily because of its "desperate character." Ben-Gurion initialed the report. It is likely that he viewed the proposal more seriously than Avi, since it corresponded with his own information that de Gaulle supported Maronite separatism so that in the future, the two states, "Jewish and Christian, [c]ould thus join forces against the vast Muslim population."[60]

Tuvia Arazi reported that Eddé, Thabit, and Naccache led that Maronite faction prepared to reduce Lebanon's size in order to rid it of much of the Muslim population and asserted that "most of Lebanon's Christians support territorial reduction."[61] While it is untrue that most Christians favored a partition of Lebanon, Eddé's support for the idea certainly came as no surprise. He had quietly proposed the same thing back in 1926 and almost twenty years later sent his son to Weizmann with a new twist on his old idea: to cede the undesirable areas of Lebanon to the Jews. Weizmann did not consider the proposal seriously, however, as evidenced by his comments at a meeting of the Jewish Agency Executive in February 1945:

> The last thing I want to say, and perhaps it will be comical—you know the confusion in Lebanon. The son of the former president came to me, a Christian under great French influence, with a proposal. And the proposal is that he wants to hand over Tyre and Sidon to us for the [Jewish] national home. It happens that they want to give us these because there are 100,000 Muslims there. I told him that I had a grandfather who used to say that he hated to receive "a gift that eats," but he didn't want to leave me alone even after I told him this, and he said that he would come again.[62]

Evidently unwilling to give up so easily, Eddé made his offer again to Arazi that July and once more in December of 1946. Arazi informed Shertok that the Vatican representative favored the proposal and that Mubarak had persuaded General Spears, the British liaison in Lebanon, of the wisdom in detaching certain Muslim areas from Lebanon.[63]

Possible great-power interest in redrawing the Palestine-Lebanon-Syria map produced a panic among this Maronite faction when a rumor developed that Britain was going to detach part of northern Palestine for annexation *to* Lebanon. Arida quickly wrote to the British foreign minister to inform him that the Lebanese utterly rejected this idea; and Mubarak followed suit, adding that

> if it is necessary to change the frontier, it would be desirable, for us Christians, to detach instead a part of south Lebanon—up to the Litani river, for example,

and reunite it with Palestine, thus diminishing the number of Muslims in Lebanon in order to restore its true character as a Christian country.[64]

Fear that British and French machinations in the region might sacrifice Maronite claims was not new. The Agency received information that at one point, Eddé, having lost faith in the French, tried to contact American authorities to propose that the United States assume responsibility for guaranteeing Lebanese independence and protecting the Christian position. According to the Agency's source, Eddé offered, in return, ports, air bases, economic opportunities, and American control over Lebanon's foreign policy.[65]

Zionist proposals proved equally startling. A private citizen in Petakh Tikva wrote repeatedly to Weizmann, claiming to have devised together with Arida a secret plan for uniting Christian Lebanon with Jewish Palestine.[66] An unsigned memo advocated playing the different regional minorities off against one another, thus exposing for the entire world the "myth" of pan-Arab unity.[67] An only slightly less hysterical version of the previous proposal recommended that the Jewish Agency defuse pan-Arab sentiment by actively helping the various minorities throughout the Middle East resist assimilation into the Sunni Muslim majority.[68]

In late 1943, Benjamin Eliav founded a political party, Tenuat Ha'am, which officially championed an alliance of minorities within the Middle East. Eliav worked closely with Ari Jabotinsky, who brought to Tenuat Ha'am the inclinations of the "mosaic of minorities" thesis espoused by his artistic circle of radical Revisionists, particularly the poet Yonathan Ratosh, another long-time associate of Eliav's.[69] Tenuat Ha'am won a seat in the Elected Assembly of 1945, but wielded no influence in mainstream Zionist policy.

These pro-Maronite proposals, submitted by individuals on the periphery of Zionist decisionmaking or beyond, generated little or no interest at the Jewish Agency. Under Ben-Gurion's firm control, the Agency made military and security matters its first priority. The obvious loss of influence of its Maronite contacts and its own problems in Palestine led the Political Department to disregard these wild plans for Zionist-Maronite collaboration.

It fell to Eliahu Epstein to perpetuate the pro-Maronite and pro-minority approach within the Political Department. In 1945, he proposed the creation of a League for the Defense of Minorities in the East, not officially linked with the Jewish Agency but serving Zionist interests as a counterweight to pan-Arab and Palestinian Arab activities.[70] Due to his personal friendships, Epstein generally looked at Lebanon through Maronite eyes and shared the view of Lebanon as the Maronites' rightful national home.[71] Whereas Sasson understood and even respected Khoury's reasoning that Christian-Muslim cooperation could preserve a considerable measure of Christian power, Epstein agreed with Eddé that growing Muslim and pan-Arab pressures constituted a mortal danger to Maronite security. He saw a clear comparison between the Zionist struggle to create a Jewish state in Palestine and Maronite efforts to make Lebanon a Christian country, although, by 1945, he thought the Maronites faced the more difficult task.[72]

But Epstein understood that those Maronites most inclined to ally with the Zionists were also least able to deliver their end of any bargain. A 1942 report filed by Epstein after meeting with Eddé shows how torn he was between the impotency of his Maronite friends and the theoretical advantages a minority alliance held out. He acknowledged that despite "all of Eddé's . . . sincerity, neither he nor any other Maronite leader . . . ever proposed an actual plan for uniting the minorities and never turned to us with an appropriate scheme."[73] Epstein, however, seemed unable to lay the Maronite card to rest. Later in the report, he resumed his familiar emphasis on the importance of active contact with the minorities, literally underlining his conviction that "We must strengthen that bond more than ever before and act according to a plan designed from the outset to tighten our relations with the Maronites, the Druze, and the rest of the minorities." His minority-defense-league idea evolved naturally from the Maronite sympathies that his involvement with Lebanon engendered, although he was also privy to the Agency's relationships with the Druze and other minority communities.[74] According to Epstein, the Political Department liked his idea; but when the Agency posted him in the United States in 1945, no one in Jerusalem pursued the plan and the league project fell by the wayside.

Although his proposal generated no more attention than did the other desperate plans for securing Maronite domination of Lebanon and creating a Maronite-Zionist front, Epstein continued to exercise considerable influence on the course of Maronite-Zionist relations from his new position in America. Making little headway in Lebanon, the extremist Maronite opposition met up with Epstein in Washington, D.C.; and they pursued their common cause from there.

ZIONIST-MARONITE COORDINATION IN THE UNITED STATES

The Zionist movement was already active in the United States, and the existence of an American Lebanese Maronite community offered possibilities for Zionist-Maronite cooperation. Was the American Maronite community interested in the power plays among al-Khoury, Eddé, and Arida? And did the latter two possess the initiative and influence necessary to rally the American Maronite community to action on their behalf? Epstein had aspired to Zionist-Maronite coordination in the United States even before coming to the Agency's political office there. Several years earlier, he pressed the subject with Charles Corm, then in charge of the Lebanese exhibit at the 1939 World's Fair in New York. Epstein arranged for a Jewish artist from the Palestine pavilion to assist with the Lebanese exhibit and offered Corm letters of introduction to Zionist friends in New York.[75] Epstein's motivation in putting his American contacts at Corm's disposal was political, not artistic. To Corm, he simply advocated contact between the two pavilions, as well as between the American Lebanese and Jewish communities, but to a Zionist in New York he added more specifically, "with his [Corm's] help you will be able to meet many Lebanese permanently residing in the United States and perhaps you will find a means of joint action against pan-Arab propaganda, which the Lebanese themselves abhor."[76]

Epstein surely found encouragement in an open letter to President Roosevelt from Elias Shamoun, president of the Maronite "Federation of Lebanese Americans in New England," urging the president to keep the gates of Palestine open for Jewish refugees from Nazi Germany. Shamoun noted the economic prosperity Palestine enjoyed due to Zionist efforts, cited Arida's invitation to Jewish refugees to find refuge in Lebanon, and concluded that "having so much in common with the persecuted Jews, we hope that the day is near when they also will become liberated and that the Jewish Homeland in Palestine will become a reality."[77] Epstein forwarded a copy of the letter to Eddé with a note declaring that "the tight bond which unites Lebanese and Jews in the United States is new testimony of the fraternal feelings unifying two peoples motivated by the same spirit and the same social and political aspirations."[78]

When Epstein arrived in Washington six years later, the mutual benefits of a coordinated Zionist-Maronite campaign in the United States seemed as relevant as ever. The Maronite nationalists, now in opposition to the Khoury regime, could use Zionist contacts and expertise in persuading the Americans to adopt a pro-Christian, anti-Arab League position, while the Zionist cause could exploit a sympathetic stance by the American Lebanese community. The Zionists also had an interest in American recognition of Lebanon as a "Christian" state, thereby establishing a precedent for a "Jewish" state. Slow to action and disorganized, however, the Maronites needed the Jewish Agency to nudge them along.

In 1941, a desperate Eddé had suggested to Sasson that with Zionist help he could rally the Maronite diaspora, but he never offered a plan of action.[79] In 1942, Bernard Joseph, then legal advisor to the Political Department, met with President Naccache and found him worried about American acquiescence in Lebanon's absorption into an Arab federation. Joseph proposed that Naccache send a Maronite envoy directly to President Roosevelt, offering the assistance of Zionist friends in the United

States.[80] Naccache never acted on Joseph's suggestion; but three years later, a Jewish Agency official traveled to Beirut to push again the idea of sending a Maronite delegation to the United States. He reported that Arida, Abdullah Khoury, Eddé, Naccache, and Thabit agreed upon the need to coordinate Maronite-Zionist activities abroad. Now desperate to reverse the erosion of their position, Eddé and Arida were persuaded to dispatch emissaries to Epstein in Washington for assistance in launching an American campaign in support of Christian Lebanon.[81]

The initial activities of the patriarch's first envoy, Monsignor Paul Akl, pleased Epstein. He reported that in speaking out against the Muslim threat to Lebanon, Akl often compared the Christians' struggle with that of the Jews in Palestine and "did not hesitate to express his sympathy toward Zionism and the Jews in Palestine publicly [and] would be glad to meet with us in order to discuss the possibilities of mutual activities in this country for the benefit of the Lebanese and Zionist causes."[82] Epstein soon soured on Akl, however, whom he accused of abandoning his mission after the first few speeches and devoting himself instead to raising funds for a Beirut charity. Epstein characterized Arida's second emissary, Habib J. Awad, as "an honest man . . . sincerely devoted to the Christian cause in the Lebanon" but lacking the personal prestige and talents necessary for the task at hand.[83] With Zionist assistance, Awad attempted to contact the White House and prominent American journalists; but he failed in his mission, as well.

The next two Christian envoys to the United States, Monsignor A. Maluf and Elias Harfoush, proved equally unsuccessful. Epstein reported that Maluf neglected the Christian cause in favor of personal interests and even made several anti-Zionist references.[84] Harfoush discussed strategy with Epstein and actively promoted the Maronite position (although without mentioning Zionism), but his call for the territorial reduction of Lebanon proved so divisive and unpopular that he soon departed.[85] Epstein endeavored to bring a more experienced delegation to the United States and appealed directly to former presidents Eddé and Naccache and Arida's top political assistant, Sheikh Tewfik Awad, explaining the seriousness of the work awaiting spokesmen of their caliber in America and assuring them "of the readiness of our office and of other Zionist institutions and persons in this country to render all possible assistance for the success of a Lebanese Christian mission to America."[86] The Lebanese responded that scheduling conflicts prohibited such a visit.

Epstein found his primary ally within the American Maronite community in Saloum Mokarzel, president of the National Lebanese Society of America and editor of *al-Hoda*, an Arabic daily published in Brooklyn. Rigidly anti-Muslim, Mokarzel used his newspaper to condemn the Arab League and Khoury's policy of Christian-Muslim rapprochement.

Believing in a natural harmony of Christian and Jewish interests in the
Middle East, Mokarzel described himself as a "friend of Zionism" and
called Epstein his "ally in a common cause."[87] Mokarzel eagerly put his
resources at the service of the Christian envoys arriving from Lebanon,
only to be bitterly disappointed by each. He and Epstein similarly despaired of the lack of organized activity among the American Maronites.
Mokarzel complained that only a prestigious patriarchal delegate could
galvanize the American Lebanese community into action, and Epstein
warned that the Zionists could not orchestrate the Christian cause but only
assist once the Christians had demonstrated the necessary initiative.[88]

Even a more capable envoy would have been hard pressed, however,
to counter the influence of the official Lebanese delegate in the United
States, Charles Malik. Upon learning of Malik's appointment, Tuvia Arazi
met with him twice in Beirut and attempted to persuade him of the need
for Zionist-Lebanese cooperation. Arazi emphasized the similarities between Christian Lebanon and Jewish Palestine and encouraged Malik to
work with the American Zionists and Jewish Agency people awaiting him
in the United States.[89] Epstein and Malik actually struck up a friendship;
but Malik never became a Zionist ally, as Arazi had hoped. Instead, Epstein
found Malik to be a "gallant opponent," a philosopher and devout Greek
Orthodox who worked zealously for his cause while maintaining respect
for his adversaries and a willingness to exchange views with them, one of
the few Arabs with "courage" enough to meet publicly with Zionists.[90] Epstein tried to persuade his friend that "the only natural allies of Christian
Lebanon are the Jews in Palestine and it is only a Jewish Palestine that
can preserve the existence of a Christian Lebanon"; but although Malik
recognized a possible Muslim threat to the Christian position in Lebanon,
he believed that Christian security depended upon cooperation with the
Muslims.[91] Epstein and the Jewish Agency were anxious to help the Maronite opposition; but Malik commanded great respect in diplomatic circles,
ably representing the Khoury government and easily overshadowing the
delegates dispatched to the United States by the church. American policy
toward the Middle East proceeded without the aid of joint Maronite-
Zionist counsel.

THE 1946 ANGLO-AMERICAN COMMITTEE OF INQUIRY

The creation of the Anglo-American Committee of Inquiry immediately after World War II offered the Jewish Agency and its Maronite
friends a chance to coordinate the expression of their shared interest in the
establishment of a Jewish state. The Lebanese performance before the Peel
Commission a decade earlier, however, suggested that Eddé and Arida
would be unwilling to voice their pro-Zionist positions—unless perhaps
their current political desperation now compelled them to act more reso-

lutely on behalf of Zionist concerns. The Political Department sent agents to Beirut to meet the Zionists' principal contacts there and encourage them to present pro-Zionist testimony before the committee.[92]

The United States and Britain set up the committee to solve the Jewish refugee problem in the wake of the war. Leading Zionists and Arab nationalists testified, vehemently debating the feasibility of Palestine as a Jewish refuge. President Khoury defended Palestinian Arab claims and beseeched the committee to halt Jewish immigration. Pierre Gemayel went before the panel to argue that augmenting Palestine's Jewish population would harm Lebanon, reflecting, according to Haddad, "the economic fear of a Jewish state, that would bring with it superior western technology and ideas."[93] In its unanimous report of 1 May 1946, the committee recommended the immediate admission of 100,000 Jewish refugees into Palestine on humanitarian grounds but rejected the idea of a Jewish state. The Arab countries condemned the proposed influx of European Jews; and Lebanon, like the others, responded to the committee's report with strikes and demonstrations. During the hearings, an American member of the committee, Judge Joseph P. Hutcheson, had recorded in his diary that all Lebanese witnesses, Christian and Muslim, presented a "violent opposition to Zionism, a determination to resist it at all costs, and an unwillingness to concede the immigration of one single Jew," concluding that while there were probably some exceptions to the overwhelming Lebanese opposition to Zionism, "the exceptions are so small as to be almost negligible."[94]

He was correct on both counts. Longrigg notes that while the majority of Lebanese decried the Anglo-American recommendations, Mubarak declared Maronite support for Zionism. In fact, Mubarak, Arida, and Abdullah Khoury obtained audiences with at least two members of the committee and tried to persuade them that the official Lebanese witnesses did not represent the true feelings of most Lebanese, especially Christians. Another American member of the committee, James McDonald, met with the three Maronites, who insisted that Lebanese Christians feared Muslim "domination" and "fanaticism" and clearly preferred a Jewish state in Palestine to an Arab one.[95] McDonald noted that Mubarak had recently stated his pro-Zionist views in an interview with an American correspondent.

Mubarak's interview with Gerold Frank appeared in the *Palestine Post* and constituted a scathing condemnation of Muslim culture, civilization, and values while praising Zionism and calling for a Christian-Zionist partnership.[96] The Zionists could ask for a more influential ally but certainly not a more passionate or articulate one. A front-page article by Itzhak Ben-Zvi in the Hebrew paper *Ha'olam* gratefully acknowledged Mubarak's declaration of support and responded in kind with a sympathetic overview of Lebanon's role as a Christian refuge.[97] Although echoing the call for an alliance among the minorities of the region, Ben-Zvi concluded that

Mubarak's statement was unlikely to alter the anti-Zionist thrust of Lebanese policy under Khoury.

The committee members and other observers overwhelmingly shared Judge Hutcheson's impression of a solid Lebanese opposition to Zionism.[98] Working closely with their Maronite friends, the Political Department failed to comprehend the same thing. Nevertheless, two striking points emerge from McDonald's experience in meeting with Mubarak, Arida, and Abdullah Khoury, and Mubarak's interview with Frank. The first is that even at this late date, some of the Jewish Agency's oldest contacts still believed in the interdependency of Maronite and Zionist destinies. The Agency welcomed their pro-Zionist testimonies even while recognizing that their motivation was desperation over the disintegration of extremist Maronite influence in Lebanon. The second point is that all three advocates were religious leaders. The fall of friends like Eddé and Naccache from power had limited Zionist political options in Lebanon; and by 1946, it appeared that any Zionists still searching for a Lebanese ally could look only to the church. Two weeks after McDonald's meetings, the church came looking for them.

THE ZIONIST-MARONITE TREATY AND THE UNITED NATIONS SPECIAL COMMITTEE ON PALESTINE

In early April 1946, Ya'akov Shimoni, a junior member of the Political Department, received word that Tewfik Attieh of Beirut was in Tel Aviv with extremely important information for the department. Attieh's brother figured prominently in Beirut's Jewish community. According to Shimoni's report, Attieh claimed to approach the Jewish Agency on behalf of "important and responsible" Maronite friends preparing to act against the pan-Arab and Muslim elements prevailing in Lebanon.[99] Attieh insisted that his Maronite friends wanted to ally with the Zionists and promised to reveal his contacts' identities and plans once the Jewish Agency committed itself, in principle, to a partnership. He hinted, however, that the Maronites might want Zionist support for Maronite newspapers and assistance in training the Phalange paramilitary corps. Shimoni brought the matter to the attention of Bernard Joseph, now acting director of the department, noting that the Agency's latest information confirmed Attieh's description of increasing Maronite agitation over Muslim gains.

Intrigued by Attieh's message, Joseph turned to David HaCohen (whose Solel Boneh firm enjoyed extensive connections in Lebanon) with the department's "pressing need to send someone . . . to Lebanon" and asked that he use his contacts there to obtain a visa for Shimoni.[100] Although HaCohen agreed, he advised against entrusting a junior official with no previous experience in Lebanon for such an important mission. HaCohen's sources reported Tewfik Attieh's displeasure that his Agency contact in Tel Aviv had been the young, unknown Shimoni.[101] Joseph wrote immediately to Amos Landman, another Palestinian Jew well connected in Beirut and Attieh's initial intermediary with the Agency, defending Shimoni and requesting Landman's assistance in nurturing Attieh's initiative. He asked that Landman prepare a detailed report of everything he knew about Attieh's mission. Another one of Landman's tasks was to encourage Attieh to return for a second meeting, bringing with him this time some of his Maronite friends. Most startling, however, is the final part of Joseph's letter:

> In conclusion, I want to inform you—and through you, Mr. Attieh—that in the meantime Mr. Joseph Awad has visited us, a cousin of the patriarch and the nephew of Sheikh Tewfik Awad . . . and he brought similar proposals [to those of Attieh]. It is desirable that Attieh meet with him in Beirut and they exchange opinions between them and help each other.[102]

It would appear, as Joseph evidently believed, that two separate Maronite cliques simultaneously decided that their desperate situation left them no choice but to seek Zionist assistance in bringing their own people to power.

Shimoni surmised that Attieh's "friends" were either in church circles or the government.[103] It is possible, however, that Attieh's initiative originated within the Phalange. Arida, Mubarak, or Eddé would not need to employ an unfamiliar intermediary like Attieh, since each had his own direct connections with the Political Department. As a leader of the Beirut Jewish community, Attieh's brother would have been more likely to have friends within the Phalange than in the church or Eddé's group; and the irregular contact between the Phalange and the Agency made the Beirut Jews a logical conduit had Gemayel wanted to reach the Political Department. Attieh's early hint to Shimoni that his friends might be interested in putting Zionist expertise at the disposal of the Phalange (perhaps drawing on the experiences of the Haganah) also implicates the Phalange. Despite the earlier argument that the Phalange threw in its lot with the popular anti-Zionist movement, in the fickle environment of Lebanese politics, it would not have been unusual or imprudent for the Phalange to explore the Zionist option even while espousing the anti-Zionist line.

For his part, Awad insinuated that his contacts were in the highest echelons of the patriarchate.[104] The fact that Attieh bowed out, once alerted to the patriarch's overture to the Agency, further supports the Phalange thesis. The point has been made that Gemayel respected the preexisting relationships among the Agency, the church, and Eddé; and it would have been characteristic of him to defer to the patriarch. It appears that once again, the Agency's long involvement with one Maronite faction

(Arida) precluded the exploration of ties with another (Gemayel), although there is certainly no assurance that a Zionist-Phalange relationship would ultimately have been any more fruitful.[105] There is no evidence that Attieh and Awad met to coordinate their colleagues' activities, but Attieh disappeared and left Awad and the Agency to pursue the topic of a Maronite-Zionist alliance.

Awad visited Palestine, ostensibly in his role as a journalist, barely a week after Attieh's meeting with Shimoni. According to his escort in the Yishuv, Awad enthused over Zionist achievements and repeatedly remarked upon Lebanon's need to undertake similar agricultural and technological activities with Zionist aid. Sasson arranged for the visitor to meet privately with Joseph, to whom Awad again emphasized the need for mutual Maronite-Zionist assistance. Joseph responded that the Agency appreciated pro-Zionist declarations and was "ready in all ways possible to help the Maronites in achieving their aspirations, but . . . they must show initiative . . . and find the way to strengthen ties with us."[106]

Awad and Sasson discussed options for Maronite-Zionist cooperation in greater detail, finally agreeing that Awad would return to Palestine with a letter from the patriarch authorizing him to represent the church in negotiations, hopefully in the company of his more influential relative Tewfik Awad, a past Lebanese minister and confidant of the patriarch.[107] Tewfik Awad next appeared in Jerusalem with the required proof that Arida had authorized him to enter into negotiations with the Jewish Agency on behalf of the church.[108]

Shimoni, Sasson, and Awad met in Jerusalem and successfully concluded a formal agreement between the Jewish Agency and the Maronite Church on 30 May 1946.[109] This treaty, which finally formalized the long relationship between the Agency and the patriarch, represented the apex of Maronite-Zionist cooperation and was signed by Joseph and Awad for Weizmann and Arida, respectively. The agreement reciprocally recognized Jewish demands for independence in Palestine and the independent Christian character of Lebanon. Vigorous application of the treaty's provisions was predicated on the Zionists' winning statehood and on the church's actually achieving political power in Lebanon. In Article 1, the church pledged its support for free Jewish immigration to Palestine and the Jewish right to establish a sovereign state there. In return, Article 2 constituted a promise by the Jewish Agency to the church that the Zionist movement had no designs on Lebanese territory and no intention of directing Jewish immigrants to Lebanon. Article 3 committed the representatives of both sides, at home and abroad and at international conferences, to oppose decisions that might compromise each other's programs and to try to prevent other parties from thwarting Maronite or Zionist objectives.

Toward the dual goals of strengthening the position of the church and realizing Jewish national aspirations, Article 4 committed the two signatories to cultural, commercial, and intelligence exchanges; joint industrial, agricultural, and tourist ventures; cooperation on security issues; and a coordinated public relations campaign. In addition, the church promised to facilitate the immigration of Jews to Palestine via Lebanon and to consider the treaty an integral feature of its government's policy as soon as it achieved political control of Lebanon. For its part, the Jewish Agency promised to respect the civil and religious rights of non-Jews in the future Jewish state, reserving special treatment for the patriarch's representatives, to include assisting them in buying land and constructing a patriarchate in Jerusalem. The Agency also pledged that its offices abroad would actively promote the church's cause. In a clause clearly aimed at the Arab bands that harassed both Jewish settlements in northern Palestine and Maronite villages in southern Lebanon, where they established their camps, both sides promised to prevent the movement of hostile elements across the border, as well as to interrupt their sources of support. Article 5 stipulated that the parties would deal directly with one another through designated representatives, naming Tewfik Awad as Arida's representative until further notice. Article 6 asserted that the treaty would become operative once signed.

With its implicit vision of a closely bound Christian Lebanon and Jewish Palestine flourishing in the face of Muslim enmity, the treaty embraced all the major assumptions of the minority alliance thesis. Its architects clearly assumed a natural harmony of political, economic, and cultural interests between Maronites and Jews and shared a common defensiveness about their respective aspirations. The clearest expression of minority alliance thinking is the belief that Christian Lebanon and Jewish Palestine could secure their positions by closing ranks against the Muslim majority in the region, instead of seeking accommodation with it. In fact, the treaty's idyllic new regional order magically reduced its Muslim Arab opponents to nameless actors likely to take "decisions or actions" contrary to Maronite and Zionist interests or "hostile elements" whose machinations could be defused by a coordinated Maronite-Zionist response. In facing its enemies and striving to fulfill its national goals, neither side could have asked for a more supportive, agreeable ally. It was, in Shimoni's words, a "splendid treaty," albeit uncharacteristic of Sasson's approach.[110]

A formal mechanism was now in place legitimizing Maronite requests for Agency assistance in financing political projects and publications. Consistent with the long history of joint Maronite-Zionist endeavors, however, the church insisted that the treaty be kept secret; and the stipulation that this "strictly confidential" accord not be made public was incorporated in identical reciprocal letters accompanying the agreement.[111] This secrecy clause denied the Agency the main benefit a Zionist-Maronite accord could offer, namely, public evidence that some Arabs could accept the creation of a Jewish state in Palestine.

Nevertheless, archival documents suggest that several attempts were made to act in the spirit of the accord. Mysterious coded correspondence between Joseph and Awad and Joseph and "Wadia" suggest that the department funneled monthly stipends to "Mother" in Beirut and clearly indicate continuing close contact between the two sides.[112] The exchange with Awad appears to be the establishment of a code whereby Joseph could summon him to Jerusalem. Wadia complained of insufficient funds, which did not arrive to "Mother" quickly enough; Joseph replied that he was unable to increase the amount or advance a loan and was not responsible for the delay. Both men refer to Wadia's visits to Jerusalem, and Joseph comments on the return of one of his people from Beirut. There is no proof as to "Mother's" identity. However, Sasson allegedly promised Joseph Awad that regardless of the outcome of Maronite-Zionist negotiations, the Agency would "give support to his newspaper *Saut al-Ahrar*, anyway."[113]

Also in line with the provisions of the treaty, Sasson cabled Shertok in Washington in April 1947 about discussions with the Maronites concerning Zionist funding for a new Lebanese office in the United States. This office, presumably patterned after the Jewish Agency's own political office in the American capital, was undoubtedly conceived of as an alternative Lebanese voice to that of the Khoury administration's official representation. Sasson informed Shertok that the Agency would pay to maintain the office, although he believed that after a few months, Lebanese American contributions would fully sustain it. In return, the new Lebanese office would "act according to our instructions."[114] According to Epstein, then representing the Agency in Washington, plans foundered on the low priority accorded the project by the Maronites despite Zionist willingness to fund the venture.[115]

In June 1947, Arida and Ben-Gurion exchanged letters reasserting their mutual respect for each other and their respective peoples. Ben-Gurion thanked the patriarch for his efforts to "maintain our reciprocal friendly relations" and assured Arida of the Agency's intentions "to collaborate with the great Maronite community in the spirit of the accord concluded [between us]."[116] The most concerted attempt to force the Maronite hand, however, was that of Avraham Lutzky, a department staff member who used his work as a journalist as his cover.

Lutzky visited Arida in July 1947 and spent several hours with him and his chief assistants. His primary question for the patriarch concerned the latter's plans for "protecting Christian Lebanon and implementing the treaty between us," to which Arida replied that he would personally see to both issues.[117] Although Lutzky confirmed that the patriarch "knows fully the text of the treaty that Sheikh Tewfik signed," his report of the meeting clearly reflects Zionist impatience with the inoperative nature of the accord and relentless efforts on his part to push Arida to action. He could not convince the patriarch to back an openly pro-Zionist party in Lebanon; but on the topic of the struggling Lebanese office in the United States he was more successful. He insisted that the demands of a modern propaganda campaign required something more sophisticated than the occasional visit of a Lebanese priest and persuaded Arida to give the task to a Maronite intellectual more familiar with America. Lutzky pressed him to act immediately and stood over his shoulder as he penned a note to Mokarzel at *al-Hoda*, persuading him to designate the Jewish Agency by name as a source of guidance and material support.[118]

Arida claimed that all the bishops approved of his ties with the Jewish Agency; but in Lutzky's opinion, the bishops felt obliged to support the patriarch's policies regardless of their own opinions. He worried that Arida's assistant, Pierre Awad, was particularly unfriendly to Zionism and recounted at length his own successful antics in thwarting Awad's efforts to undo the positive results of his conversation with Arida. By the time he left, Lutzky also had in his possession a souvenir picture of the patriarch and a copy of a second letter lamenting the continuation of the anti-Zionist boycott, which he had persuaded Arida to write to Mount Lebanon's representative in parliament.[119]

In February 1947, Britain had turned the Palestine problem over to the United Nations, which designated an eleven-nation investigative board to research the conflict and suggest a solution. The United Nations Special Committee on Palestine (UNSCOP) retraced the footsteps of the previous year's Anglo-American Committee of Inquiry. Although the Maronite-Zionist treaty had been signed in the interim, nothing changed when the new committee reached Beirut: official Lebanese testimony proved uniformly anti-Zionist, Eddé and Arida presented pro-Zionist testimony only secretly, and Mubarak alone spoke out unequivocally in favor of the establishment of a Jewish state in Palestine.

Maronites Camille Chamoun, chief Lebanese delegate to the United Nations, and Hamid Franjieh, Lebanon's foreign minister, took the lead in expressing the pro-Palestinian Arab, anti-Zionist perspective when UNSCOP met with the official Arab League delegation in Beirut.[120] Unofficially, several UNSCOP delegates met with members of Eddé's primarily Maronite National Bloc. The National Bloc group described Khoury's recent reelection as fraudulent and charged that the majority of Lebanese accepted Lebanon's Christian, Western heritage and deplored Lebanon's membership in the Arab League. Several people spoke out in favor of the establishment in Palestine of a Jewish state, warning that "it is wrong to think of all this area as uniformly Moslem and Arab."[121] Eddé himself proved reticent. Lutzky claimed to have briefed Eddé prior to the committee's arrival and to have extracted from him a promise that he would speak frankly in support of the creation of a Jewish state. Secluded in an adjoining room, however, Lutzky reported that

> several minutes before the guests arrived, and with the arrival of the [National Bloc's] Muslim member, [Eddé] was stricken with terrible fear and informed me . . . that the appearance of the latter made frankness difficult . . . and that he would be forced to speak diplomatically in the beginning and only privately could he give his true opinion.[122]

According to Lutzky's report, once the meeting began and when asked for his solution to the Palestine problem, Eddé requested more time to study the issue while his colleagues readily called for the partition of Palestine into Jewish and Arab states. Even the Muslim member of the National Bloc, whose presence had so unnerved Eddé, agreed that "there is nothing to research; partition is necessary."[123] Concerned about the security of his position within his own party, Eddé had quickly rebuffed an earlier suggestion by Lutzky that he negotiate a treaty between the National Bloc and the Jewish Agency along the lines of the Agency's accord with the church and now hesitated to speak out even in this closed forum.[124] Jorge Garcia Granados, the Guatemalan UNSCOP delegate, recorded that Eddé did draw him aside later in order to express his "very warm" feelings toward a Jewish state, although by then, the committee members already understood that support existed for Jewish sovereignty in Palestine within the Lebanese opposition, particularly among the Christians.[125]

Two UNSCOP delegates visited Arida the next day; and although he and his attending bishops spoke of the need create a Jewish state by partitioning Palestine, Lutzky lamented the fact that the patriarch did not seem to make a very forceful impression upon his guests.[126] The secrecy surrounding Arida's pro-partition testimony is evident in Maronite historian Matti Moosa's own confusion over what he calls a "startling statement" by Lebanese writer Anis Sayigh to the effect that Arida demanded the creation of a Zionist state in Palestine when UNSCOP visited Beirut.[127]

Despite the long relationship with Eddé and the treaty with Arida, the Zionists discovered, once again, that only Mubarak would publicly support the creation of a Jewish state. Epstein reported that the "ruling clique [had succeeded in] forcing Msgr. Mubarak to leave the Lebanon, at least temporarily."[128] Unwilling to be muffled, Mubarak expressed his opinions from abroad in a letter to UNSCOP that constituted his most passionate and explicit demand ever for the establishment of a Jewish state in Palestine. Denying any Arab claims to Palestine, contrasting the enlightened Jews (and Christians) with the "backward and unprogressive" Muslim Arabs, and citing the need for cooperative minority havens in the Middle East,

Mubarak closed his missive with the capitalized assertion, "THE LEBANON DEMANDS FREEDOM FOR THE JEWS IN PALESTINE — AS IT DESIRES ITS OWN FREEDOM AND INDEPENDENCE."[129]

A storm of protest erupted throughout Lebanon when *al-Diyar* published the letter. According to Agency Intelligence, Camille Chamoun had procured a copy of the letter and turned it over to the government, which appealed to Mubarak personally and then to the Vatican to pressure him into withdrawing his statement. Failing that, the government released the letter to the press.[130] Mubarak's letter struck Lebanon "like a bomb," igniting demonstrations and eliciting calls for everything from his arrest to his deportation.[131] Panicky Maronite deputies in the Lebanese parliament led the attack, introducing a resolution denouncing his narrow vision of a Christian Lebanon, rejecting the partition of Palestine and the establishment of a Jewish state, and emphasizing that Mubarak spoke only for himself and not for the Maronite community.[132] Nevertheless, Mubarak's small band of extremist followers spurned the call for a general strike and exhorted the other minorities to keep their shops open, as well. Ironically, the strike day coincided with the Jewish festival of Sukkot; and Beirut's Jewish community found itself shuttering its businesses along with Mubarak's detractors.[133] Despite overwhelming condemnation, Mubarak stood by his statement in its entirety.

After years of private assurances and public demurrals, Arida's reaction surely did not surprise the Agency. Initial reports suggested that the patriarch condemned Mubarak, withheld funds from the Beirut diocese, and voiced his opposition to partition and the creation of a Jewish state.[134] In an interview in *al-Hayat* Arida adopted a neutral tone, repeating his belief that Lebanon should strive for friendly relations with all its neighbors and refrain from taking sides in others' affairs, including those of Palestine.[135] Lutzky reported, however, that the Beirut papers published a statement by Arida emphasizing that Mubarak had written the UNSCOP letter in his name alone and not that of the patriarch or the Maronite community.[136] Some scholars contend that as a result of this episode, Mubarak was reprimanded by the patriarch, relieved of his duties, and exiled to a monastery, while others credit his increasingly threatening opposition to the Khoury government with causing his fall from grace.[137] Only three weeks after writing his letter to UNSCOP, Mubarak called publicly for a civil insurrection against Khoury's "tyrannical government" and allegedly approached Lutzky to ask for Agency funds and assistance in overthrowing the government.[138] Regardless of the catalyst, with Mubarak gone the Jewish Agency lost its most vocal supporter in Lebanon.

In distancing himself from Mubarak's openly pro-Zionist position, Arida prefigured the demise of the Zionist-Maronite treaty. A quarrel between Arida and Tewfik Awad in January of 1948 deteriorated into a slanderous campaign. Although the controversy did not involve the Jews, in his effort to defame the patriarch, Awad publicly accused Arida of having sent him to negotiate a treaty with the Jewish Agency. In response, the patriarch immediately accused Awad of libel and denied the charge of having any dealings with the Zionists.[139] The exchange apparently remained within a small circle at the patriarchal seat, because there is no evidence of its causing the type of public outcry one would imagine. Nevertheless, Arida never again approached the Agency either to activate the accord or to confirm his commitment to it privately. Over a decade in the making, the treaty quickly became but a secret, dormant testimony to the vision of a shared Zionist-Maronite destiny.

In the wake of the Mubarak affair, even those allies which had privately voiced pro-Zionist opinions fell silent. The angry response from most Maronite quarters to Mubarak's letter to UNSCOP challenged the Zionist notion of a friendly, Christian Lebanon, as did subsequent Lebanese contributions to the Arab campaign to thwart the partition of Palestine and the creation of a Jewish state. Haddad credits Lebanon's UN representative, the Greek Orthodox Charles Malik, with serving as the "unofficial annunciator in the West of Arab opposition to the creation of the state of Israel."[140] Malik portrayed Lebanon as a leading force in the Arab League, while Camille Chamoun, a Maronite, worked with delegates from the other Arab states to try and block passage of the partition resolution. Nevertheless, on 29 November 1947 the required two-thirds majority of the United Nations General Assembly approved the partition of Palestine and the establishment of a Jewish state, with a reluctant France deciding to vote in favor only at the last moment.[141] Charles Hélou, another Maronite and Lebanon's ambassador to the Vatican, was instrumental in persuading the pope to withhold diplomatic recognition from the new state of Israel.[142]

In the face of this Lebanese enmity, Weizmann recalled Mubarak's unfailing support and sent him greetings on the occasion of the United Nations vote, expressing an eagerness for neighborly relations with "our friends in the Lebanon, of whom you are so distinguished a representative."[143] Among the Zionists' other faithful supporters, Corm and Naccache had already died; but Mubarak, Arida, and Eddé lived to see Israeli independence. Epstein learned from a mutual friend that only the lack of peaceful relations between the Jewish state and his own tempered Eddé's delight at the Zionists' success.[144] Israel came into being without the assistance of its Lebanese allies and in spite of the efforts of its Lebanese foes.

CONCLUSION

World War II and its aftermath dictated the pre-state Zionist relationship with Lebanon in its final decade. Zionist influence in Lebanon waned continually throughout the forties, as did the potential for a Maronite-Zionist alliance. Under Vichy, British, and then nationalist pressure, pro-Zionist leaders in both political and religious circles in Lebanon lost much, if not all, of their authority. The deterioration of the relationship between the president and patriarch reflected the downward spiral of Zionist fortunes in Lebanon. In Eddé and Arida the Agency enjoyed a pro-Zionist alliance between the highest echelons of the political and religious establishments. The conflict between Naccache and Arida, both Agency friends, shattered this political-religious symbiosis and weakened the overall strength of pro-Zionist forces in Lebanon. Under Bishara al-Khoury's guidance, Lebanon proceeded steadily along a course of Christian-Muslim rapprochement, earning the president Arida's unbridled enmity and terminating Zionist political options in Lebanon.[145]

The Agency's friends did not accept their defeat quietly. They and their Zionist supporters offered wild proposals for returning pro-Zionist Maronites and the Maronite community to positions of predominance. Their hysterical plans never commanded a significant base of support or engendered serious debate. Anyone desperate enough to come up with such ideas was already in too desperate a situation to follow through with them. Only Epstein had the potential resources and credibility to promote joint Zionist-Maronite interests. Although he could not advance his minority-defense-league idea on his own, he used his connections to assist the Maronite opposition in its American campaign. In America, apathy kept the pro-Zionist Maronite opposition from effectively expressing its views; in Lebanon, fear served the same purpose. Pro-Zionist testimony before the Anglo-American and United Nations committees in Beirut was secretive and weak.

With the political option closed, the church emerged as the only Lebanese actor with the inclination and ability to try and salvage Christian privilege in Lebanon through an alliance with the Yishuv and access to Zionist resources. Although a formal accord was finally committed to paper, it proved ultimately no more effective than any of the failed alliance attempts that preceded it. The "splendid treaty," predicated on the unlikely scenario of the church's imposing its political will on Lebanon's many factions and the (also uncertain) prospect of the establishment of a Jewish state, was doomed to failure. By ignoring the numbers and influence of anti-Zionist Muslim and Christian Arab nationalists, the church envisioned a "Christian Lebanon" that did not truly exist. The Zionist side proved equally eager to engage in wishful thinking, deluding itself that it could win security for a Jewish state by negotiating around the Palestinian Arabs, with whom it was locked in an apparently intractable conflict.

The treaty with Arida constituted a logical step in the continuing relationship between the two sides, particularly since the idea of a special

Jewish-Maronite partnership had long been ingrained in Zionist thinking. Of dubious political advantage to its signatories, the treaty is nonetheless invaluable as an explicit expression of the minority alliance thesis. In many ways, the treaty epitomized the strengths and weaknesses of the Zionist-Maronite relationship. It was easily and quickly negotiated because Zionists and Maronites of Arida's political persuasion did share common interests. In practical terms of Zionist relations with the Lebanese polity, however, it was useless. The Lebanese signatories represented only one segment of the Maronite community, itself but one of many Lebanese factions. At the height of its power, the church had no authority to commit Lebanon to a political agreement but did wield political influence; the church that signed the treaty, however, allied with the Zionists out of weakness, not strength. The desperate situation that finally propelled Arida into a formal alliance guaranteed that he would be an ineffective ally. In denying Tewfik Awad's revelation of the treaty's existence, Arida appears to have confirmed the suspicions of those Zionists who never believed in a minority alliance: in the end, no Maronite would dare risk rupturing Lebanon's fragile Christian-Muslim relationship by openly pursuing a pro-Zionist policy.

Mubarak's experiences reconfirm this theory. Condemned and ridiculed, he suffered for his repeated pro-Zionist proclamations, possibly losing his parish as a result. Unlike an appointed church leader, a politician dependent upon wide public support would have lost his position immediately for espousing Mubarak's views. The consolidation of Greater Lebanon meant that Maronite politicians had to try to develop Muslim constituencies. This, of course, accounts in part for Eddé's refusal to act on his personal pro-Zionist proclivities.

Mubarak's activities also demonstrate the impotence of the 1946 treaty. Despite negotiating the pact with the Agency in the interim, Arida proved no bolder in his pro-Zionist testimony before UNSCOP than he had been a year earlier before the Anglo-American committee. Only Mubarak, who had no hand in the treaty, spoke out forcefully in favor of a Jewish state.[146] With Arida the Agency had a reticent ally and a treaty; with Mubarak the Agency had no treaty but an outspoken ally. Both, however, were ultimately ineffective. Mubarak battled on alone, slowly stripped of any influence that might have furthered Maronite-Zionist interests, and the extensive cooperation outlined in Arida's treaty was never realized. The treaty of 1946 remains important, however, as testimony to that tempting perception of Lebanon that figured so prominently in the early Zionist imagination: the vision of a natural harmony of interests between the minority Jewish and Christian communities in the Muslim Middle East and the interlocking of their destinies.

~ 6 ~

CONCLUSION

THE SUCCESSFUL CONCLUSION of a formal Zionist-Maronite treaty and the absolute failure of that treaty to produce a meaningful political alliance succinctly reflect the history of pre-state Zionist interests in Lebanon and the results of the minority alliance approach. Although pursuit of that policy proved unproductive, a study of Zionist efforts to make it work produces useful information about the bureaucratic process of decision making and how (mis)perceptions, once introduced into the policy-making system, persist. More specifically, an analysis of the course of Zionist involvement with Lebanon and the Maronites in the pre-state era reveals a great deal about the Zionists' vision of the Middle East and the future they perceived for a Jewish state. Early Zionist thoughts about the integration of a Jewish political entity into the Muslim Middle East are still relevant, since that process has yet to be completed satisfactorily. An analysis of the minority alliance program is particularly important if this notion retains any influence in Israeli thinking about Lebanon, especially because it proved unsuccessful.

Zionists involved with the treaty's genesis contend that while the achievement of an official friendship pact pleased them, its uselessness did not surprise them and, for that reason, did not disturb the normal flow of policymaking. By 1946, they say, the Agency had learned not to anticipate great dividends from its dealings with the Maronites. One would think, however, that the repeated Maronite inability to provide practical political assistance over the years would have taught the Political Department this

147

lesson much sooner. The failure to act upon the plan to resettle German Jews in Lebanon, to consummate the numerous proposals for both apolitical and political associations, and to effect a coordinated campaign before the Peel Commission, all of which occurred a decade before the pact with Arida, come immediately to mind. A thorough examination of pre-state Zionist policy toward Lebanon, particularly as concerns the minority alliance idea, begs the question: Why was a policy that should have been seen as misguided, surely by the late 1930s, not discredited and discarded at that time?

This study pulls together incidents in Zionist policy toward Lebanon to create a seamless flow of events. In analyzing that policy, however, one should remember that the Jewish Agency never enjoyed the luxury of examining a linear summary of its efforts in Lebanon as a whole. Time elapsed between letters exchanged with its Lebanese contacts, between proposals, and between attempted operations. In the interim, the Agency grappled with far more serious conditions posed by Palestinian Arab resistance and British obstacles to the realization of Zionist aspirations in Palestine. Even in the arena of Zionist interests in the larger Arab world, Lebanon often lost out to countries, such as Syria, that were seen as more important and more threatening.[1] In the hierarchy of pre-state Zionist priorities, relatively friendly Lebanon held only minor significance, commanding the most attention during the period of Hajj Amin's activity there.

The ad hoc nature of the Political Department's decision-making process combined with the Zionists' pressing British and Palestinian problems to work against a coherent, carefully determined policy toward Lebanon. In the intervals between activity with its Maronite friends in Lebanon, the department pursued operations elsewhere, generally encountering more hostile interlocutors. Each new plan for Zionist-Maronite cooperation must have appeared as a welcome relief and a fresh possibility worth exploring. The repeated failures of the Maronites to translate their kind words into deeds did not have as negative an effect on Zionist perspectives over time as one might have expected for several reasons. For one thing, the harried, understaffed, underbudgeted, and overworked Political Department did not have a specific Lebanon policy to effect (whose failure after a few years would have been obvious) but, rather, responded to overtures and possibilities as they arose. It never undertook the careful retrospective analysis that would have highlighted the pattern of Maronite initiative and interest but ultimately inaction that marked Zionist efforts to coordinate activity. Also, tiny successes here and there obscured the overall failure of the Zionist-Maronite relationship to bear fruit. The cumulative effect of years of ongoing negotiations and the movement from early wild alliance proposals to draft treaties and ultimately a formal accord created the illusion of progress. When one considers the difficulties the Agency encountered in its dealings with the rest of the other Arab countries, it is not surprising that it did not judge the actual value of its Lebanese policy more harshly.

It is also necessary to ask what the department realistically expected of its activities in Lebanon before determining whether they succeeded or failed. With respect to intelligence gathering and making contact with a variety of Arab circles, for instance, the department could certainly chalk up significant successes. But were the terms of the 1946 treaty widely known, and did the Zionists really anticipate that a tangible political alliance would become operative? Ya'akov Shimoni, who participated in the drafting of the treaty, contends that Weizmann, Ben-Gurion, Shertok, and the members of the executive knew of the treaty and agreed with the basic tenet that if a possibility existed for allying with Lebanon, or even just the Maronite church, the Jewish Agency should respond positively.[2] This was, after all, a logical outcome to more than a decade's worth of meetings and negotiations with both Eddé and Arida. Shimoni insists, however, that while a formal alliance and the prospect of potential political benefit pleased the department, continuing Zionist policy toward Lebanon did not depend on the treaty. In light of the hostility facing the Jewish Agency elsewhere, it would have as foolish to rebuff the patriarch's overture as to predicate continuing activities in Lebanon on the basis of that alliance. According to Shimoni, the department wisely concluded the best possible accord with Arida and then carried on as if the treaty did not exist.

The 1936–39 Arab uprising in Palestine convinced the Jewish Agency of the futility of attempting to reach an accommodation with the Palestinian Arabs and led the Political Department to focus its attentions on the surrounding Arab countries, instead. The ex-mufti's success in turning Beirut into a Palestinian stronghold and southern Lebanon into a staging ground for attacks against the Yishuv obviously brought Lebanon to the fore. The Maronite option became all the more appealing in light of the Zionist interest in finding an ally behind the mufti's Lebanese lines and once the intractable nature of the Arab-Jewish conflict over Palestine confirmed the Zionist impetus to circumvent the Palestinians by reaching an agreement with other Arabs. The likelihood of actually consummating an effective Zionist-Maronite alliance probably appeared no less than that of reaching a modus vivendi with the Palestinian Arabs, and the former constituted a much more pleasant effort.

Willingness to cut a separate deal with the Maronites was consistent with the general Zionist effort to negotiate agreements with non-Palestinian Arab leaders in the years immediately preceding the 1948 war, as evidenced by parallel understandings reached by the Jewish Agency with the prime minister of Egypt, Ismail Sidqi, and the king of Transjordan,

Abdullah.[3] Efforts to formalize a Druze-Zionist alliance perhaps most mirror the experience with the Maronites. Both the Druze and the Maronites constituted non-state minority communities in the Middle East, with whom the Agency maintained decades-long relationships of intermittent intensity. In both cases, the department could point to some small successes in managing isolated events to the Zionist advantage; but ultimately the payoffs proved meager when compared with the Zionist expenditure of energy and capital in nurturing the relationships and in light of the Zionists' need for useful political alliances in the region. In the spring of 1946, at the same time the department and the Maronite Church were negotiating their treaty, the department made a similar effort to come to a formal agreement with the Palestinian Druze.[4] In the last years of the mandate, Zionist diplomacy in the Arab world was the unhappy midwife of the abortive attempt to conclude a Druze-Zionist alliance, the stillborn Maronite-Zionist treaty, and the short-lived agreements with Sidqi and Abdullah.

The pan-Arabization of the Palestine conflict emerged as one of the most important results of the disturbances in Palestine. As the Arab states increasingly involved themselves in the issue of Arab Palestine, the Zionist movement adopted an increasingly hostile attitude toward pan-Arabism. Ian Black contends that in their effort to discredit pan-Arabism, Zionists got caught up in an absolutist dichotomy between their movement and their opponents'. For them, the battle became a black-and-white struggle between what they saw as the destructive forces of pan-Arabism and those of progressive Zionism.[5] Black argues that, seeing no legitimate or redeeming quality in pan-Arabism, Zionists underestimated the importance of the Palestine issue throughout the Arab world. It is true that Zionist strategists proved persistently unable to appreciate the strength of Arab nationalism and Arab solidarity. Familiar with Arab rivalries, Zionists tended to see pan-Arabism, and Palestinian Arab nationalism as well, as corrupt, temporary, political tools used by Arab leaders for their own purposes. Exaggerating the weaknesses and underestimating the strengths of pan-Arabism and Arab nationalism, Zionist policymakers deluded themselves as to the likelihood of finding an Arab partner prepared to take a pro-Zionist position apart from the rest of the Muslim Arab world. In the case of Lebanon, in particular, the general consensus held that anti-Zionism did not reflect a genuinely hostile attitude toward the Yishuv on the part of the Lebanese but, rather, the temporary effect of Palestinian Arab propaganda and intimidation. It followed that effective Zionist counterpropaganda and the eventual end of the disturbances in Palestine would permit the natural Lebanese and Maronite receptivity toward a cooperative relationship with the Yishuv to reassert itself.

Eddé and Arida understood better than their contacts at the Jewish

Agency the depth of Arab solidarity, although they persisted in believing that at some future point they could hold power so firmly as to withstand Muslim-Arab fury at a pro-Zionist policy. In the meantime, however, they were not above trying to harness Zionist resources and influence for their own benefit. The Maronites were more successful in their quest for quiet material and diplomatic assistance from the relationship, while the Zionists were generally frustrated in their attempts to attain open declarations of support for the creation of a Jewish state. The Maronites' insistence that joint ventures remain secret probably saved their lives even while it nullified the political benefit of those ventures. Public knowledge of the 1946 treaty, for instance, would have cost the Maronite Church its remaining legitimacy as a political force in Lebanese politics, and might very well have led to an all-out Muslim/Arab assault on the Maronite principals.

Glenn E. Perry discusses the fact that although pragmatic politics alone suggest that the Arab states should find a strong Israel a desirable ally in their conflicts among themselves ("My enemy's enemy"), popular anti-Israel attitudes inhibit regimes from entering into an Israeli alliance and make them reluctant to risk the appearance of being openly supported by Israel even in moments of desperation.[6] Perry notes that even the Maronites, who generally do not share the ardent anti-Zionist attitudes of other Arabs and Muslims, have been constrained by broader regional considerations. Although he is primarily discussing the post-state period of Israeli involvement in inter-Arab politics, Perry's comments hold true for the pre-state era, as well. Despite repeated Maronite demands for secrecy and public Maronite disavowals of pro-Zionist sentiments expressed privately, most Zionist policymakers did not appreciate the extent to which their movement had become a regional pariah by the eve of Israeli statehood.

Perhaps the freedom with which Zionist representatives moved through the Middle East conferring with leading Arabs of all political persuasions obscured this unhappy development. Pursuit of the Zionist dream initially demanded a significant degree of single-mindedness and idealism at times when an objective review of the obstacles to Jewish sovereignty suggested that this was an unrealistic goal. By disregarding those factors which indicated they were doomed to fail, the Zionists succeeded. This strategy did not yield similarly positive results regarding the Zionist-Maronite alliance. By downplaying the obstacles facing the pro-Zionist Maronites, the department kept alive an idea that should have been laid to rest long before. In the early thirties, Zionists, particularly Ben-Gurion, discussed with Arab leaders creative solutions by which an autonomous Jewish national home would participate in a regional federation of Arab states. By the early forties, the Arab world had adopted a pro-Palestinian Arab stance, which ensured that a Jewish state would stand against its Arab neighbors, not among them. The Zionist goal of encouraging significant

Arab factions to support the creation of a Jewish state foundered on the successful pan-Arabization of the Palestine conflict, which even fervent Maronite anti-pan-Arabists could not overcome.

Were the Zionists deluded in their whole approach to Lebanon? Why did interest in doing business with the Maronites persist long after the Maronites had repeatedly proven themselves unreliable allies? Part of the responsibility lies with Eliahu Epstein and others like him, whose objectivity suffered due to their personal affinity for their Maronite friends. Having come to share Eddé's and Arida's outlook on the Lebanese situation, Epstein overestimated the strength of the Maronite opposition to Khoury and of general Maronite resistance to the "Arabization" of Lebanon.

Although the department did not base its perception of Lebanon on Epstein's reports alone, its reliance on that narrow Maronite clique represented by Eddé and Arida contributed to this same misjudgment of the relative strength of the various Lebanese groups vying for power. Treading cautiously among Lebanon's many factions, the Jewish Agency confined its serious relations to one particular group. Although it maintained irregular contact with other Maronite (and non-Christian) parties, the Agency reserved its primary intercourse with Lebanon for those Maronites who shared Eddé's and Arida's orientation. It is clear from Agency and department documents that Zionists spoke of "Maronite" support and encouragement when they actually meant that Maronite *faction* which espoused a pro-Zionist view. Was this merely verbal shorthand? Or did it reflect the misperception that significant sectors of the large and powerful Maronite community as a whole, not merely one small faction of dubious influence, saw Zionism as an ally against a Muslim enemy?

Gideon Raphael, who served the Jewish Agency in various capacities during the pre-state period, asserts that Ben-Gurion, for instance, rarely distinguished among Maronite factions or between Maronites and the many other Christian denominations in Lebanon and persisted in lumping all "Christians" together in "Christian" Lebanon.[7] Interpreted as "Lebanese Christian," a "Maronite" alliance would have seemed truly significant for the Yishuv; and evidence suggests that Ben-Gurion, to the extent he considered the idea, did find it appealing. He had indicated as much in 1937; and three times in his 1948 war diaries he recorded his belief that the emergence of a strong Christian state in Lebanon allied with Israel would be a logical and positive outcome of the war.[8] Preoccupied with more pressing problems, however, Ben-Gurion never seriously pushed the Maronite option and never ordered the more sophisticated investigation which would have revealed the divisions within the Christian and Maronite communities.

Eddé's and Arida's close relations with the Jewish Agency meant that their extremist, anti-Muslim position received a hearing disproportionate to its influence among competing Lebanese and even Maronite doctrines. Although Shertok and Sasson recognized that their contacts did not speak for all Maronites, that the Maronites did not represent all Lebanese Christians, and that Lebanon's Christians were losing predominance, the department found it hard to resist the inclination to pursue the friendly relationship offered by the Maronite ultranationalists while its overtures elsewhere were coming to naught. The consequences of the Zionists' exclusive ties with that particular Maronite faction manifested themselves when Eddé fell from power and the Agency found itself cut off from Lebanese political circles and left with only the church as a potential ally.

It was a curious feature of Lebanese life that apparently powerful individuals occupying some of the highest positions in the political, religious, and private sectors actually commanded very small followings and limited influence. At that time, could the Jewish Agency really discern that two presidents of the republic, the Maronite patriarch, the archbishop of Beirut, a leading industrialist, and a prominent poet were actually aberrations, who could not persuade their constituents and colleagues to share their pro-Zionist views? William Haddad dubs the outlook of Eddé, Alfred Naccache, Arida, Mubarak, Albert Naccache, and Corm "Mubarakism," after its most colorful and strident proponent.[9] He argues that "Mubarakism" never found an audience among non-Maronite Christians and claimed only a small following within the Maronite community, citing the outcries that ensued among the Maronites after each of the archbishop's pro-Zionist proclamations. In a secret meeting shortly after Israeli independence, one of Eddé's Maronite rivals, Hamid Franjieh, explained to an Israeli visitor why Lebanese Christians (including most Maronites) did not profess a "Mubarakist" philosophy. Israel must understand the Christians' position in Lebanon, asserted Franjieh:

> Either they declare a holy war against the Muslims, or live in peace with them. . . . The bishop Mubarak and the patriarch [Arida] . . . preach holy war. That is an immature policy forgivable from people who have spent all their lives in monasteries without contact with the real world. The time for holy wars has passed, and although the bishop and the patriarch have religious prestige, we listen to a higher religious authority, and that is his holiness the pope, who counsels restraint and peace with the Muslims. Eddé and his followers clashed [with the Muslims] and that was possible when French bayonets were here to protect them. [But] every Christian . . . businessman recognizes in his daily life his bond with his Muslim neighbors. . . . Bishara al-Khoury and his followers are the only Christian party pursuing a Christian policy, the only one possible: to live in peace with the Muslims and protect the integrity of Lebanon.[10]

The idea of a Zionist-and-Maronite-led alliance of minorities persisted throughout the pre-state period because seemingly influential

Maronite leaders repeatedly proposed it; because Zionists involved with Lebanon came to identify with that Maronite perspective; because the Political Department never established a fixed, alternative policy for Lebanon or effectively scrutinized the overall pattern of its activities there over time; and because circumstances intervened time and again to preclude an actual test of the two sides' ability to commit themselves to a collaborative relationship anathema to most Arabs and Muslims. On those occasions when the Jewish Agency did ask for Maronite assistance and the Maronites refused, the Zionists proved exceptionally understanding as to the domestic and mandatory constraints facing their friends.

Although identified here as "pro-Zionist Maronites," one must realize that for these men, thoroughly immersed in the daily domestic politics of Lebanon, support for Jewish aspirations in Palestine was but a minor element of wide-ranging political platforms focused first and foremost on internal Lebanese rivalries and affairs. A relationship with the Jewish Agency was only one of many means to a larger, Lebanese goal (such as establishing firm Maronite control over Lebanon), not an end in itself. The search for outside resources and assistance in the context of their internal political power struggles propelled Maronites like Eddé and Arida toward a Zionist alliance; the same concern for their standing and legitimacy within the Lebanese body politic inhibited their willingness to pursue a pro-Zionist agenda actively.

Maronites often claimed that French opposition to their participation in joint Maronite-Zionist ventures prevented them from taking steps they truly wanted to take. French objections stemmed from reasonable fears of wholesale rebellion in the Arab and Muslim areas under French control, as well as more exaggerated fears of Zionists as British agents. Files of the Quai d'Orsay and the high commission in Beirut reveal that overwhelmed by crises in French-Maronite, intra-Maronite, Maronite-Muslim, and French-Muslim affairs, the French mandatory authority devoted only a miniscule amount of attention to Maronite-Zionist relations. In fact, although French officials were aware of Maronite sympathies for Zionism and understood the appeal of a minority alliance, the documentary record suggests that they were largely oblivious to most of the Zionist-Maronite activities afoot from time to time. The French archives are remarkable largely for a conspicuous silence regarding Maronite relationships, meetings, and plans with Political Department representatives. It is not surprising that anticipated mandatory protestations coupled with domestic political disincentives caused the Agency's Maronite allies to hide their Zionist connections. Repeated Maronite complaints that active French interference had frustrated joint Maronite-Zionist plans they were otherwise prepared to pursue appear somewhat disingenuous, however, in light of general French ignorance as to specific Maronite-Zionist dealings. Underestimating the strength of anti-Zionism in Lebanon and focusing too closely on the obstacles posed by the French mandatory authorities, many in the Political Department let themselves believe that an independent Lebanon ruled by their Maronite contacts would finally join forces with the Yishuv.

Zionist policy toward Lebanon also suffered from a series of gaps: between theory and practice, between the larger Jewish Agency Executive and the Political Department, between Zionist observers in the field and the decisionmakers in Jerusalem, and between the Maronite elite and masses. Theoretically, pragmatic politics almost dictated a Zionist-Maronite alliance; but in practice, popular Arab anti-Zionism restrained the Maronites in their dealings with the Agency. By and large, Zionists who most favored a pro-minority policy were those agents most narrowly involved with Lebanon, not policymakers. On the small Lebanese stage, players such as Arida, Mubarak, and Eddé loomed large; and their value as allies appeared inflated. For those concerned with the broader drama of the Zionist struggle within Palestine and with the Arab world without, the Christians constituted only minor characters. The persistence of the alliance-of-minorities option surely benefited from the fact that the Political Department carried out its activities "almost totally without prior consultation with the Jewish Agency Executive, to which it was, at least formally, responsible."[11] Finally, the department did not pay sufficient attention to those field reports which did note a discrepancy between the clear pro-Zionism of the Francophile, Maronite elite, with whom the department conducted most of its business, and the more ambiguous, sometimes anti-Semitic tendencies of the common Maronite people. A thoughtful analysis of this phenomenon would have forced the Zionists to ask themselves how far the Maronite leadership could go in committing itself to an alliance unpopular with much of its constituency.

Perhaps if Maronites and Zionists had crossed paths at a different time, they could have effected a more productive relationship. Although observers at the time might not have been able to discern it, the Zionist star was rising and the Maronite star sinking throughout the period of the Zionist-Maronite romance. Immigration swelled Jewish numbers in Palestine; land purchasing proceeded unabated; and Kenneth Stein contends that by 1939, "the question really was not if a Jewish state was to come into being; rather the question was when."[12] In contrast, the Muslim population overtook the Christian population in Lebanon; extremist Maronite nationalists lost out to their more conciliatory brethren; and the Maronites as a whole lost a large measure of their political supremacy. Reflecting upon the 1937 Weizmann-Eddé meeting at which the Lebanese head of state toasted the Zionist leader, Epstein (Elath) pointed out, "Weizmann became president, as Eddé foresaw, but Eddé disappeared."[13] The concept of

"Christian Lebanon," not entirely irrelevant in the twenties and early thirties, became but a figment of Zionist and Maronite imaginations by the
time the National Pact of 1943 formally initiated the "Arabization" of
Lebanon.

Not entirely unaware of the increasingly difficult position facing Lebanon's Christians, general Zionist wisdom held that this would propel
them toward a defensive partnership with other non-Muslim communities
in the region.[14] Themselves unable to strike an agreement with the Palestinian Arabs, Zionists placed little faith in Christian-Muslim cooperative
efforts in Lebanon, as pursued by Khoury. Desperation, in fact, did finally
drive Arida to conclude the treaty of 1946. Nevertheless, the department's
assumption that if a Maronite alliance failed, the cause would be a Maronite, not Zionist, inability to hold up its end of the bargain, hinted at the
truth: with their position weak and steadily deteriorating, the pro-Zionist
Christians simply could not afford an open relationship with the Zionists.
The same conditions that led Arida to ally with the Jewish Agency guaranteed that the alliance would remain inoperative.

But what if the two sides had thrown caution to the wind and committed themselves to a minority alliance program? What if the Maronites, in
an effort to better the chances for the program's success, had ceded those
Muslim areas of Lebanon and retreated, in Itamar Rabinovich's words, into
"'Fortress Lebanon,' a small Christian-Maronite Lebanon in conflict with
Muslims and Arabs"?[15] Hamid Franjieh told his Israeli interlocutor that
without Sidon, Tyre, Tripoli, and Beirut, Christian Lebanon would be
nothing but "a few miserable villages in the mountains."[16] Walid Khalidi
identifies a series of problems that argue against the creation a tiny Christian state in Lebanon. According to Khalidi, opposition to the partition of
Lebanon by the Lebanese Muslims, the non-Maronite Christians,
the Syrians, all the Arab states, the superpowers, France and the rest
of the European countries, and the Vatican make such a premise purely
hypothetical:

> But even if it were feasible, it would not be to the benefit of the Maronites,
> the non-Maronite Christians of Lebanon, or the Christian communities in the
> Arab world. Apart from the additional suffering it would bring . . . in the pro-
> cess of its implementation, it would seal off the state from all contact with the
> Arab world. In one stroke it would deprive the Maronites from reaping any
> advantages from the entrepot role of Lebanon and Beirut in the Middle
> East. . . . Partition would preclude Arab financial aid to the Maronite state. It
> would block access for the Maronite entrepreneurial talent to the oil-rich Arab
> states. It would impose an intolerable strain on the Christian communities
> throughout the Arab world. It would start the Maronite state on a via dolorosa
> of endless strife with its Arab hinterland.[17]

In retrospect, Eliahu Elath agreed with the somber picture Khalidi paints.[18] Would this truncated Christian Lebanon have made for a powerful Jewish-Christian bulwark in a hostile Muslim Middle East? At the very best, the two minorities together would have remained a minority; and their partnership would not have significantly altered the course of the Arab-Israeli and Palestinian-Israeli conflicts. It is more likely that the inhabitants of this economically impoverished and regionally isolated Lebanon would have eventually replaced their extremist Maronite leadership with a more conciliatory government, perhaps choosing to finally reunite with their Muslim countrymen in a Greater Syria. Most probably, however, Muslim Arab refusal to accept the partition of Lebanon would have led to an all-out assault on the weak new state, and perhaps its Zionist ally, as well. It does not seem that an alliance between the Yishuv and a diminutive Christian Lebanon would have enhanced the security of either.

The preceding discussion stretched the Zionist-Maronite alliance concept to its extreme conclusion; but it is necessary to remember, once again, that the Political Department did not. To be fair to Eliahu Epstein, who has emerged in this study as the most prominent proponent in the Agency of a pro-Maronite orientation, his primary goals for Zionist-Maronite cooperation focused on the practical assistance the two sides could render each other, not on a grand and formal alliance as such.

Concentrating on more pressing issues, the Political Department's fitful attention to Lebanon resulted in a fitful policy toward Lebanon. The alliance-of-minorities idea persisted because the Department never decided categorically *against* it, not because a decision was made *in its favor*. Although illogical to *pursue*, the Maronite option was not necessarily illogical to *consider*. Lebanon did differ from the other Arab states, primarily because of the Maronites. The periodic resurgence of interest in a Zionist-Maronite alliance throughout the mandate period reflects the natural appeal of the concept. The archives reveal that each time a new individual joined the political department's research division, he would inevitably "discover" the Maronites and excitedly produce a "new" plan for Zionist-Maronite collaboration. Institutional memory kept alive the idea that the friendly Maronites might be useful allies; institutional amnesia accounted for the failure to recall that all past alliance attempts had failed.

Having dismissed the efficacy of a Zionist-Maronite-led minority alliance policy, is it appropriate to label pre-state Zionist policy toward Lebanon misguided, short-sighted, and unsuccessful? Not necessarily. Most of the Zionist assumptions about Lebanon proved accurate. Lebanon did differ from the rest of the Arab countries; its prominent Maronite community did serve as the source of its uniqueness; Lebanon did prove friendlier to Zionism than any other Arab state. The rapid development of lucrative commercial ties, Lebanese offers to sell property, proposals for joint projects, appeals to Jewish tourists, and cordial Zionist-Lebanese relations along the border confirmed a special Lebanese receptivity toward a relationship with Jewish Palestine on the part of both Muslims and Christians. Warm personal relationships between Jewish Agency members and ranking Maronite Christians appeared to attest to a special Jewish-Maronite bond. Similar backgrounds, outlooks, and aspirations served as positive inducements to a Zionist-Maronite tie, while the struggle against a common Muslim enemy constituted a negative force drawing the two sides closer together: my enemy's enemy is my friend.

Zionist policy, to the extent it can be called policy, failed, however, on three key assumptions, all of which proved faulty: (1) the conviction that these friendly, informal, apolitical ties could be pushed to produce political advantages; (2) the belief that a pragmatic, healthy, economic relationship between Lebanon and the Yishuv could offset pan-Arab and anti-Zionist pressures stemming from the conflict in Palestine; and (3) Zionist hopes that Lebanon, on the basis of its mutually rewarding relations with the Yishuv, could separate itself from the other Arab countries in adopting a pro-Zionist position. Zionists thought they had accounted for Lebanon's weakness with the oft-repeated adage that Lebanon would be the *second* Arab country to make peace with Israel; but with this, they underestimated both the sway of pan-Arab, pro-Palestinian sentiment and the precarious Christian position in Lebanon.

Despite the Jewish Agency's misjudgments, however, and the failure to achieve a working alliance with its Lebanese Maronite partners, "the depth and extent of the contacts between them [proceeded] on a far greater scale than with any other of the countries surrounding Palestine. . . . The ideological basis for Maronite friendship with the Zionists promised, at least potentially, a far more stable ally" than any other Zionist contact in the pre-state era.[19] Relatively speaking, the Zionists' most significant achievements in ingratiating themselves with an Arab community, finding common ground for coexistence and cooperation, and winning Arab support for Zionism came among the Maronites.

With Israeli independence, David Ben-Gurion became the Jewish state's first prime minister. Although he raised the question of an alliance with the Christians of Lebanon several times in the first few years of his tenure, he never tried to make the idea operational, channeling his apparent interest in regional minority communities into the "policy of the periphery" instead, focusing Israeli foreign policy on other non-Arab and non-Sunni states on the periphery of the Arab-Israel conflict region, such as Turkey, Iran, Ethiopia, and Cyprus. Moshe Shertok (Sharett), always dubious as to the wisdom of a pro-Christian policy toward Lebanon, became Israel's foreign minister. Appointed first Israeli ambassador to the

United States, Eliahu Epstein abandoned his Maronite interests for more pressing American-Israeli issues. Eliahu Sasson, the new director of the Foreign Ministry's Middle East Department, set out to change the traditional Zionist approach to Lebanon. Sasson doubted whether the Christian opposition in Lebanon could seize power even with Israeli assistance and recommended that Israel not support the Lebanese Christians (or any other faction) until Jerusalem had defined for itself broad policy objectives. He listed his imperatives for a successful Israeli policy, among them (and with special implications for Lebanon) a well-thought-out, predetermined plan of action, instead of hand-to-mouth reactions to events as they arose, and a serious attempt to make peace with the Arab world, not just one Arab state.[20] Gideon Raphael, involved in 1948–51 discussions with the Phalange, pinpointed the major problem that had plagued Zionist-Maronite relations from the beginning:

> In the present circumstances in the Middle East, I cannot imagine that a Christian movement, when it reaches power in Lebanon, will dare enter into a conflict with the Muslim world by maintaining friendly ties with Israel. On the contrary, my opinion is that as long as the other Arab states persevere in their stubborn policy toward Israel, Lebanon will not be able, even under a friendly Christian government, to give concrete expression to its friendly proclivities.[21]

Shortly after Israeli independence, both Mubarak and Eddé contacted their old acquaintances in the new Israeli government to request backing for separate coup schemes and the Phalange appealed to Jerusalem for assistance in its struggle for power, as well.[22] Rabinovich contends that by then, however, the Israeli Foreign Ministry had come to understand that "most Maronites had accepted the post–1943 pluralistic Lebanese system and that Israel, too, ought to accept it as an established fact. . . . This, indeed, was done for the next twenty years, during which Israel's relations with Lebanon were a marginal aspect of its Middle Eastern policies."[23]

The Zionists' isolation and Lebanese demographics prior to 1948 made it logical for the Jewish Agency to consider a pro-Christian policy vis-à-vis Lebanon. The failure of the Zionist-Maronite relationship to produce significant political benefits proves, however, that it was an unwise policy to pursue. Although not necessarily harmful to Zionist interests, continuing delusions about the feasibility of a Zionist-Maronite entente served as a faulty premise for a resultantly faulty policy. Should Zionist strategists at the time have been able to see that factors inhibiting an effective alliance with the Maronites outweighed those promoting it? Hindsight responds in the affirmative, but an analysis of the situation from a pre-state Zionist perspective suggests that the answer is not so clear-cut.

Proponents of a special relationship with the Maronites correctly identi-fied an unusual harmony of interests between their two communities. While they misjudged the potential for turning those shared interests to mutual political advantage, these Zionists were not wrong in imagining that of all their enemy's enemies, the Maronites offered the most willing candidates for friendship.

APPENDICES

Antoine Pierre Arida to
Chaim Weizmann,
24 May 1946

Békerké, le 24 mai 1946

A Son Excellence Monsieur le Professeur Weizman [*sic*]
Président de l'Agence Juive
Jérusalem

Monsieur le Professeur,

Notre cher Fils, Cheikh Toufic Aouad, ancien ministre et notre fondé de pouvoirs permanent, nous a rapporté les détails de l'entretien qu'il a eu avec Monsieur le Docteur Bernard Joseph, votre représentant. Appréciant les sentiments de sympathie que nous avons toujours eu pour la Nation Juive, vous avez bien voulu venir en aide à l'oeuvre nationale et patriotique que nous organisons.

Nous avons été très sensible à l'intérêt que vous prenez pour nos oeuvres et nous vous témoignons notre reconnaissance.

Il est bien entendu que nos relations avec la Nation Juive ont été toujours fondés sur l'esprit de justice et les sentiments humains; elles n'ont jamais été intéressées. Poussé par ces même sentiments nous continuerons toujours à poursuivre la même conduite que nous avons eu jusqu'ici.

Nous avons autorisé notre fils Cheikh Toufic Aouad de conclure avec vous tous accords utiles aux intérêts de votre Pays et du nôtre. Il est autorisé de même par nous de recevoir éventuellement toutes sommes d'argent.

Dans l'espoir de vous revoir parmi nous, nous prions Votre Excellence d'agréer l'expression de nos sentiments distingués.

Le Patriarche Maronite
d'Antioche et de tout l'orient
Antoine Pierre Arida

Source: Ben Gurion Archives

B:
Tewfik Awad to Bernard Joseph,
30 May 1946

Jérusalem, le 30 mai 1946

M. le Dr. B. Joseph,
Agence Juive pour la Palestine,
Jérusalem.

Cher Docteur Joseph,
    Me référant à l'accord conclu en date de ce jour entre vous, en votre qualité
de représentant de l'Agence juive et moi, en ma qualité de représentant de S.B. le
Patriarche Maronite du Liban, j'ai l'honneur de vous confirmer par la présente
notre accord verbal sur le point suivant:

> "L'accord conclu doit être considéré pour le moment comme strictement confidentiel
> et il ne pourra être publié que lorsque, de commun accord, les deux parties auront re-
> connu l'opportunité de procéder à sa publication."

La présente est à considerer comme une annexe au dit accord.
Veuillez agréer, cher Docteur Joseph, l'assurance de ma haute considération,

Toufic Aouad

Source: Ben-Gurion Archives

Bernard Joseph to Tewfik Awad,
30 May 1946

Jérusalem, le 30 mai 1946

Cheikh Toufik Aouad,
Jérusalem.

Cher Cheikh Toufik,
    Me référant à l'accord conclu en date de ce jour entre vous, en votre qualité
de représentant de S.B. le Patriarche Maronite du Liban, et moi, en ma qualité
de représentant de l'Agence juive, j'ai l'honneur de vous confirmer par la présente
notre accord verbal sur le point suivant:

"L'accord conclu doit être considéré pour le moment comme strictement confidentiel
et il ne pourra être publié que lorsque, de commun accord, les deux parties auront re-
connu l'opportunité de procéder à sa publication."

La présente est à considerer comme une annexe au dit accord.
Veuillez agréer, cher Cheikh Toufik, l'assurance de ma haute considération,

B.J.
Bernard Joseph

Source: Ben-Gurion Archives

D:
Bernard Joseph to
Antoine Pierre Arida,
30 May 1946

Jérusalem, le 30 mai 1946.

S.B. Le Patriarche Maronite
Antoine Pierre Arida,
Patriarcat d'Antioche et
de tout l'Orient,
Békerké.

Votre Béatitude,

Notre Président, Professeur Weizmann, m'a chargé de vous accuser reception de votre lettre du 24 mai et de vous remercier vivement des sentiments d'ami-
tié pour la nation juive que vous y avez exprimés.

Nous avons toujours apprécié l'attitude bienveillante de Votre Béatitude en-
vers nos aspirations nationales. Dr. Weizmann m'a prié de vous assurer que nous,
de notre part, entretenons toujours des sentiments et de haute considération pour
le peuple libanais et en particulier pour la Communautée Maronite. Il a été heu-
reux de voir la réalisation de l'indépendance libanaise et désire vous souhaiter le
meilleur succès pour l'avenir de votre pays. Il est bien content de l'accord qui a
été fait entre Votre Béatitude par l'entremise de votre représentant Cheikh Toufic
Aouad et l'Agence Juive par mon entremise et il espère que cet accord ouvrira
une époque de pleine coopération entre les peuples Juif et Libanais.

Il m'a également chargé de vous exprimer ses meilleurs voeux de bonne
santé et l'espoir qu'il aura le plaisir de vous voir quand les circonstances le permet-
tront.

Veuillez agréer, Votre Béatitude, l'expression de ma haute considération et
de mes salutations distinguées,

Bernard Joseph
AGENCE JUIVE POUR LA PALESTINE

Source: Ben-Gurion Archives

E:
Treaty between the Jewish Agency for Palestine
and the Maronite Church,
30 May 1946

Nous soussignés:

1. S.B. le Patriarche Maronite, Antoine Arida, agissant au nom de l'Eglise et de la Communauté Maronite, la plus grande des communautés de la République Libanaise, — laquelle Communauté compte des ressortissants aussi dans d'autres pays, représenté par Cheikh Toufic Aouad, ancien ministre, en vertu d'une procuration adressée au Président de l'Agence Juive, le Professeur Weizman [sic], en date du 24 mai 1946,
> ci-après dénommé: "la première partie"

2. Dr. Bernard Joseph, agissant au nom de l'Agence Juive pour la Palestine, reconnue en droit international comme le représentant du peuple Juif dans le monde entier à l'effet de l'établissement du Foyer National juif en Palestine

> ci-après dénommé: "la seconde partie"

> avons arrêté et convenue ce qui suit:

ART. 1er: La première partie déclare reconnaître pleinement le lien historique unissant le peuple Juif à la Palestine, les aspirations du peuple Juif en Palestine, ainsi que le droit du peuple Juif à une immigration libre en Palestine et à s'établir librement dans le pays, et il déclare être d'accord sur le programme politique actuel declaré de l'Agence Juive, comprenant notamment l'établissement de l'Etat Juif.

ART. 2: La seconde partie déclare reconnaître pleinement l'indépendance du Liban et le droit de ses habitants de fixer le régime de leur pays dans la forme qu'ils considèrent opportune.
La seconde partie déclare également qu'il n'est pas dans son programme de

Source: Central Zionist Archives S25/3269

s'élargir en s'étendant dans le Liban mais au contraire elle déclare respecter l'état libanais dans sa forme actuelle. L'immigration juive ne comprend pas le Liban.

ART. 3: Les deux parties prennent l'engagement de s'abstenir de porter atteinte à leurs aspirations et status respectifs; le dit engagement comporte l'obligation que les représentants de chacune des deux parties — officiels ou non officiels, — à l'intérieur du pays, à l'étranger et dans les conférences internationales, occidentales ou orientales, — s'abstiennent de fournir n'importe quel support dans des décisions ou des actions susceptibles de porter atteinte à l'autre partie; non seulement mais aussi qu'ils fassent tout ce qui est en leur pouvoir pour empêcher que de telles décisions soient prises ou de telles actions soient entreprises.

ART. 4: Les deux parties s'engagent à s'entre-aider aux points de vue: politique, commercial, de la sécurité et social, dans le but de soutenir la position de la première partie et de réaliser les aspirations de la seconde. Cet engagement comprend:

a) éclairer l'opinion publique en Orient et en Occident sur la cause de chacune des deux parties; dans l'esprit du présent accord.

b) effort des deux parties dans le but d'ouvrir les portes de chacun des deux pays à l'autre partie afin de resserrer les liens culturels et sociaux, les échanges commerciaux, l'échange d'agents de liaison, et cultiver les rapports de bon voisinage.

c) la première partie, qui reconnait à tout juif le droit d'immigrer en Palestine, s'engage à aider cette immigration au mieux de ses possibilités, dans la mesure où les immigrants devraient passer par le Liban.

d) la seconde partie s'engage, — pour le moment où elle formera l'Etat juif, — à respecter pleinement les droits civils et religieux des communautés non-juives et le caractère sacré de leurs lieux saints en Palestine. La première partie s'engage, — pour le moment où elle arrivera au pouvoir dans son pays, — de considèrer le présent accord comme partie intégrante du programme de son gouvernement.

e) las deux parties s'engagent à s'aider réciproquement, — dans la mesure où l'une serait requise par l'autre, — à maintenir la sécurité dans leurs pays. Cet engágement comporte l'obligation de prendre toutes les mesures nécessaires pour empêcher l'entrée ou la sortie d'éléments hostiles susceptibles de troubler l'ordre public, — ainsi que l'obligation d'empêcher toute aide à de pareils éléments.

f) les deux parties s'engagent à échanger entre elles des informations sur tous les sujets, — par exemple sur la politique de leurs pays, leur économie, leur sûreté, leurs liens avec des tiers, etc.

g) les deux parties s'engagent sur le plan industriel, agricole et des recherches scientifiques, à échanger des informations et des conseils pour synchroniser les efforts des juifs et des Libanais, afin d'assurer le meilleur developpement de leurs industries (tourisme compris), agricultures et recherches respectives sur la base d'une collaboration mutuelle.

h) la seconde partie, quand elle formera l'Etat Juif, s'engage à réserver aux représentants du Patriarche Maronite un trâitement amical; à lui faciliter l'achat d'un terrain et la construction d'un Patriarcat digne de la Communauté Maronite.

i) la seconde partie s'engage à ce que ses bureaux dans les differents pays donnent leur soutien à la cause de la première et appuyent ses représentants à Washington, Londres et Paris et dans les conférences internationales.

ART. 5: Sur les moyens de réaliser les obligations quì précédent, et sur les moyens pratiques supplémentaires de collaboration et d'entre-aide, les deux parties délibéreront directement ou par représentants, au fur et à mesure et suivant les circonstances.

La première partie nomme d'ores et dèja comme représentant attitrè Cheikh Toufic Aouad, sauf nouvelle notification à l'avenir.

ART. 6: Le présent accord entrera en vigueur aussitôt signé. Chacune des parties aura le droit d'y mettre fin moyennant un préavis de six mois.

En foi de quoi, les deux parties ont signé le présent accord.

Fait en double original pour un seul et même effet, à Jérusalem, le 30 mai 1946.

Au nom de Sa Béatitude	For the Jewish Agency
Msgr. Antoine Pierre Arida	for Palestine
Toufic Aouad	Bernard Joseph

ABBREVIATIONS

AD   Centre des Archives Diplomatiques de Nantes, Ministère des Affaires Étrangères, Nantes

AE   Archives du Ministère des Affaires Étrangères, Quai d'Orsay, Paris

BGA   Ben-Gurion Archives, Sede Boqer

CZA   Central Zionist Archives, Jerusalem

ED   Archive for Jewish Education in Israel and the Diaspora, Tel Aviv University

HA   Haganah Archives, Tel Aviv

ISA   Israel State Archives, Jerusalem

JAE   Jewish Agency Executive

LCW   *Letters and Papers of Chaim Weizmann*

SC   Schwadran Collection, Shiloah Institute, Tel Aviv University

WA   Weizmann Archives, Rehovot

Note to Reader: Two of the primary characters in this study changed their names in 1949. Moshe Shertok became Moshe Sharett and Eliahu Epstein became Eliahu Elath. Both the early and later names appear in the notes, depending upon the date of reference.

NOTES

PREFACE

1. Walid Khalidi, *Conflict and Violence in Lebanon* (Cambridge: Center for International Affairs, Harvard University, 1979), pp. 13–14.

CHAPTER 1

1. Eder to Weizmann, 21 June 1920, Central Zionist Archives (CZA), Z4/16033.

2. Weizmann to Eder, 27 October 1921, in *The Letters and Papers of Chaim Weizmann* (*LCW*), vol. 10, letter 266.

3. Kalvarisky's willingness to grant far more concessions to the Arabs than did mainstream Zionist thinking ultimately estranged him from the Zionist leadership. See Neil Caplan, *Futile Diplomacy* (London: Cass, 1983–86), vol. 1, pp. 65–68; idem, *Palestine Jewry and the Arab Question* (London: Cass, 1978), pp. 40–45; Aharon Cohen, *Israel and the Arab World* (New York: Funk & Wagnalls, 1970), pp. 153–60, 322–29; Yehoshua Porath, *The Palestinian Arab National Movement, 1929–1939* (London: Cass, 1977), pp. 67–69.

4. Kisch to Kalvarisky, 26 March 1931, CZA, S25/3039.

5. Kisch to Selim Mann, 20 January 1928, CZA, S25/9947. Kisch explained to Mann, editor of a pro-Zionist journal published independently in Beirut, why the executive could no longer afford to subsidize his paper.

6. For an analysis of the institutions of the Yishuv as a quasi state, see Moshe Lissak and Daniel Horowitz, *Origins of the Israeli Polity* (Chicago: University of Chicago Press, 1978); J. C. Hurewitz, *The Struggle for Palestine* (New York: Norton, 1950), chap. 3.

7. Arlosoroff to Selig Brodetsky, 17 November 1931, and Arlosoroff to Louis Brandeis, 8 May 1932, both in CZA, S25/3061.

8. Shertok changed his name to Sharett in 1949. I employ both names in citing him, based on the date.

9. Ya'akov Sharett, interview with author, 1 April 1987, Tel Aviv.

10. For a comparison of the personalities and political perspectives of Ben-Gurion and

Shertok, see Michael Brecher, *The Foreign Policy System of Israel* (New Haven: Yale University Press, 1972), chap. 12; Gabriel Sheffer, "The Confrontation Between Moshe Sharett and David Ben-Gurion," in *Zionism and the Arabs*, ed. Shmuel Almog (Jerusalem: Zalman Shazar Center, 1983), pp. 95–147; Itamar Rabinovich, *The Road Not Taken: Early Arab-Israeli Negotiations* (Oxford: Oxford University Press, 1991), pp. 5–6, 31–34; Amos Perlmutter, *Israel: the Partitioned State* (New York: Charles Scribner's Sons, 1985), pp. 145–58; Ya'acov Bar-Simon-Tov, "Ben-Gurion and Sharett: Conflict Management and Great Power Constraints in Israeli Foreign Policy," *Middle Eastern Studies* 24 (July 1988): 330–56; and Avi Shlaim, "Conflicting Approaches to Israel's Relations with the Arabs: Ben-Gurion and Sharett, 1953–1956," *Middle East Journal* 37, no. 2 (Spring 1983): 180–202.

11. Epstein changed his name to Elath in 1949. I employ both names when citing him, based on the date.

12. Eliahu Epstein to the Jewish Agency Executive (JAE), 3 November 1932, Weizmann Archives (WA).

13. Eliahu Sasson, *Baderekh el Hashalom* [On the road to peace] (Tel Aviv: Am Oved, 1978), pp. 11–16.

14. Although his Damascene upbringing generally stood Sasson in good stead within the Arab world, it backfired in 1949 when he was dispatched to meet the Maronite candidate for the Lebanese presidency, Hamid Franjiyeh. Franjiyeh complained that "he had hoped to have dealings with Western Jews [who are gifted] with a broad vision, [but instead Israel] sent an Eastern element in the form of Sasson, and [Franjiyeh] was not particularly pleased thereby, . . . he was even disappointed." (Report to Foreign Ministry, 15 December 1949, Israel State Archives [ISA], 184/7, quoted in Amikam Nachmani, "Middle East Listening Post: Eliahu Sasson and the Israeli Legation in Turkey, 1949–1952," *Studies in Zionism* 6, no. 2 [Autumn 1985]: 280). For evidence of a possible rivalry between Sasson and Epstein, see Sasson to Bernard Joseph, 12 January 1940, CZA, S25/5568 (Heb.).

15. Neil Caplan, "Negotiation and the Arab Israeli Conflict," *Jerusalem Quarterly* 6 (Winter 1978): 13.

16. See e.g., N. Goldmann to Itzhak Ben-Zvi, 5 June 1936, CZA, S25/9164 (Heb.).

17. Chaim Weizmann to Felix M. Warburg, 11 February 1937, CZA, Z4/17026B.

18. Caplan, "Negotiation," p. 13.

19. Testimony of David Ben-Gurion Before the Palestine Royal Commission, 7 January 1937, CZA, S25/4642.

20. Ian Black, "Zionism and the Arabs, 1936–1939," Ph.D. diss., University of London, 1978, pp. 205–6.

21. Caplan, "Negotiation," p. 10.

22. Ibid., pp. 14–15. For an analysis of the impact of great power considerations on Zionist-Arab negotiations see Caplan, *Futile Diplomacy*, esp. vol. 1, pp. 117–19, and vol. 2, pp. 169–72.

23. For an examination of Zionist land purchasing activities in Palestine, see Kenneth W. Stein, *The Land Question in Palestine, 1917–1939* (Chapel Hill: University of North Carolina Press, 1984).

24. A excellent example of the wide-ranging activities under consideration by the Political Department is Sasson's "Plan for Activity Among the Arabs," Eliahu Sasson to David Ben-Gurion, 21 April 1939, CZA, S25/8163 (Heb.).

25. The principal Jewish Agency players discussed here all left accounts of their many meetings with some of the most prominent leaders in the Arab world. See esp., David Ben-Gurion, *My Talks with Arab Leaders* (Jerusalem: Keter, 1972); Moshe Sharett, *Yoman Medini* [Political diary], 5 vols. (Tel Aviv: Am Oved, 1968–79); Sasson, *Baderekh*; Eliahu Elath, *Shivat Tzion Ve'arav* [Zionism and the Arabs] (Tel Aviv: Dvir, 1974).

26. See, e.g., David Ben-Gurion, 11 October 1938, *Zikhronot* [Memoirs] (Tel Aviv: Am

Oved, 1971–87), vol. 5, p. 320. For a general discussion of this phenomenon over time, see Caplan, *Futile Diplomacy*, vol. 2, pp. 68–105, 142–64.

27. For a breakdown of the distribution of the Lebanese population by religious confessions and districts in 1944, see Albert Hourani, *Minorities in the Arab World* (London: Oxford University Press, 1947), chap. 9.

28. Amnon Yonai, interview with author, 12 May 1987, Netanya, Israel.

29. See Arthur Ruppin's comments during the JAE meeting, 20 May 1936, CZA, Minutes of the JAE, vol.25/3 (Heb.); and Anon., "Letter from Beirut," 1 July 1945, CZA, S25/4556 (Heb.).

30. Eliahu Elath, interview with author, 14 October 1986, Jerusalem.

31. Glenn E. Perry, "Israeli Involvement in Inter-Arab Politics," *International Journal of Islamic and Arabic Studies* 1 (1984): 16.

32. Ya'akov Shimoni, interview with author, 4 March 1987, Jerusalem; idem, lecture at the Shiloah Institute, Tel Aviv University, 7 December 1983; Yehoshua Porath, interview with author, 10 March 1987, Jerusalem; idem, *Shelah ve'et Beyado* [The life of Uriel Shelah (Yonathan Ratosh)] (Tel Aviv: Machbarot Lesifrut, Zmora, 1989), pp. 75, 81, 90–91.

33. Cohen, *Israel and the Arab World*, pp. 90–98; Barry Rubin, *The Arab States and the Palestine Conflict* (Ithaca: Syracuse University Press, 1982), p. 26; Walter Laqueur, *A History of Zionism* (New York: Schocken Books, 1976), p. 212.

34. Amos Elon, *The Israelis: Founders and Sons* (New York: Bantam Books, 1972), p. 214.

35. Shertok to Epstein, 15 November 1931, CZA, S25/3561 (Heb.).

36. Chaim Arlosoroff, *Yoman Yerushalayim* [Jerusalem diary] (Tel Aviv: Mifleget Poale Eretz Yisrael, 1941), 14 November 1931, pp. 112–13.

37. Arlosoroff to Selig Brodetsky, 17 November 1931, CZA, S25/3061.

38. Arlosoroff to Victor Jacobson, 2 January 1933, CZA, Z4/20177.

39. Epstein, "The Character of the Pan-Arab Movement: Its Political and Social Value," 4 February 1938, CZA, S25/5682.

40. Weizmann to Ignatius Mubarak, 5 December 1947, in *LCW*, vol. 23, letter 87.

41. Bernard Joseph's Report to the Mapai Center, 18 September 1937, CZA, S25/10.475 (Heb.); Epstein, "Conversation with the President of the Lebanese Republic, Mr. Emile Eddé" (Beirut), 22 September 1936, CZA, S25/5581 (Heb.).

42. Bernard Joseph's Office Diary, 28 December 1942, CZA, S25/4549.

43. Shimoni, lecture at the Shiloah Institute, Tel Aviv University, 7 December 1983.

44. Regarding treaty proposals, see Abba Hushi to Shertok, 3 July 1936, CZA, S25/9165 (Heb.); Yoav Gelber, "Antecedents of the Jewish-Druze Alliance in Palestine," *Middle Eastern Studies* 28, no. 2 (April 1992): 352–73; "Proposal for a Treaty with a Group of Lebanese: Not Executed: Negotiations conducted with a Lebanese Named Iliya Halbi," April 1947, CZA, S25/9025 (Arab.).

45. Sasson to Shertok, 12 June 1938, CZA, S25/5568 (Heb.); idem, *Baderekh*, pp. 123–25; Abba Hushi, "Negotiations with Sultan Pasha al-Atrash," 14–17 March 1939, CZA, S25/8221 (Heb.).

46. Aharon Cohen, "The Fate of Our Relations with the Druze People," 2 November 1937, CZA, S25/6638 (Heb.).

47. Michael Hudson, *The Precarious Republic: Political Modernization in Lebanon* (New York: Random House, 1968), p. 6.

48. Epstein, "Conversation with Mr. George Hakim, Counselor of the Lebanese Legation, Washington, D.C.," 3 February 1947, CZA, A263/18.

49. Fouad Ajami, *The Arab Predicament* (Cambridge: Cambridge University Press, 1981), p. 159.

50. Rubin, *Arab States and the Palestine Conflict*, p. 140. The Christian attempt to divorce the Arab identity from the Islamic one did not entirely displease many Muslims. Christian

identification with a secular Arab nationalism would deprive Europeans of dissident Christian clients and deprive Zionists of minority alliance partners by closing Christian and Muslim ranks. Regarding Christian Arab nationalism, see George Antonius, *The Arab Awakening* (Philadelphia: Lippincott, 1939), esp. chap. 3; David C. Gordon, *The Republic of Lebanon: Nation in Jeopardy* (Boulder: Westview, 1983), pp. 24, 44–45, 50; Sylvia Haim, *Arab Nationalism* (Berkeley: University of California Press, 1962); Kamal S. Salibi, *The Modern History of Lebanon* (New York: Praeger, 1965), pp. 151–59; Albert Hourani, *Arabic Thought in the Liberal Age, 1798–1939* (London: Oxford University Press, 1962), pp. 95–102, 245–59, 319–23.

51. See William W. Haddad, "The Christian Arab Press and the Palestine Question: A Case Study of Michel Chiha of Bayrut's *Le Jour,*" *Muslim World* 65, no. 2 (April 1975): esp. pp. 128–29.

52. Hadad, "Hasbarah Activity Among the Christians of Lebanon: A Conversation with the Representative of the Pope in Lebanon," 24 June 1943, CZA, S25/5577 (Heb.). Others contend that while political enmity motivated Muslim anti-Jewish sentiment, Christians, especially Maronites, often expressed traditional anti-Semitic beliefs (Chaim Levkov, interview with author, 11 May 1987, Holon, Israel; Michael Sasson to author, 24 April and 23 June 1987; Shula Cohen-Kishik, interview with author, 20 May 1986, Jerusalem).

53. JAE to the Sephardic Association, 5 February 1936, CZA, S25/5576 (Heb.); [Shertok?] to Ben-Zvi, 26 October 1937, CZA, S25/5812 (Heb.).

54. Minutes of the JAE meeting, 26 October 1941, CZA, vol. 35/1 (Heb.).

55. Sasson, "Comments on Our Relations with the Druze," 5 November 1937, CZA, S25/6638 (Heb.).

56. Porath, interview with author, 10 March 1987; Shimoni, interview with author, 4 March 1987; Yehoshua Palmon, interview with author, 26 March 1987, Kfar Shmariyahu, Israel.

57. Minutes of the JAE meeting, 20 May 1936, Jerusalem, CZA, vol. 25/3.

CHAPTER 2

1. Concerning the imprecision of geographical terms in the Levant, see Kamal Salibi, *A House of Many Mansions: The History of Lebanon Reconsidered* (Berkeley: University of California Press, 1988), pp. 60–71. For a detailed analysis of the various interpretations of the biblical boundaries of Eretz Yisrael, see Yehezkel Kaufmann, *The Biblical Account of the Conquest of Canaan* (Jerusalem: Magnes, 1953).

2. Weizmann to Vera Weizmann, 8 September 1907, in *LCW,* vol. 5, letter 54.

3. Weizmann to Johann Kremenetzky, 26 September 1907, in *LCW,* vol. 5, letter 60. Nothing came of these projects.

4. B. Shlichover to the Odessa Committee, 20 Nisan 5668 [21 April 1908], CZA, A24/51/II (Heb.). See also Joseph Katz, "Tokhniyot Tziyoniyot Lerekhishat Karka'ot Balevanon Batchilat Hamaya Ha'esrim" [Zionist plans for purchasing properties in Lebanon in the early twentieth century], *Cathedra* 35 (April 1985): 53–57.

5. M. Ussishkin to David Wolfson, 4 Iyar 5668 [5 May 1908], CZA, Z2/647 (Heb.).

6. Petition from the Jewish Community of Sidon, [ca. 1919?], Archive for Jewish Education in Israel and the Diaspora (ED), file 1138 (Heb.). See also Pinchas Na'aman, "The Jewish Community of Sidon on the Threshold of Its Demise," *al-Hamishmar,* 23 May 1948, ED, file 1630 (Heb.); David Sitton, *Kehilot Yehudai Sefarad Vehamizrach Ba'olam Beyameinu* [Jewish communities of Spain and the East in the world in our days] (Jerusalem: Ahva Cooperative, 1974), p. 59; and Norman A. Stillman, *The Jews of Arab Lands in Modern Times* (Philadelphia: Jewish Publication Society, 1991), pp. 197–98.

7. Deuteronomy 1:7, 3:25, 11:24; Joshua 1:4; "The Northern Boundary of Biblical Palestine," 1 January 1920, CZA, Z4/16024; Kaufmann, *Biblical Account.*

8. Fox report quoted by Chaim Weizmann to David Lloyd George, 7 January 1920, in *LCW*, vol. 9, letter 252.

9. Zionist Organization to David Lloyd George, 29 December 1919, and Chaim Weizmann to David Lloyd George, 7 January 1920, in *LCW*, vol. 9, letters 251 and 252; [Aaron Aaronsohn?], "A Memorandum on the Boundaries of Palestine" and "The Boundaries of Palestine," 1919, CZA, Z4/16024; Lewis Namier to Louis Brandeis, 3 October 1919, CZA, Z4/16024.

10. "Statement of the Zionist Organization Regarding Palestine," 3 February 1919, in *LCW*, vol. 9, app. 2, pp. 392, 397.

11. Shabtai Teveth, *Ben-Gurion and the Palestinian Arabs* (Oxford: Oxford University Press, 1985), p. 34.

12. [Aaronsohn?], "A Memorandum on the Boundaries of Palestine," 1919, CZA, Z4/16024.

13. Frederic Hof, *Galilee Divided: The Israel-Lebanon Frontier, 1916–1984* (Boulder: Westview, 1985), pp. 7–8. For a detailed account of the Franco-British negotiations over the Palestine-Lebanon border and an analysis of the political, security, and economic implications of the placement of the border, see chaps. 1–5. See also Howard M. Sachar, *A History of Israel* (New York: Knopf, 1981), pp. 116–17.

14. Hof, *Galilee Divided*, pp. 17–20; Mayor Yossi Goldberg, David Sandler, and Shalom Fein, interviews with author, 28 April 1987, Metulla, Israel.

15. Pinchas Na'aman to Zionist Commission, 8 July 1920 and 13 July 1920, CZA, L3/625 (Heb.); L. K. Weiss to Kadmi-Cohen concerning land for sale near Tyre and Sidon, [ca. 1921–1924?], CZA, A174/20/5 (Heb.).

16. Gaston Maugras to Ministry of Foreign Affairs, 29 July 1925, and Ballereau (consul general in Palestine) to Ministry of Foreign Affairs, 1 October 1925, Archives du Ministère des Affaires Étrangères (AE), série E—Levant 1918–29/Palestine (LE 18–29/PAL) vol. 28 (Fr.); see also Weygand (High Commission in Beirut) to Ministry of Foreign Affairs, 27 September 1924, and Ministry to Weygand, 4 October 1924, LE 18–29/PAL 28 (Fr.); Ministry of Foreign Affairs to G. Sarrail (High Commission in Beirut), 2 June 1925 and 17 August 1925, and Sarrail to Ministry, 30 September 1925, Centre des Archives Diplomatiques de Nantes (AD), serie Mandat Syrie-Liban (MAN)/1064 (Fr.).

17. Jouvenel to Aristide Briand, 27 April 1926, WA (Fr.); Jouvenel to Briand, 8 May 1926, AE, LE 18–29/PAL 29 (Fr.); Chaim Weizmann, *Trial and Error: The Autobiography of Chaim Weizmann* (New York: Harper & Brothers, 1949), pp. 366–67.

18. Kisch, "Visit to Syria," 18 April 1926, Diary Notes, CZA, S25/9022; Weizmann to Philippe Berthelot, 2 August 1926, in *LCW*, vol. 13, letter 71.

19. Jouvenel to Briand, 27 April 1926, WA; Kisch, "Visit to Syria," 18 April 1926, Diary Notes, CZA, S25/9022; Weizmann to Philippe Berthelot, 2 August 1926, in *LCW*, vol. 13, letter 71; Barnet Litvinoff, ed., *The Essential Chaim Weizmann* (New York: Holmes & Meier, 1982), pp. 226–27; Chaim Arlosoroff, *Yoman Yerushalayim* [Jerusalem diary] (Tel Aviv: Mifleget Poale Eretz Yisrael, 1941), p. 111.

20. Jouvenel to Briand, 27 April 1926, WA; Ministry of Foreign Affairs to Jouvenel, 4 May 1926, and Jouvenel to Ministry, 6 May 1926, AE, LE 18–40/PAL 29 (Fr.).

21. British Foreign Office, remarks concerning Jouvenel's scheme to settle Jews in northern Syria, May and June 1926, FO/371/11518 E3112, held in ISA.

22. Weizmann to Sir John Shuckburgh, 28 May 1926, in *LCW*, vol. 13, letter 24.

23. JAE meeting, 24 June 1926, CZA, Z4/302/13; Kisch, Diary Notes, 18 April 1926, CZA, S25/9022; Minutes of the Actions Committee meeting (London), 26 July 1926, quoted in Jon Kimche, *There Could Have Been Peace* (New York: Dial, 1973), pp. 314–15.

24. Kimche, *There Could Have Been Peace*, pp. 314–15.

25. JAE meetings, 24 June 1926 and 15 July 1926, CZA, Z4/302/13.

26. Reports of Weizmann's and Jacobson's visits to Philippe Berthelot and M. Canet, 2 and 4 May 1927, AE, LE 18–40/PAL 29 (Fr.); d'Aumale (French consul general in Jerusalem) to Henri Ponsot (high commissioner in Beirut), 12 February 1930; Foreign Ministry to Berthelot, 12 March 1930; Foreign Ministry to St. Quentin, 3 April 1930; Ponsot to Ministry of Foreign Affairs, 5 June 1930; and Report of Leon Blum's visit to Berthelot, 21 November 1930, all in AE, LE 18–40/PAL 69 (Fr.). See also "Syria and Zionism," 30 May 1930, LE 18–40/PAL 64 (Fr.). Contrary to the documentary evidence, Weizmann suggests in his autobiography that he never took Jouvenel's proposal seriously.

27. Ussishkin to Rabbi Israel Levy, 21 April 1926, and Levy to Ussishkin, 6 May 1926, both in CZA, S25/590.

28. Kisch to Weizmann, 10 June 1926, CZA, S25/590; Weizmann to Kisch, 24 June 1926, in *LCW*, vol. 13, letter 34. See also Shmuel Dayan, *Biyemai Chazon Umatzor* [In days of vision and siege] (Tel Aviv: Massada, 1953), pp. 16–41,54–56.

29. "Visit of the Chief Rabbi of France," 2 May 1930, AE, LE 18–40/PAL 64 (Fr.).

30. See multiple letters and reports in AE, LE 18–40/PAL 69 (Fr.).

31. Jewish National Fund to French Consulate in Jerusalem, 9 December 1929; Jerusalem Consulate to French High Commission in Beirut, 11 December 1929; d'Aumale to Ministry of Foreign Affairs, 20 December 1929; and Ministry of Foreign Affairs to Ministry of Finances, 6 January 1930, all in AD, MAN/808 (Fr.).

32. Bollack to Weizmann, 23 May 1930, WA.

33. Dr. Joseph's Office Diary, 24 September 1937, CZA, S25/1511.

34. Hudson, *The Precarious Republic: Political Modernization in Lebanon* (New York: Random House, 1968), pp. 25–26; David C. Gordon, *The Republic of Lebanon, Nation in Jeopardy* (Boulder: Westview, 1983), p. 5. See also Kamal Salibi, *A House of Many Mansions: The History of Lebanon Reconsidered* (Berkeley: University of California Press, 1988), chap. 5.

35. Matti Moosa, *The Maronites in History* (Syracuse: Syracuse University Press, 1986), p. 284.

36. Albert Hourani, "Ideologies of the Mountain and the City," in *Essays on the Crisis in Lebanon*, ed. Roger Owen (London: Ithaca, 1976), pp. 36–37.

37. Hourani, "Ideologies," pp. 36–37.

38. Ibid.

39. Itamar Rabinovich, *The War for Lebanon, 1970–1983* (Ithaca: Cornell University Press, 1984), pp. 18–19.

40. Moosa, *Maronites in History*, pp. 286–87; Rabinovich, *War for Lebanon*, p. 19.

41. See "Memorandum Presented by the Maronite Patriarch Hawayik to the Paris Peace Conference," 25 October 1919 (Fr.), text in Meir Zamir, *The Formation of Modern Lebanon* (London: Croom Helm, 1985), pp. 269–78. Zamir's book is the definitive analysis of the creation of Greater Lebanon and the implications thereof.

42. Hof, *Galilee Divided*, p. 25. See also Rabinovich, *War for Lebanon*, pp. 19–21; Zamir, *Formation of Modern Lebanon*, p. 97.

43. Zamir, *Formation of Modern Lebanon*, pp. 76–77, 91–93, 118–19; idem., "Smaller and Greater Lebanon—The Squaring of a Circle?" *Jerusalem Quarterly* 23 (Spring 1982): 35–37; Rabinovich, *War for Lebanon*, p. 21.

44. Clemenceau to Hawayik, 10 November 1919 (Fr.), text in Zamir, *Formation of Modern Lebanon*, pp. 279–80.

45. Hudson, *Precarious Republic*, p. 127. See also Zamir, "Smaller and Greater Lebanon," p. 39; idem, *Formation of Modern Lebanon*, pp. 70–72, 78.

46. Zamir, "Smaller and Greater Lebanon," pp. 38–40; idem, *Formation of Modern Lebanon*, pp. 117–20. For extensive discussions on the consequences of the formation of Greater Lebanon see Zamir, *Formation of Modern Lebanon*, chap. 3; Hof, *Galilee Divided*.

47. George Samne, quoted in Zamir, "Smaller and Greater Lebanon," p. 40.

48. Amin Sa'id, *Al-Thawra al-Arabiya al-Kubra* [The great Arab revolt], vol. 3 (Cairo: Matba'a Issa al-Babi al-Halabi, 1934), p. 433.

49. Zamir, "Smaller and Greater Lebanon," p. 40; idem, "Emile Eddé and the Territorial Integrity of Lebanon," *Middle Eastern Studies* 14, no. 2 (May 1978): 232–35; idem, *Formation of Modern Lebanon*, p. 119–20, 125; Rabinovich, *War for Lebanon*, pp. 21–22.

50. Hof, *Galilee Divided*, pp. 25–26, 113.

51. Hourani, "Ideologies," p. 38.

52. Albert Hourani, *Minorities in the Arab World* (London: Oxford University Press, 1947), pp. 71–73.

53. Tewfik Khalaf, "The Phalange and the Maronite Community: From Lebanonism to Maronitism," in *Essays on the Crisis in Lebanon*, ed. Roger Owen, pp. 44–46.

54. Hof, *Galilee Divided*, pp. 44–45; Zamir, *Formation of Modern Lebanon*, pp. 169–78; Stephen Longrigg, *Syria and Lebanon under French Mandate* (London: Oxford University Press, 1958), p. 161.

55. Hof, *Galilee Divided*, p. 45.

56. Itzhak Ben Gad, "Israel's Concern for the Christians in Lebanon," *Hatzofeh*, 1 September 1978, p. 3 (Heb.).

57. Sachar, *History of Israel*, p. 22.

58. Eliahu Elath, *Shivat Tzion Ve'arav* [Zionism and the Arabs] (Tel Aviv: Dvir, 1974), p. 303; Eliahu Elath, interview with author, 29 July 1986, Jerusalem; Arida's letter to the Jews of Beirut, quoted in Epstein to Shertok, 1 June 1933, CZA, l9/350B (Heb.); Uri M. Kupperschmidt, "Tmikhat Hapatriarch Hamaroni Arida Bayehudim Nirdafai Hanatzim" [The Maronite Patriarch Arida's support for Jews persecuted by the Nazis], *Pa'amim* 29 (1986): 74.

59. Barry Rubin, *The Arab States and the Palestine Conflict* (Syracuse: Syracuse University Press, 1981), p. 26; Aharon Cohen, *Israel and the Arab World* (New York: Funk & Wagnalls, 1970), pp. 90–98; Hochberg to Jacobson, quoted in Walter Laqueur, *A History of Zionism* (New York: Schocken Books, 1976), p. 212; Neville J. Mandel, *The Arabs and Zionism Before World War I* (Berkeley: University of California Press, 1976), pp. 154–56.

60. Cohen, *Israel and the Arab World*, p. 92.

61. Abraham Elmaleh, "Report of August 1919", CZA, L4/794.

62. David Tidhar, *Entziklopedia Lechalutzai Hayishuv Ubonav* [Encyclopedia of the Yishuv's pioneers and its builders] (Tel Aviv: Sifriyat Rishonim, 1947–71), pp.4664–66.

63. Na'aman to Zionist Commission, 13 July 1920, CZA, L3/625 (Heb.).

64. Na'aman to Zionist Commission, 8 July 1920, CZA, L3/625 (Heb.).

65. Village of Deir Mimus to Zionist Organization in Jerusalem, 7 July 1920, CZA, L3/625 (Arab.). See also thank-you letters from Jedida and Marjyoun of 5 July 1920, Abel al-Kumh of 7 July 1920, Deir Mimus of 8 July 1920, and Marjyoun of 8 July 1920, all in CZA, L3/625 (Arab.). A letter from Rashid Jumblatt, the mutassarif, also impressed Na'aman. As per Na'aman's request, Jumblatt drew up a list of the most needy Christian refugees, ending with a prayer that God "give to the Zionist Society all the good fortune which it deserves." Na'aman reported to Jerusalem that Rashid was the nephew and political heir of Druze leader Nasif Jumblatt and that it would serve Zionist interests well to maintain close relations with this soon-to-be Druze chieftain. See Rashid Jumblatt to Pinchas Na'aman, 3 July 1920 (Fr.), and Na'aman to Zionist Commission, 8 July 1920 (Heb.), both in CZA, L3/625.

66. Na'aman to Zionist Commission, 8 July 1920, CZA, L3/625 (Heb.).

67. Zionist Commission to Na'aman, 1 and 22 July 1920, CZA, S2/579 and L3/625 (Heb.).

68. Pinchas Na'aman, "In Syria," [ca. July or August 1927?], ED, File 1630 (Heb.).

69. J. J. Caleb to Weizmann, 6 June 1920, CZA, Z4/16078 (Fr.).

70. Ibid.

71. Draft Treaty, n.d., CZA, Z4/16078 (Heb.); Treaty, 26 March 1920, CZA, S25/9907 (Heb., Fr., Arab.).

72. Treaty, 26 March 1920, CZA, S25/9907; Yehoshua Porath, "History of Friendship," *Jerusalem Post*, 22 May 1981, p. 7; Benny Morris, "The Phalange Connection," *Jerusalem Post Magazine*, 1 July 1983, p. 7.

73. Caplan, *Futile Diplomacy*, vol. 1 (London: Cass, 1983–86), p. 69; Elath, interview with author, 29 July 1986.

74. Sfeir to Weizmann, 3 May 1920, CZA, Z4/16078 (Fr.); Eder to Weizmann, 17 May 1920, CZA, Z4/16033. S. Felman, a Zionist activist in Damascus to whom Eder apparently forwarded a report received from Sfeir and company, warned Eder about Sfeir even prior to Hankin's signing the accord. Felman informed Eder that the report was full of untruths, called its authors charlatans, and advised against doing business with them. See Felman to Eder, 21 February 1920, CZA, L3/278 (Fr.); see also Neil Caplan, *Futile Diplomacy*, vol. 1, p. 68.

75. "Information," 30 January 1930, AD, MAN/1064 (Fr.).

76. Moshe Sharett, *Yoman Medini* [Political diary] (Tel Aviv: Am Oved, 1968–79), 17 February 1936, vol. 1, p. 65, and 23 May 1937, vol. 2, p. 141.

Chapter 3

1. Stephen Longrigg, *Syria and Lebanon Under the French Mandate* (London: Oxford University Press, 1958), pp. 203–5, 252.

2. Eliahu Elath, interview with author, 29 July 1986, Jerusalem; E. Epstein, "Meetings and Conversations During My Visit to Syria, October 1934," December 1934, CZA, S25/10225 (Heb.).

3. Matti Moosa, *The Maronites in History* (Syracuse: Syracuse University Press, 1986), pp. 288–92.

4. Arida to Weizmann, 4 April 1934, WA (Fr.).

5. Mubarak, "The Archbishop Mubarak Witnesses the Truth: An Open Letter to His Excellency the Sheikh Bishara al-Khoury," 26 May 1947, and "From the Bishop Mubarak to the Honorable Lebanese People," 24 August 1947, both in ISA, 2569/19 (Arab.); "Report of a Speech by Bishop Mubarak," 2 March 1938, CZA, S25/6639 (Heb.).

6. William W. Haddad, "Christian Arab Attitudes Toward the Arab-Israel Conflict," *Muslim World* 67, no. 2 (April 1977): 141.

7. Eliahu Elath, *Shivat Tzion Ve'arav* [Zionism and the Arabs] (Tel Aviv: Dvir, 1974), p. 308.

8. Ibid., pp. 308–9.

9. Quoted in Joseph D. Farhi to I. Ben-Zvi, 19 October 1937, CZA, S25/5580.

10. Eliahu Elath, "Hatziyonut Hafanikit Balevanon" [Phoenician Zionism in Lebanon], *Cathedra* 35 (April 1985): 109; idem, "Phoenician Zionism in Lebanon," *Jerusalem Quarterly* 42 (Spring 1987): 38–56.

11. Elath, "Hatziyonut Hafanikit," pp. 109–10; Elath, interview with author, 29 July 1986.

12. "Letter From E. Epstein to the Executive" (Beirut), 3 November 1932, WA. His description of Maronite Francophilia held truer for the Maronite elite than for the Maronite population at large.

13. Elath, "Hatziyonut Hafanikit," p. 111.

14. Elath, "Hatziyonut Hafanikit," pp. 110–16; Elath, *Shivat Tzion Ve'arav*, pp. 306–8; I. Ben-Zvi, "Zones of the Arab World," *Palestine Post*, 24 July 1936, p. 5; Moosa, *Maronites in History*, p. 303; Albert Hourani, "Ideologies of the Mountain and the City," in *Essays on the Crisis in Lebanon*, ed. Roger Owen (London: Ithaca, 1976), p. 39; Kamal Salibi, *A House of Many Mansions* (Berkeley: University of California Press, 1988), pp. 87–107, 167–81. Salibi

challenges the Phoenician theory and suggests a Yemenite origin for the Maronites (ibid., pp. 88–89).

15. Eliahu Elath, *Zionism at the UN* (Philadelphia: Jewish Publication Society, 1976), p. 255; idem, *Shivat Tzion Ve'arav*, p. 308.

16. E. Epstein, "Meetings and Conversations During My Visit to Syria, October 1934," December 1934, CZA, S25/10225 (Heb.).

17. Elath, *Zionism at the UN*, p. 256; idem, *Shivat Tzion Ve'arav*, p. 306. According to the Hebrew Bible, Solomon and Hiram cooperated on several occasions, most notably during the building of the Holy Temple in Jerusalem, when Hiram in Tyre provided Solomon with all the cedar and cypress wood he required and received, in return, regular deliveries of wheat and oil. On the basis of that successful mutual enterprise, the two kings later embarked together on a "joint maritime venture of great magnitude and not inconsiderable risk" (Alexander Flinder, "Is This Solomon's Seaport?" *Biblical Archaeology Review* 15, no. 4 [July/August 1989]: 32–35). Solomon provided access to the Red Sea and unlimited labor, and Hiram contributed his seafaring skills and the renowned Cedars of Lebanon for the construction of a fleet. The partnership prospered and continued for many years.

Heskel Haddad proposes a genealogical link between Phoenicians and biblical Israelites. According to Haddad's interpretation of biblical history, Abraham crossed into Canaan and finally settled with most of his followers in the countryside around Hebron; but some of his company "went to dwell in the north between the mountains of Lebanon and the Mediterranean; the latter became the Phoenicians and even until the time of Solomon were considered Hebrews and cousins" (Heskel M. Haddad, *Jews of Arab and Islamic Countries* [New York: Shengold, 1984], p. 15).

Right-wing Zionists (the radical Revisionists) and the anti-Zionist Canaanite movement sometimes adopted the Hebrew-Phoenician connection for their own purposes. See Avraham Stern, "Ha'ivrim Kekolonizatorim Velochamim" [The Hebrews as colonialists and fighters], in *Lohmei Herut Yisrael, Ktavim Alef* (Tel Aviv: 1959), copy in CZA; Ya'akov Shavit, "Hebrews and Phoenicians: An Ancient Historical Image and Its Usage," *Studies in Zionism* 5, no. 2 (Autumn 1984): 157–80.

18. E. Epstein, "Meetings and Conversations During My Visit to Syria, October 1934," December 1934, CZA, S25/10225 (Heb.). Zionists who spent time in Lebanon remember the Young Phoenicians (if they remember them at all) as a tiny group of no political consequence. Some even suggest that their lack of influence propelled them toward the Zionists: "We seemed strong and they wanted to benefit from our strength" (Chaim Levkov, interview with author, 11 May 1987, Holon, Israel; Shula Cohen-Kishik, interview with author, 20 May 1987, Jerusalem; Yehoshua Palmon, interview with author, 26 March 1987, Kfar Shmariyahu, Israel). Elath insisted that the Young Phoenicians, regardless of their influence, were genuine believers, dreamers, rich men who neither needed nor accrued personal gain from their pro-Zionist position but were, in fact, true friends of the Zionist movement (Interview with author, 29 July 1986).

19. Weizmann to Victor Jacobson, 25 December 1924, in *LCW*, vol. 12, letter 220; Yoav Gelber, "Antecedents of the Jewish-Druze Alliance in Palestine," *Middle Eastern Studies* 28, no. 2 (April 1992): 352–73; Elath, interview with author, 29 July 1986.

20. Gelber, "Antecedents of the Jewish-Druze Alliance"; Shimoni, interview with author, 4 March 1987.

21. Eder to Weizmann, 19 March and 20 May 1922, CZA, Z4/16056; Weizmann to Eder, 21 and 30 March 1922 and 3 June 1922, in *LCW*, vol. 11, letters 75, 76 and 109; Yehoshua Porath, *The Palestinian Arab National Movement* (London: Cass, 1977), pp. 112–14; Howard M. Sacher, *A History of Israel* (New York: Knopf, 1981), p. 168; Neil Caplan, *Futile Diplomacy* (London: Cass, 1983–86), vol. 1, pp. 54, 60, 113.

22. Itamar Ben-Avi to Weizmann, 10 January 1930, and multiple other reports from

1930, WA. For Weizmann's impressions of al-Sulh and what he thought the man could do for the Zionist movement, see Weizmann to Felix M. Warburg, 15 May 1930, in *LCW*, vol. 14, letter 272.

23. Weizmann to Warburg, 15 May 1930, in *LCW*, vol. 14, letter 272; "Discussion at the Meeting of the Political Advisory Committee" (London), 25 June 1936, CZA, S25/6326. See also Caplan, *Futile Diplomacy*, vol. 1, pp. 17, 49.

24. Elath, interviews with author, 29 July and 14 October 1986; "Discussion at the Meeting of the Political Advisory Committee" (London), 25 June 1936, CZA, S25/6326.

25. Victor Jacobson, "Report on My Trip to Eretz Yisrael and Syria," 12 May 1933, WA (Heb., orig. Ger.); E. Epstein, "Meetings and Conversations During My Visit to Syria, October 1934," December 1934, CZA, S25/10225 (Heb.); Neil Caplan and Ian Black, "Israel and Lebanon: Origins of a Relationship," *Jerusalem Quarterly* 27 (Spring 1983), p. 53.

26. E. Epstein, "Meetings and Conversations During My Visit to Syria, October 1934," December 1934, CZA, S25/10225 (Heb.).

27. E. Epstein, "Meetings and Conversations During My Visit to Syria, October 1934," December 1934, CZA, S25/10225 (Heb.); Epstein to Ya'akov Franco, 21 January 1935, CZA, S25/3143 (Heb.).

28. Epstein to Shertok, 17 May 1933, CZA, L9/350B (Heb.).

29. Weizmann to Elie Aad, 30 December 1935, in *LCW*, vol. 17, letter 117.

30. Harry Zehenny to Weizmann, 20 December 1935, WA; see also Weizmann to Monsignor Joseph Rahme, 29 October 1935, WA; Rahme to Weizmann, 12 November 1935, CZA, S25/6560; Zehenny to Weizmann, 3 December 1935, CZA, S25/6560. Other Maronite clergymen similarly directed Maronites with business in Palestine to the Jewish Agency and furnished them with letters of introduction. See Paul Akl to Weizmann, 17 July 1938 and subsequent letters concerning Albert Chidiac, CZA, S25/3042 (Heb., Fr.).

31. Rahme to Weizmann, 12 November 1935, CZA, S25/6560.

32. Zehenny to Weizmann, 3 December 1935, CZA, S25/6560.

33. Epstein to Naccache, 31 October 1934, CZA, S25/3143.

34. Shertok to Bernard Joseph, 7 October 1937, CZA, Z4/17032. Naccache also availed himself of Epstein's offer of assistance. He invented a new type of motor and prevailed upon Epstein to have the device evaluated by experts at the Technion in Haifa. There ensued an extensive correspondence concerning the testing of the motor; and Epstein specifically instructed the Technion faculty to address Naccache through the Jewish Agency, with Epstein as middleman. See correspondence between Epstein and Naccache and between Epstein and various professors at the Technion, 1939–40, CZA, S25/5580 (Eng., Heb., Fr.).

35. Elath, "Hatziyonut Hafanikit," pp. 118–22; Frederic Hof, *Galilee Divided: The Israel-Lebanon Frontier, 1916–1984*, (Boulder: Westview, 1985), p. 30.

36. French Delegate General to Department of Public Works and Public Works to Delegate General, 27 and 31 January 1942; Delegate General to Cabinet, 10 February 1942; and "Information," 10 October 1942, all in AD, MAN/808 (Fr.).

37. The rise to power of Bishara al-Khoury's anti-Zionist Maronite group in Lebanon and the increasingly bitter conflict in Palestine in the years following the end of the war and prior to Israeli independence made it impossible to pursue Naccache's project.

38. Shertok to S. Horowitz, 27 November 1933, CZA, S25/4552I.

39. [?] to Shertok, 7 June 1933, CZA, S25/6560 (Heb.).

40. Ian Black, "Zionism and the Arabs, 1936–1939," Ph.D. diss, University of London, 1978, p. 276.

41. Epstein to Farhi, 11 November 1937, CZA, S25/5812 (Heb.).

42. "Report of the Visit to Beirut by an Economic Delegation From Palestine, 21–26 January 1940," CZA, S25/5630 (Heb.).

43. Epstein to Shertok, 12 January 1944, CZA, S25/4556 (Heb.).

44. Sasson to Shertok, 12 and 24 September 1939; Sasson to Kaplan, 25 September 1939; Sasson to Luzia, 24 September 1939; Sasson to Harfouche, 21 September 1939, all in CZA, S25/3500 (Heb.). See also Harfouche to Sasson, 11 October 1939, and G.A. to Sasson, 8 November 1939, both in CZA, S25/5580 (Heb.).

45. Rafael Sverdlov, *Halevanon: Tziyorai Mas'a, Im Mapah Vetaish'a Tmunot* [The Lebanon: Travelogue with a map and nine pictures] (Tel Aviv: Kupat Hasefer, 1930), copy in ED.

46. *Halevanon: Eretz Hatayarut Vehakitanot* [The Lebanon: Land of tourism and resorts] (Paris: Economic Department of the Government of Lebanon, 1935), copy in ED.

47. Black, "Zionism and the Arabs," p. 276; Shertok, "Diary of the Political Department," 21 July 1936, CZA, S25/443 (Heb.).

48. "The Patriarch and the Zionists" (French Administrative Advisor for Northern Lebanon to High Commissioner in Beirut), 31 August 1935, AD, MAN/595 (Fr.).

49. Rafael Turgman to Political Department of Jewish Agency, 23 June 1939, CZA, S25/3183 (Heb.).

50. Epstein, "Ties with Lebanon," 9 July 1939; Sasson, "Neighborly Relations with the Resorts of Lebanon," 27 June 1939; Epstein, report of 12 July 1939, all in CZA, S25/3183 (Heb.).

51. Epstein to Shertok, 19 February 1936, CZA, S25/10121 (Heb.).

52. Epstein to Eddé, 24 January 1940, and Director of the President's Cabinet to Epstein, 7 February 1940 (Fr.), both in CZA, S25/5581; Frank Anthony to I. Elazari-Volcani, 24 January 1945, CZA, S25/3561.

53. Epstein to M. Sherman, 29 April 1938 (Heb.); Epstein to George Vayssie, 6 May 1938 (Fr.); Hadassah Medical Organization to Shertok, 15 May 1938 (Heb.); Epstein to H. Yeski, 17 May 1938 (Heb.), all in CZA, S25/5580.

54. Epstein to Shertok, 17 April 1938, CZA, S25/3668 (Heb.).

55. Epstein to Joseph, 19 April 1936, CZA, S25/436, in Black, "Zionism and the Arabs," p. 278; Epstein to Shertok, 17 April 1938, CZA, S25/3668 (Heb.); Black, "Zionism and the Arabs," pp. 276–78.

56. The proposal so impressed Shertok that he approached Arida personally in an attempt to move the idea along. See Shertok to Arida, 3 June 1935, and M. Policar to Shertok, 6 June 1935, both in CZA, S25/4552 II (Fr.).

57. Epstein to Corm, 24 and 31 October 1934 and 24 February 1935, all in CZA, S25/3143.

58. Director of French Intelligence in the Levant, "Information," 7 April 1930, AD, MAN/1064 (Fr.).

59. Elath, "Hatziyonut Hafanikit," pp. 116–18, 122. Elath expended considerable energy on the case of Nahum Slouschz, whose lecture to the Young Phoenician group was repeatedly postponed over a period of three years. Epstein to Slouschz, 22 December 1937, and Epstein to Shertok, 22 March 1938, both in CZA, S25/5580 (Heb.); Corm to Epstein, 23 February 1938, CZA, S25/5580 (Fr.); Epstein to M. Gordon, 17 June 1940, CZA, S25/5580 (Heb.); Gordon to Epstein, 17 June 1940, and Epstein to Gordon, 17 July 1940, both in CZA, S25/4549 (Heb.).

60. Black, "Zionism and the Arabs," p. 278.

61. Sasson contracted with one M.N. in Lebanon for the publication of 75 articles over a period of three months in one Syrian Paper, *al-Istiqlal*, and four Beirut papers, *al-Nahar*, *al-Ahwaal*, *al-Hadis*, and *al-Sharq*; this was a typical arrangement. See Sasson to Shertok, [1937?], CZA, S25/5568 (Heb.). Sasson also succeeded in placing articles in *al-Ahrar*, *La Syrie*, and *L'Orient*, also published in Beirut. See Epstein to Shertok, 24 July 1936, CZA, S25/10121 (Heb.); Sasson to Shertok, 29 December 1937, CZA, S25/5568 (Heb.); Epstein to Vayssie, 13 May 1938, CZA, S25/5580.

62. Sasson, "Activities of the Political Department in Syria and Lebanon," 19 July

1939, CZA, S25/3500; see also Sasson to Shertok, 29 December 1937, CZA, S25/5568 (Heb.); Epstein to Shertok, 24 July 1936, CZA, S25/10121 (Heb.); Sasson to Shertok, [1937?], CZA, S25/5568 (Heb.).

63. Epstein to JAE, 3 November 1932, WA; Epstein to Directorship of the Levant Fair (Tel Aviv), 16 June 1938, CZA, S25/5814 (Heb.); Black, "Zionism and the Arabs," pp. 281–82.

64. Sasson, "Activities of the Political Department in Syria and Lebanon," 19 July 1939, CZA, S25/3500.

65. Eliahu Sasson, *Baderekh el Hashalom* [On the road to peace] (Tel Aviv: Am Oved, 1978), p. 185.

66. Sharett, *Yoman Medini* [Political Diary] (Tel Aviv: Am Oved, 1968–79), 2 July 1939, vol. 4, p. 326.

67. Leo Kohn to Bernard Joseph, 2 January 1939, CZA, S25/3183.

68. Palestine Land Development Company to Jewish Agency, 14 January 1934, CZA, Z4/17024A (Heb.); Epstein to Shertok, 1 June 1933, CZA, L9/350B (Heb.); Weizmann to Adelaide Cohen, 30 April 1934, in *LCW*, vol. 16, letter 273.

69. Minutes of the JAE meeting (Jerusalem), 22 April 1934, CZA, (Heb.). Kenneth Stein documented a similar willingness to sell land privately to the Zionists among some Palestinian Arab leaders who publicly opposed Jewish land acquisition (*The Land Question in Palestine, 1917–1939*, [Chapel Hill: University of North Carolina Press, 1984], pp. 66–69).

70. Nossif Sahadi to Jewish Agency, 13 November 1933, and A. Fellman to Sahadi, 8 January 1934, both in CZA, S25/6560. For the case of Aref Bey Namani, see Ben Bigio to Brodetsky, 28 November 1934; Epstein to Lourie, 18 December 1934; and Lourie to Shertok, 14 January 1934, all in CZA, S25/3143; Elia Simantob to Jewish Agency, 15 September 1935, and J. Gaulan to Simantob, 17 September 1935, both in CZA, S25/6560 (Fr.); Selim Malouf to Ben-Gurion, 14 April 1937, and Jewish Agency to Malouf, 19 April 1937, both in CZA, S25/3500; J. Jammal to Jewish Agency, 3 May 1937, CZA, S25/6560; J. D. Farhi to Weizmann, 3 May 1938, and Robert Cirbeau to Weizmann, 4 May 1938, both in CZA, S25/ 6560 (Fr.).

71. Palestine Land Development Company to Jewish Agency, 14 January 1934, CZA, Z4/17024A (Heb.).

72. Weizmann to Adelaide Cohen, 30 April 1934, in *LCW*, vol. 16, letter 273.

73. The issue of the German Jews transcended Zionist concerns and became a matter of Jewish survival. The proposal to bring German Jews to Lebanon focused on saving Jewish lives, not Jewish state building. To those Zionists who despaired of diverting funds or energy toward a project other than the creation of a Jewish state, Epstein suggested that the growth of a Jewish presence in Lebanon held great national, political and economic importance for the Yishuv in Palestine in that it would create a Jewish hinterland for the future Jewish state. See Epstein, "Letter from Beirut," 16 May 1933, CZA, L9/350B (Heb.).

74. Shertok to Epstein, 15 May 1933, and Epstein to Shertok, 17 May 1933, both in CZA, L9/350B (Heb.).

75. Weizmann to Felix Warburg, 5 November 1933, in *LCW*, vol. 16, letter 116.

76. Weizmann to Gabriel Arnou, 25 September 1935, in *LCW*, vol. 17, letter 23.

77. Multiple correspondence, 1933–35, AE, LE 18–40/PAL 68, 69 (Fr.); see also correspondence, April 1934, in AE, Série Société des Nations/Mandats [SDN/MAND] 571 (Fr.); Gourevitch to de Martel and de Martel to Foreign Ministry, 10 October and 16 November 1934, both in AD, MAN/617 (Fr.). See also Weizmann to Alexis Leger, 17 June 1933, in *LCW*, vol. 15, letter 426; Weizmann to Ruppin, 24 October 1933 and 21 November 1933, and Weizmann to Warburg, 20 November 1933, all in *LCW*, vol. 16, letters 94, 134, 137.

78. Helleu to Ministry of Foreign Affairs, 25 September 1933, AE, LE 18–40/PAL 65

(Fr.); de Martel to Ministry of Foreign Affairs, 11 May 1934; Multiple "Notes," June–July 1934; Ministry of Foreign Affairs to de Martel, 27 September 1934; and multiple correspondence, autumn 1934, all in AE, LE 18–40/PAL 69 (Fr.); de Martel to Ministry of Foreign Affairs, 16 January 1935, AE, LE 18–40/PAL 68 (Fr.).

79. Summary of offers coming in, Epstein to Shertok, 17 May 1933, CZA, L9/350B (Heb.); "Communiqué" (Beirut), 13 April 1934, AE, LE 18–40/PAL 69 (Fr.); Michel Faragh to Association of German Jews, 17 August 1933, and Dr. Loe to Faragh, 30 August 1933, both in CZA, S25/6560 (Fr.); Faragh to Jewish Agency, 22 December 1934 (Fr.), and Epstein to Faragh, 31 December 1934, both in CZA, S25/3143; Fidelity Emun Investment and Trust Company to Eliezer Kaplan, 11 October 1935, and JAE to Fidelity Emun, 13 November 1935, both in CZA, S25/6560 (Heb.); "Jewish Settlement in Syria, 1934–35," CZA, S25/5567. Gabriel Arnou, a French Christian industrialist, teamed up with a French Jew, Michel Rubinstein, to form a company to bring Jews to Lebanon and build settlements, schools, factories, irrigation systems, and hospitals. Their proposals advanced to quite a detailed stage of development. See Rubinstein to Weizmann, 24 May 1934, CZA, Z4/17024A (Fr.); Rubinstein to de Martel, 31 December 1934, CZA, S25/5567 (Fr.); Proposed contract between Arnou and Weizmann [December 1934?] (Fr.), and Weizmann to Arnou, 24 May 1935, both in CZA, Z4/17024A; Arnou to French Ministry of Foreign Affairs, 24 April 1935, AE, LE 18–40/PAL 69 (Fr.); Weizmann to Arnou, 25 September 1935, in *LCW,* vol. 17, letter 23; Arnou to Weizmann, 30 September 1935, CZA, Z4/17024A (Fr.); Weizmann to Rubinstein, 2 February 1936, in *LCW,* vol. 17, letter 156. See also Epstein to A. Dana (director of Bank Misr, Beirut), 28 February 1935; Dana to JAE, 12 March 1935 (Fr.); and Dana to Jewish Agency, 10 April 1935 (Fr.), all in CZA, S25/3143.

80. Epstein to Shertok, 17 May 1933, CZA, L9/350B (Heb.).

81. Shertok to Weizmann, 2 October 1936, CZA, S25/6327; Epstein to Shertok, 17 May 1933, CZA, L9/350B (Heb.).

82. "Note of Discussion at the Meeting of the Political Advisory Committee" (London), 25 June 1936, CZA, S25/6326; JAE meeting (Jerusalem), 26 July 1936, CZA, vol. 25/3; Shertok, "Diary of the Political Department," 21 July 1936, CZA, S25/443. Weizmann allegedly acknowledged that Lebanon was certainly not Palestine but thought that Jewish refugees might look upon it as the next best thing, especially the district near Tyre and Sidon. See Arthur Wauchope, "Report on a Conversation with Weizmann," 13–14 December 1936, CO 733/297, File 75156/V, held in ISA.

83. Shertok to Epstein, 15 May 1933, CZA, L9/350B (Heb.).

84. Corm to Epstein, 11 April 1938, CZA, S25/5580 (Fr.).

85. Sharett, *Yoman Medini,* 17 February 1936, vol. 1, pp. 64–65; Black, *Zionism and the Arabs,* p. 273.

86. High Commissioner Ponsot to Minister of Foreign Affairs, 16 June 1933, AE, LE 18–40/PAL 68 (Fr.); Epstein to Shertok, 1 June 1933, CZA, L9/350B (Heb.). The patriarch's letter is translated into Hebrew in Uri M. Kupperschmidt, "Tmikhat Hapatriarch Hamaroni Arida Bayehudim Nirdafai Hanatzim" [The Maronite Patriarch Arida's support for Jews persecuted by the Nazis], *Pa'amim* 29 (1986): 72–75; the letter is translated into English in Norman A. Stillman, *The Jews of Arab Lands in Modern Times* (Philadelphia: Jewish Publication Society, 1991), p. 370.

87. Arida to Weizmann, 4 April 1934, WA; Arida to Weizmann, 12 May 1934, CZA, Z4/17024A (Fr.).

88. Quoted by Edmund Meir, "The Maronites: With Special Regard to Their Political Development Since 1860," 24 June 1942, CZA, S25/6639, pp. 21–22. See also Elath, *Shivat Tzion Ve'arav,* pp. 295–96; French Criminal Investigation Department, "Visit of the Maronite Patriarch to Beirut," 23 April 1937, AD, MAN/596 (Fr.); Stillman, *Jews of Arab Lands in Modern Times,* pp. 376–77; Kupperschmidt, "Tmikhat Hapatriarch Hamaroni Arida," p. 77.

89. Arthur Ruppin to Weizmann, 1 June 1936, CZA, Z4/17024B. The Agency conducted negotiations through an intermediary in Beirut, George Mouchawar.

90. Arthur Ruppin to Weizmann, 1 June 1936, CZA, Z4/17024B; Weizmann to Ruppin, 11 June 1936, in *LCW,* vol. 17, letter 245. For a minority Zionist position advocating the immediate conclusion of the deal and the beginning of German Jewish immigration to Lebanon, see Hankin to Thon, 2 June 1936, CZA, Z4/17024B (Heb.).

91. Sasson to Ben-Gurion, 16 April 1937, CZA, S25/5568 (Heb.).

92. Epstein, "Letter From Beirut," 16 May 1933, CZA, L9/350B (Heb.).

93. Weizmann to Adelaide Cohen, 30 April 1934, and Weizmann to Arida, 3 May 1934, both in *LCW,* vol. 16, letters 273, 280.

94. Concerning Weizmann's discussions with the high commissioner, see de Martel to Weizmann, 6 April 1934, and Weizmann to de Martel, 11 May 1934, both in CZA, Z4/17024A (Fr.); Weizmann to Ruppin, 29 April 1934, in *LCW,* vol. 16, letter 272; Weizmann to Arida, 3 May 1934, in *LCW,* vol. 16, letter 280; and Arida to Weizmann, 12 May 1934, CZA, Z4/17024A (Fr.); L. Mansell-Jeune to Weizmann, 7 April 1935, CZA, S25/6560; Weizmann to Shertok, 11 September 1936 and 14–18 October 1936, both in *LCW,* vol. 17, letters 312 and 336. See also [de Martel?], "Visit to the British High Commissioner in Palestine," 11 January 1934, AE, LE 18–40/PAL 65 (Fr.).

95. "Note for the Ministerial Cabinet," 29 April 1933, AE, LE 18–40/PAL 64 (Fr.); French Consul General in Jerusalem to Minister of Foreign Affairs, 6 June 1933, AE, LE 18–40/PAL 65 (Fr.).

96. Meir, "The Maronites: With Special Regard to Their Political Development Since 1860," 24 June 1942, CZA, S25/6639, pp. 21–22.

97. Epstein to Shertok, 17 May 1933, CZA, L9/350B (Heb.).

98. "Extracts from the Minutes of the Twenty-Fifth Session of the Permanent Mandates Commission, 1934," CZA, S25/4552 II; "Decree of 18 January 1934," AE, LE 18–40/PAL 68.

99. Summary of telegrams in "Protests Against the Pro-Jewish Speech by Mgr. Mubarak," 24 April 1937; Association for Muslim Civilization to high commissioner, 26 April 1937; "Lebanese Politics," 27 April 1937; "Review of the Lebanese and Syrian Press" and "Situation in Lebanon," de Martel to Ministry of Foreign Affairs, 28 April 1937; "Demonstrations Against Mgr. Mubarak," 3 May 1937; and French Consulate in Jerusalem to High Commission in Beirut, 4 May 1937, all in AD, MAN/596 (Fr.). See also Sasson, *Baderekh,* p. 40; "The Question of Zionists Immigrating to Syria," 14 March 1935, CZA, S25/10121 (Heb.); Kupperschmidt, "Tmikhat Hapatriarch Hamaroni Arida," p. 78.

100. Director of French Criminal Investigation Department to High Commissioner's Advisor on Foreign Relations, 31 August 1933, AD, MAN/615 (Fr.).

101. J. Attieh and J. D. Farhi to de Martel, 10 May 1935, and Committee for the Defense of the Rights of Israelites in Central Europe and the East to de Martel [1935?], both in CZA, S25/5567 (Fr.). For their detailed advice on how to minimize local objections to the plan, see Attieh to Gourevitch, 15 March 1935, AD, MAN/617 B (Fr.). See also Kupperschmidt, "Tmikhat Hapatriarch Hamaroni Arida," p. 76.

102. Albert Hourani, *Minorities in the Arab World* (London: Oxford University Press, 1947), p. 63; Michael Sasson to author, 24 April 1987 (from Kibbutz Hanita, Israel). Sasson is a native of Beirut, where he grew up, and a relative of Eliahu Sasson. For further descriptions of Lebanese Jewry, see Haddad, *Jews of Arab and Islamic Countries,* pp. 59–60; David Sitton, *Kehilot Yehudai Sefarad Vehamizrach Ba'olam Beyameinu* [Jewish communities of Spain and the East in the world in our days] (Jerusalem: Ahva Cooperative, 1974), pp. 59–64; Stillman, *Jews of Arab Lands in Modern Times,* pp. 80, 83–84; and Irit Avramski-Bleiyi, "Yehudai Suriya Velevanon Takhat Shilton Vishi" [The Jews of Syria and Lebanon under Vichy rule], *Pa'amim* 28 (1986): 131–57.

103. For some of Farhi's complaints about the Jewish community in Beirut, see Farhi to Greenbaum, 14 January 1935, and Farhi to Epstein, 28 January 1935, both in CZA, S25/3143. For Farhi's protestations that a pro-Zionist position would endanger the Jews of Lebanon, see Frederick H. Kisch, *Palestine Diary* (London: Gollancz, 1938), p. 123; Farhi to the Histadrut, 27 January 1937, CZA, S25/2204 (Heb.); Farhi to Epstein, 4 May 1937, CZA, S25/6319 (Heb.). When Farhi caught wind of a proposal for the Agency to establish a Beirut office he squelched it in no uncertain terms: "The idea is close to my heart and I would love to be part of it but conditions now absolutely prohibit any such undertaking." See Farhi to Histadrut, 27 January 1937; A. Borak to JAE [late 1936?]; and Keren Kayemet to Political Department, 10 January 1937, all in CZA, S25/2204 (Heb.).

The Farhi-Agency connection was sufficiently close that when it appeared that new elections in Lebanon might allow for Jewish representation in Parliament, the Agency tried to use its influence to ensure his election. Its representative in Paris spoke with officials at the Quai d'Orsay and with Premier Léon Blum in an attempt to have Paris encourage Eddé to set aside a seat for a Jewish delegate. See Ben-Zvi to Marc Jarblum, 1 September 1937 (Heb.) and Farhi to Ben-Zvi, 19 October 1937 (Fr.), both in CZA, S25/5580.

104. "Note of Interview with Dr. Attieh From Beirut," 8 December 1929, CZA, S25/ 4552 I; Cohen-Kishik, interview with author, 20 May 1986; Michael Sasson to author, 24 April 1987. On several occasions, young Lebanese Jews contacted the Agency directly with proposals for extensive Zionist activities, requesting guidance and funding from the Agency. For a polite demurral, see Provisional Committee to Kisch, early October 1930 (Heb., Arab.), and Kisch to JAE, 19 October 1930, both in CZA, L9/350B; Kisch to J. Azar, 19 October 1930; Provisional Committee to Kisch, 23 November 1930 (Fr.); and Kisch to Provisional Committee, 4 December 1930, all in CZA, S25/4552 I.

105. Elath, interview with author, 14 October 1986; Palmon, interview with author, 26 March 1987; Amnon Shamosh, interview with author, 29 April 1987, Kibbutz Ma'ayan Bar-uch, Israel. At one point, Sasson recommended briefing Jewish leaders in Arab countries with regard to Zionist aims and encouraging them to report any conversations with influential Arabs; but he clearly did not envision employing them as spies. "Plan for Activity Among the Arabs" (Sasson to Ben-Gurion), 21 April 1939, CZA, S25/8163 (Heb.).

An exception was Shula Cohen-Kishik, a Jerusalemite who married a Lebanese Jew and moved to the Jewish quarter of Beirut in 1936. Of her own initiative, she became deeply involved in smuggling illegal Jewish refugees and arms to the Yishuv; and in 1948, the Israeli government began using her as a full-fledged spy. The Lebanese originally condemned her to death upon her apprehension and conviction in 1962. She remained in prison pending appeal until Lebanon returned her to Israel in the prisoner exchange following the Six Day War of 1967. Shula Cohen-Kishik, interview with author, 20 May 1986, Jerusalem; Aviezer Golan and Danny Pinkas, *Shem Tzofen: Hapeninah* [Code name: the Pearl] (Tel Aviv: Zmora/ Bitan, 1980); idem, *Shula: Code Name "The Pearl"* (New York: Delacorte, 1980). Yishuv military (as opposed to political) institutions did try to place Jewish spies in Arab countries. Regarding Gamliel Cohen, a Syrian Jew sent in January 1948 by Palmach intelligence to spy in Beirut, see Avner Avrahami, "The First Israeli Mole," *Ma'ariv*, 6 October 1992, pp. 6–9 (Heb.); Gamliel Cohen, interview with author, 7 May 1993, Tel Aviv.

106. Itzhak Ben-Zvi to Shertok, 8 September 1938, CZA, S25/3500.

107. Shamosh, interview with author, 29 April 1987.

108. Mubarak to Dr. Attieh, "Receipt for Money Donated by the Jewish Community to the Schools in the Maronite Parish," 21 August 1947, CZA, S25/4029 (Arab.); Elath, interview with author, 14 October 1986; Epstein, "A Letter From Beirut," 3 February 1939, CZA, Z4/17024 B.

Regarding the Phalange, see Tewfik Khalaf, "The Phalange and the Maronite Commu- nity: From Lebanonism to Maronitism," in *Essays on the Crisis in Lebanon*, ed. Roger Owen;

Frank Stoakes, "The Super Vigilantes: The Lebanese Kataeb Party as Builder, Surrogate and Defender of the State," *Middle Eastern Studies* 11, no. 3 (October 1975): 215–36; Itamar Rabinovich, *The War for Lebanon, 1970–1983* (Ithaca: Cornell University Press, 1984); Walid Khalidi, *Conflict and Violence in Lebanon* (Cambridge: Center for International Studies, Harvard University, 1979); and any history of modern Lebanon.

109. Michael Sasson to author, 24 April 1987; Cohen-Kishik, interview with author, 20 May 1986.

110. "News From the Lebanon" [December 1949?], ISA, 2531/12 (Heb.); Cohen-Kishik, interview with author, 20 May 1986; Ya'akov Shimoni, interview with author, 4 March 1987, Jerusalem; Michael Sasson to author, 23 June 1987; Michael Hudson, *The Precarious Republic: Political Modernization in Lebanon* (New York: Random House, 1968), pp. 48–49; Kamal Salibi, interview with author, 31 October 1992, Portland, Oregon.

111. Epstein, "Letter From Beirut," 3 February 1939, CZA, S25/5574; Elath, interview with author, 14 October 1986; Ya'akov Shimoni, interview with author, 4 March 1987; Shimoni, lecture at the Shiloah Institute, Tel Aviv University, 7 December 1983; Porath, interview with author, 10 March 1987.

112. Yitzhak Ben Ya'akov, "The Christians in Lebanon—Between the Hammer and the Anvil," *Davar,* 6 April 1946 (Heb.). William Haddad agrees that the Phalange "did not wish to have a Jewish state on its borders . . . not for any altruistic motives but for economic ones, [namely, the] economic fear of a Jewish state, that would bring with it superior western technology and ideas" ("Christian Arab Attitudes," p. 134).

113. Notes of a meeting with Pierre Gemayel, quoted in S. Kharali, "A Visit in Lebanon and Syria" [late 1936 or early 1937?], CZA, S25/5570 (Heb.).

CHAPTER 4

1. Victor Jacobson, "Report on My Trip to Eretz-Yisrael and Syria," 12 May 1933, WA (Heb., orig. Germ.). An extract is translated in Neil Caplan and Ian Black, "Israel and Lebanon: Origins of a Relationship," *Jerusalem Quarterly* 27 (Spring 1983): 53–54.

2. Shertok to Arida, 3 June 1935, and M. Policar to Shertok, 6 June 1935, both in CZA, S25/4552 II (Fr.); Elath, "Hatziyonut Hafanikit Balevanon" [Phoenician Zionism in Lebanon], *Cathedra* 35 (April 1985): 116–18, 122–24.

3. Constitution of the Lebanon-Palestine Society [1938?], CZA, S25/4552 II (Fr.).

4. Elath, "Hatziyonut Hafanikit," p. 124. Eliahu Sasson mentions receiving a proposal similar to Corm's Lebanon-Palestine Society from a Maronite notable in Beirut in June of 1938 (*Baderekh el Hashalom* [On the road to peace] [Tel Aviv: Am Oved, 1978], pp. 126–27).

5. [Bernard Joseph?] to Eddé, 21 January 1936, CZA, S25/5581.

6. Quoted in Weizmann, "Note of Discussion at Meeting of Political Advisory Committee" (London), 25 June 1936, CZA, S25/6326.

7. Weizmann to Shertok, 11 September 1936, CZA, Z4/17032, quoted in Ian Black, "Zionism and the Arabs, 1936–1939," Ph.D. diss., University of London, 1978, p. 285.

8. Shertok to Weizmann, 2 October 1936, CZA, S25/6327.

9. Epstein, "A Conversation with the President of the Republic of Lebanon, Emile Eddé," 22 September 1936, CZA, S25/5581 (Heb.).

10. Ibid. See also Moshe Sharett, *Yoman Medini* [Political diary] (Tel Aviv: Am Oved, 1968), 27 September 1936, vol. 1, pp. 316–17.

11. Shertok to Weizmann, 2 October 1936, CZA, S25/6327.

12. Shertok to Lourie, 22 September 1936, CZA, S25/6327; E. E[pstein] to Amos Landman, 29 September 1936, CZA, S25/10121.

13. "Draft of a Pact Submitted the Twenty-Third of December 1936 to Mr. Eddé and Communicated by Him to Mr. de Martel," CZA, Z4/17024B (Fr.); also in AE, LE 18–40/

PAL 67 and AD, MAN/617B (Fr.). An extract is translated in Caplan and Black, "Israel and Lebanon," pp. 54–55.

14. Isaac Kadmi-Cohen's reports of his meetings with Eddé [first week of January 1937?] and 9 January 1937, both in CZA, Z4/17024B (Fr.).

15. Isaac Kadmi-Cohen's report of his meeting with de Martel, 7 January 1937, CZA, Z4/17024B (Fr.).

16. Ibid.; de Martel to French Minister of Foreign Affairs, 13 January 1937, AE, LE 18–40/PAL 67 (Fr.).

17. Weizmann to Kadmi-Cohen, 20 April and 3 November 1937, AE, LE 18–40/PAL 67 (Fr.); Sasson, *Baderekh*, p. 106; See also *LCW*, vol. 17, pp. xxii, 352.

18. Weizmann to Shertok, 11 and 26 September and 2 October 1936, in *LCW*, vol. 17, letters 312, 318, 327.

19. Shertok to Weizmann, 2 October 1936, CZA, S25/6327. Others in the department felt that time and experience reflected poorly on Kadmi-Cohen. Two years after Shertok's wary estimate, Bernard Joseph reported that the Agency representative in Paris, Marc Jarblum, was complaining that Kadmi-Cohen's activities were "fraught with danger as he is hopelessly uninformed, and a bluffer to boot" (Joseph to Shertok, 11 January 1938, CZA, S25/5476).

20. De Martel to French Minister of Foreign Affairs, 13 January 1937, AE, LE 18–40/PAL 67 (Fr.).

21. Testimony of Chaim Weizmann Before Palestine Royal Commission, 8 January 1937, CZA, S25/4642.

22. Weizmann, "Summary Notes of Two Meetings with M. Léon Blum" (Paris), 27 and 30 January 1937, WA.

23. M. Meyrier (aide to the high commissioner) to Minister of Foreign Affairs, 3 July 1936, AE, LE 18–40/PAL 66 (Fr.); Multiple reports, 1938, AD, MAN/648, 649 (Fr.).

24. "News from the Arab Bureau," 29 April 1936, CZA, S25/10121 (Heb.); A. Shenkar to Shertok, 19 June 1936, CZA, S25/9783 (Heb.); JAE meeting (Jerusalem), 26 July 1936, CZA, vol. 25/3 (Heb.).

25. Epstein to A. Shenkar, 2 July 1936, CZA, S25/10121 (Heb.).

26. Report from David HaCohen, 22 October 1936, CZA, S25/9783 (Heb.).

27. Quoted in Dr. Joseph's Office Diary, 7 October 1937, CZA, S25/1511; Sasson, *Baderekh*, p. 78.

28. [?] to I. Ben-Zvi, 28 October 1937, CZA, S25/5580 (Fr.).

29. Furlonge dismissed the possibility that Arab nationalist support for the Palestinian revolt would result in serious anti-British sentiment with classic imperialist reasoning: "Their attitude at present seems more like that of a child whose venerated father has suddenly and incomprehensibly beaten him; he is resentful and a little bewildered that the injury should have been done to him, but would not wish to change his father for anyone else's" (Furlonge to Anthony Eden, 14 August 1936, FO371/20023, held in ISA). The thought that the child might feel he is ready to lead an independent life did not occur to him.

30. Consul general Harvard to Sir Oliphant, May 1938, FO371/21876, held in ISA.

31. "Information: Anti-Semitic Campaign," 8 April 1938, AD, MAN/615 (Fr.); Tract Distributed by the Higher Committee of Students and the Christian and Muslim Youth (Beirut), 28 July 1938, AD, MAN/652 (Arab. and Fr.).

32. E. Epstein, "Letters from Beirut," 3 and 28 September and 14 October 1938, all in CZA, S25/5574 (Heb.).

33. E. Epstein, "Letters from Beirut," 3 September and 8 October 1938, both in CZA, S25/5574 (Heb.).

34. Frederic C. Hof, *Galilee Divided: The Israel-Lebanon Frontier 1916–1984* (Boulder: Westview, 1985), p. 48.

35. Kenneth W. Stein, *The Land Question in Palestine, 1917–1939* (Chapel Hill: University of North Carolina Press, 1984), pp. 207–8. Ya'akov Sharett recalls a proposal from a private Maronite-Zionist group to set up a Maronite version of the Jewish National Fund to buy land along the Lebanese side of the border and slowly displace and/or subsume the Shi'a population with Maronite settlements. According to Sharett, the Agency never took the plan seriously (Ya'akov Sharett, interview with author, 1 April 1987, Tel Aviv).

36. Quoted in A. C. C. Parkinson, Note of a Meeting with Weizmann and Ben-Gurion, 30 June 1936, CO 733/297, file 75156/III, held in ISA. See also Weizmann to Yvon Delbos (Quai d'Orsay), 29 June 1937, AE, LE 18–40/PAL 67 (Fr.). See also Neil Caplan, *Futile Diplomacy* (London: Cass, 1983–86), vol. 2, p. 52.

37. David Ben-Gurion, *Zikhronot* [Memoirs] (Tel Aviv: Am Oved, 1971–1987), 28 October 1938, vol. 5, p. 373; Ben-Gurion to Lord Lloyd, October 1938, quoted in Moshe Pearlman, *Ben-Gurion Looks Back in Talks with Moshe Pearlman*, (New York: Simon & Schuster, 1965), p. 92.

38. Ben-Gurion, *Zikhronot*, 27 July 1937, vol. 4, p. 331.

39. Ben-Gurion, *Zikhronot*, 29 July 1937, vol. 4, p.367. Regarding Ben-Gurion's evolving conception of the Jewish state's borders and Israeli-Arab relations, see Avi Bar-Ayal, "Gvulot Eretz-Yisrael Batfisato Shel David Ben-Gurion" [David Ben-Gurion's Perception of the Borders of the Land of Israel], *Kivunim* 21 (November 1983): 5–15.

40. Shertok to Wauchope, 21 June 1937, CZA, S25/5474; Sharett, *Yoman Medini*, 15 June 1937, vol. 2, p. 197; Shertok to Weizmann, 22 April 1937, CZA, Z4/17032.

41. Epstein, "Conversation with A. Arida, the Maronite Patriarch, on the Ship Marco Polo," 2 May 1937, CZA, S25/5576 (Heb.); Eliahu Elath, *Shivat Tzion Ve'arav* [Zionism and the Arabs] (Tel Aviv: Dvir, 1974), p. 297.

42. Quoted in Joseph to Shertok, 12 January 1938, CZA, S25/5476.

43. Elath, *Shivat Tzion Ve'arav*, pp. 298, 310. Sasson noted that an outcry ensued when Eddé did advise a visiting representative of the Arab Higher Committee that the Palestinians should accept partition. (*Baderekh*, pp. 73–74).

44. Eliahu Elath, *Hama'avak al Hamedinah* [The battle for statehood] (Tel Aviv: Am Oved, 1982), pp. 23–24; idem, *Shivat Tzion Ve'arav*, pp. 311–12; idem, *Zionism at the UN* (Philadelphia: Jewish Publication Society, 1976), p. 240; Caplan and Black, "Israel and Lebanon," p. 56. Elath attended the Weizmann-Eddé meeting and described the incident in great detail. He wrote that at one point in the friendly and rambling discussion, Weizmann paused, produced his pocket watch, and announced that in one half-hour, the Peel report recommending partition and the establishment of a Jewish state would be signed. Curiously enough, Eddé appeared to ignore Weizmann's statement and continued chatting until suddenly he paused, consulted his own watch, and rose to pronounce the Peel recommendation official and offer his congratulations to Weizmann. Elath noted that both men seemed quite moved by their little dramatics and raised their glasses to toast the future friendship between their countries. In subsequent discussions with Elath, Weizmann and Eddé both recalled that meeting with great fondness and excitement and expressed the belief that they had forged a bond of historic consequences. The two men never met again.

45. Shertok to Weizmann, 22 April 1937, CZA, Z4/17032.

46. Quoted in Epstein, "Conversation with A. Arida, the Maronite Patriarch, on the Ship Marco Polo," 2 May 1937, CZA, S25/5576 (Heb.); part of the text is reproduced in Elath, *Shivat Tzion Ve'arav*, p. 296. See also Sharett, *Yoman Medini*, 2 May 1937, vol. 2, p. 118; Epstein to Shertok, 7 June 1937, CZA, S25/3163 (Heb.).

47. Quoted in Elath, *Shivat Tzion Ve'arav*, p. 299. See also Epstein to Shertok, 7 June 1937, CZA, S25/3163 (Heb.). Weizmann and Arida met at the Hotel Luzia in Paris on 6 June 1937. The patriarch's entourage insisted that the Zionists not publish anything concerning the meeting or Arida's friendly remarks. See Elath, *Zionism at the UN*, p. 137.

48. Multiple correspondence, 1937, AD, MAN/650 (Fr.).

49. Epstein to Shertok, 12 May 1937, CZA, S25/3163 (Heb.).

50. Shertok to Epstein, 25 May 1937, CZA, S25/5810 (Heb.). Shertok complained that Sfeir had appeared recently with wild plans for joint Maronite-Agency activities and, despite being summarily dismissed, proceeded to relay all sorts of fictitious promises from the Jewish Agency to his circle in Lebanon. See also Sharett, *Yoman Medini*, 23 May 1937, vol. 2, pp. 141–42.

51. Shertok to Epstein, 25 May 1937, CZA, S25/5810 (Heb.). See also Sharett, *Yoman Medini*, 23 May and 8 June 1937, vol. 2, pp. 142, 174–75.

52. Khoury to Blum, 18 May 1937, CZA, S25/3775 (Fr.). See also Black, "Zionism and the Arabs," p. 297.

53. For the debate over whether to coordinate activity with Abdullah Khoury and his faction, see Shertok to Epstein, 25 May 1937, CZA, S25/5810 (Heb.); Epstein to Shertok, 7 June 1937, CZA, S25/3163 (Heb.). See also Black, "Zionism and the Arabs," p. 298.

54. Minutes of Bernard Joseph's Interview with President of the Lebanese Government, 6 August 1937, CZA, S25/5581; Dr. Joseph's Office Diary, 3 August 1937, CZA, S25/1511.

55. Stephen Longrigg, *Syria and Lebanon Under French Mandate* (London: Oxford University Press, 1958), p. 257. See also multiple reports about the recruitment of Arab volunteers to fight in Palestine, 1938, AD, MAN/649 (Fr.).

56. Sharett, *Yoman Medini*, 6 February 1938, vol. 3, p. 33.

57. British consul general in Beirut to Gabriel Puaux (French high commissioner in Lebanon), 26 July 1939, FO371/23239 E5729, held in ISA; Sasson, *Baderekh*, pp. 72–102, esp. pp. 85–97. See also Michael J. Cohen, *Palestine 1936–1945: Retreat from Mandate: The Making of British Policy 1936–1945* (New York, Holmes & Meier, 1978), p. 55; Philip Mattar, *The Mufti of Jerusalem: Al-Hajj Amin al-Husayni and the Palestinian National Movement* (New York: Columbia University Press, 1988), pp. 83, 122.

58. E. Epstein, "Letters from Beirut," 8 October and 5 November 1938, both in CZA, Z4/17024B (Heb.).

59. Weizmann to Ormsby-Gore, 7 April 1938, CZA, S25/5476.

60. That the British plan to crush the rebels' campaign against them by removing Hajj Amin from office failed miserably is evident from the fact that anti-Zionist and anti-British violence in Palestine increased dramatically in the month following the mufti's ouster and flight and that the uprising reached its fiercest proportions in the summer of 1938, ten months after the mufti went into exile. Howard M. Sachar, *A History of Israel* (New York and Oxford: Knopf and Oxford University Press, 1981–87), vol. 1, p. 212; Mattar, *Mufti of Jerusalem*, p. 83.

61. Sasson, *Baderekh*, esp. 81–85, 97, 127–29.

62. Report from David HaCohen, 22 October 1936, CZA S25/9783 (Heb.).

63. Sasson to Shertok, 8 July 1938, CZA, S25/5568 (Heb.).

64. "Meeting with the Editor of *al-Ayaam*" (Sasson to Shertok), 7 September 1939, CZA, S25/5568 (Heb.).

65. See multiple correspondence, 1938–39, AD, MAN/446 (Fr., Eng.).

66. De Martel to Ministry for Foreign Affairs, 30 March 1938, AD, MAN/446 (Fr.).

67. Furlonge to British Secretary of State for Foreign Affairs, July 1938, FO371/21878 E4309, held in ISA.

68. Shertok, Political Department Diary, 21 July 1936, CZA, S25/443 (Heb.); Shertok to Weizmann, 2 October 1936, CZA, S25/6327.

69. "Plain Speaking," *Palestine Post*, 30 May 1938, quoted in Black, "Zionism and the Arabs," p. 309; "Our Neighbors to the North," *Ha'aretz*, 13 May 1938, CZA, S25/3500 (Fr., orig. Heb.). See also "A Word to Our Neighbors," *Palestine Post*, 4 April 1938; "Another

Word to Our Neighbors," *Palestine Post*, 21 April 1938, both quoted in Black, "Zionism and the Arabs," p. 308.

70. Sasson to Shertok, 5 and 6 May 1938, CZA, S25/10571 (Heb.).

71. Epstein, "Letters from Beirut," 11 and 18 September 1938, CZA, Z4/17024B.

72. Weizmann to Ormsby-Gore, 7 April 1938, CZA, S25/5476.

73. Weizmann to Isaac Naiditch, 4 April 1938, and Weizmann to Malcolm MacDonald, 12 July 1938, both in *LCW*, vol. 18, letters 318, 367.

74. Shertok to Lourie, 15 March 1938, CZA, S25/3156. See also Weizmann to Blum, telegram, n.d., AE, LE 18–40/PAL 67 (Fr.).

75. Weizmann to Ormsby-Gore, 7 April 1938, CZA, S25/5476.

76. Weizmann to Blanche Dugdale, 4 April 1938, in *LCW*, vol. 18, letter 317.

77. Weizmann to Ormsby-Gore, 7 April 1938, CZA, S25/5476.

78. Multiple correspondence, 1939, AD, MAN/653 (Fr.). See also Cohen, *Palestine 1936–1945*, pp. 54–62.

79. Report of meeting with Epstein, de Martel to Ministry of Foreign Affairs, 15 December 1937, AE, LE 18–40/PAL 69 (Fr.).

80. Assistant to French consul general (Jerusalem) to Minister of Foreign Affairs, 29 April 1938, AD, MAN/648 (Fr.).

81. Report from David HaCohen, 22 October 1936, CZA, S25/9783 (Heb.).

82. Sasson, *Baderekh*, p. 89; "Affaires Palestiniennes," 18 July 1938, CZA, Z4/17024B, N.52; Sharett, *Yoman Medini*, 17 August 1938, vol. 3, p. 247.

83. Regarding French troop assignments, see Pierre Bart to high commissioner, 24 February 1938, and Sandfort to Havard, 4 March 1938, both in AD, MAN/649 (Fr.). For border clashes, incidents, and evidence of Franco-British cooperation, 1936–39, see esp. "Franco-British Relations," 19 December 1937; high commissioner to Diplomatic Service (Paris), 10 March 1938; high commissioner to Minister of Foreign Affairs, 15 October 1938, all in AD, MAN/653 (Fr.). See also high commissioner to Minister of Foreign Affairs, 7 June 1938, AD, MAN/653 (Fr.).

84. Epstein, "Letter from Beirut," 25 November 1937, CZA, S25/5574; "Report on the Activities of the Ex-Mufti in Lebanon," 25 September 1938, CZA, S25/3156.

85. Aviel Roshwald, *Estranged Bedfellows: Britain and France in the Middle East During the Second World War* (New York: Oxford University Press, 1990), p. 9; Report of meeting with Epstein, de Martel to Ministry of Foreign Affairs, 15 December 1937, AE, LE 18–40/PAL 69 (Fr.).

86. Hof, *Galilee Divided*, p. 46.

87. Sachar, *History of Israel*, vol. 1, pp. 214–16; Christopher Sykes, *Crossroads to Israel, 1917–1948* (Bloomington: Indiana University Press, 1965), pp. 182–83; Chaim Levkov, interview with author, 11 May 1987, Holon, Israel.

88. Hof, *Galilee Divided*, pp. 47–48.

89. Shertok to Weizmann, 2 October 1936, CZA, S25/6327.

90. Quoted in Shertok, Political Department Diary, 21 July 1936, CZA, S25/443 (Heb.).

91. Vilenski to Shertok, 22 November 1936, CZA, S25/9790 (Heb.). As a rule, however, the Jewish Agency made no serious attempt to distinguish between the Christian and Muslim communities in Palestine and perceived no natural convergence of interests with the Palestinian Christians, as it did in Lebanon. If anything, Zionists generally saw the Christian Arabs of Palestine as fervent anti-Zionists, as represented by the eloquent and articulate Greek Orthodox George Antonius.

92. Sasson, quoted in Dr. Joseph's Office Diary, 7 November 1938, CZA, S25/1511.

93. Epstein to B. Joseph, "The Relations Between the Muslims and the Christians in Southern Lebanon" [late 1938?], CZA, S25/5580 (Heb.).

94. JAE meeting (Jerusalem), 26 July 1936, CZA, vol. 25/3 (Heb.); Sasson, *Baderekh*, p. 120. See also Dr. Joseph's Office Diary, 18 February 1937, CZA, S25/50; Sharett, *Yoman Medini*, 23 May 1937, vol. 2, p. 141; Sfeir to Weizmann, 22 September 1937, CZA, S25/5580 (Fr.); Caplan, *Futile Diplomacy*, vol. 2, p. 48.

95. For a Zionist request that the Palestinian Druze warn their Lebanese brethren not to support the Palestinian Arab rebels, see Y. Nahmani to Sheikhs of the Druze community, 26 September 1936, CZA, S25/9165 (Heb., orig. Arab.); for Palestinian Druze appeals to the Lebanese Druze, see Report by Sheikh Zayid Abu Rukn, 4 October 1936, CZA, S25/9165; Sheikh Zayid Abu Rukn to Notables of Bayyadah, Autumn 1938, S25/4960 (Heb. orig. Arab.). See also Yoav Gelber, "Antecedents of the Jewish-Druze Alliance in Palestine," *Middle Eastern Studies* 28, no. 2 (April 1992): 353–55, 358–59; Yehoshua Porath, *The Palestinian Arab National Movement, 1929–1939* (London: Frank Cass, 1977), pp. 271–73; idem, interview with author, 10 March 1987, Jerusalem; Shertok, Political Department Diary, 5 July 1936, CZA, S25/443 (Heb.); Ben-Zvi to Abba Hushi, 20 October 1936, CZA, J1/6184 (Heb.); Report of a meeting with a Lebanese Druze gang leader, 4 January 1937, CZA, S25/9165 (Heb.); Dr. Joseph's Office Diary, 16 February 1937, CZA, S25/1511; Sasson to Shertok, 6 June 1938, CZA, S25/5568 (Heb.); idem, *Baderekh*, pp. 123–25; Ya'akov Shimoni, interview with author, 4 March 1987, Jerusalem.

96. JAE meeting (Jerusalem), 13 February 1938, CZA, vol. 27/2 (Heb.); Sharett, *Yoman Medini*, 7 March 1938, vol. 3, p. 78. Ahdab spelled out his objections to the mufti's presence and activities in Lebanon in two letters to Weizmann, one of which Weizmann described as having been written by "a very prominent Moslem personality in the Lebanon" and passed along to the British as proof of strong anti-mufti feelings by responsible persons in Lebanon. See Weizmann to Ormsby-Gore, 7 April 1938, CZA, S25/5476. See also Ahdab to Weizmann and Shertok, 23 August 1938, CZA, S25/5580 (Fr.).

97. Epstein to Jarblum, 17 May 1938, CZA, S25/5814 (Heb.). See also Sasson, *Baderekh*, pp. 115–16, 122–23; Sasson to Shertok, 27 July 1938, CZA, Z4/17024B (Heb.).

98. Proposals on King David Hotel stationery, Jerusalem, [February/March 1938?], CZA, S25/2960b (Arab.); An extract is translated in Caplan and Black, "Israel and Lebanon," pp. 51, 56–57.

99. Zionist activity against the mufti continued unabated, however. Chaim Levkov and a companion disguised themselves as Palestinian Arabs and worked undercover in Lebanon as saboteurs for the British and the Haganah. Levkov contends that sometime in 1938, he and his companion received joint British-Haganah instructions to assassinate the mufti. According to Levkov, they caught up with the mufti in Aleppo, ingratiated themselves with his men, and procured weapons for the attack. The mufti departed Aleppo suddenly in the night, however, unwittingly foiling the plot against him. Levkov, interview with author, 11 May 1987.

100. Shertok to Ahdab, 16 March 1938, CZA, S25/5581 (Fr.). Shertok requested that Ahdab use his authority to advance neighborly relations and security from the Lebanese side

by giving the necessary instructions to the district authorities and by reinforcing the police posts in the area. It is highly desirable that the inhabitants of the neighboring villages be made to understand that the Jews who are coming to establish themselves in the vicinity are motivated by the finest sentiments of peace and friendship. . We would like this new enterprise . . to be carried out with perfect cooperation between the Government of the Lebanese Republic and ourselves.

He assured Ahdab that the Jewish settlers had been carefully chosen for their familiarity with local customs and proficiency in Arabic, both of which would facilitate good relations across the border.

Ahdab responded immediately with a pledge to maintain order, ensure security in the Lebanese area neighboring the new settlement, and encourage the local Lebanese to establish "the best of neighborly relations" with Hanita (Ahdab to Shertok, 18 March 1938, CZA, S25/5588 [Fr.]). Ironically, this letter constituted one of Ahdab's final official acts as prime minister, since he wrote it on his last day in office. See also Caplan and Black, "Israel and Lebanon," pp. 57–58. Regarding Zionist preparations for establishing Hanita, see Sharett, *Yoman Medini*, vol. 3, pp. 79–91, 318–19.

101. Weizmann to Malcolm MacDonald, 12 July 1938, in *LCW*, vol. 18, letter 367. See also Caplan and Black, "Israel and Lebanon," p. 58.

102. Yonah Ben-Azar and Itamar Ben-Barak, interviews with author, 9 April 1987, Kibbutz Hanita, Israel; Mayor Yossi Goldberg and Dina Rudalinski, interviews with author, 28 April 1987, Metulla, Israel; Achiam Kroll, interview with author, 27 April 1987, Kibbutz Kfar Giladi, Israel; Amnon Yonai, interview with author, 12 May 1987, Netanya, Israel. All of the interviewees lived on the Lebanese border during the mandate period, and most still reside there.

103. Kroll, interview with author, 27 April 1987; Levkov, interview with author, 11 May 1987; Shalom Fein, interview with author, 28 April 1987, Metulla, Israel.

104. Ben-Azar and Ben-Barak, interviews with author, 9 April 1987; Yonai, interview with author, 12 May 1987; David Sandler, interview with author, 28 April 1987, Metulla, Israel; Nahum Hurwitz, interview with author, 27 April 1987, Kibbutz Kfar Giladi, Israel.

105. Ben-Azar and Ben-Barak, interviews with author, 9 April 1987; Fein, interview with author, 28 April 1987; Hurwitz and Kroll, interviews with author, 27 April 1987; Rudalinski and Sandler, interviews with author, 28 April 1987; Yonai, interviews with author, 12 May 1987. Gunrunning and illegal Jewish immigration to Palestine via Lebanon caught the attention of the *New York Times* as late as 1945. See A. C. Sedgwick, "Levant Arabs Act To Shut Palestine," *New York Times*, 15 October 1945.

106. Ben-Azar, interview with author, 9 April 1987.

107. Ben-Azar and Ben-Barak, interviews with author, 9 April 1987; Fein and Sandler, interviews with author, 28 April 1987; Kroll, interview with author, 27 April 1987; Yonai, interview with author, 12 May 1987. Each of the interviewees maintains that Lebanese villages never actively assisted the Arab gangs and relate instances in which Lebanese neighbors tipped off Jewish settlements about imminent rebel operations. For French reports of attacks along the border, see "Information No. 182" [1938?], AD, MAN/653 (Fr.).

108. Goldberg and Sandler, interviews with author, 28 April 1987; Kroll, interview with author, 27 April 1987.

109. See esp. Yosef Fein to Shertok, 10 and 12 June 1938, and n.d., all in CZA, S25/2957 (Heb.). In June of 1938, he reported that Arab bands were harassing the settlement but also that the Lebanese villagers came to Hanita for the funeral of a kibbutznik killed in a skirmish with the rebels. He confirmed that Hanita residents traveled easily to Lebanon and maintained good relations with the people and authorities in Tyre and Sidon. He acknowledged that some Lebanese resented what they saw as Jewish encroachment on Arab Palestine but suggested that many more were anxious to develop commercial relations with the Jews.

110. Fein to Shertok, 10 June 1938, CZA, S25/2957 (Heb.). See also Fein to Shertok, 12 June 1938 and n.d., CZA, S25/2957 (Heb.); Sharett, *Yoman Medini*, vol. 3, pp. 319–20.

CHAPTER 5

1. Kamal Salibi, *The Modern History of Lebanon* (New York: Praeger, 1965), pp. 183–84.

2. Eliahu Sasson, *Baderekh el Hashalom* [On the road to peace] (Tel Aviv: Am Oved, 1978), p. 186.

3. Sasson, *Baderekh*, p. 220.

4. Moshe Sharett, *Yoman Medini* [Political diary] (Tel Aviv: Am Oved, 1979), 26 August 1940, vol. 5, p. 110; see also Stephen Longrigg, *Syria and Lebanon Under French Mandate* (London: Oxford University Press, 1958), p. 304; and Irit Avramski-Bleiyi, "Yehudai Suriya Velevanon Takhat Shilton Vishi" [The Jews of Syria and Lebanon under Vichy rule], *Pa'amim* 28 (1986): 131–57.

5. Sharett, *Yoman Medini*, 4 and 11 May 1941, vol. 5, pp. 197, 202.

6. Longrigg, *Syria and Lebanon*, p. 304; Albert Hourani, *Syria and Lebanon: A Political Essay* (London, Oxford University Press, 1946), pp. 231–33.

7. Longrigg, *Syria and Lebanon*, pp. 304–20; Frederic C. Hof, *Galilee Divided: The Israel-Lebanon Frontier, 1916–1984* (Boulder: Westview, 1985), pp. 49–51; Hourani, *Political Essay*, pp. 237–40; A.B. Gaunson, *The Anglo-French Clash in Lebanon and Syria, 1940–1945* (London: MacMillan, 1987), pp. 44–45; Aviel Roshwald, *Estranged Bedfellows: Britain and France in the Middle East During the Second World War* (New York: Oxford University Press, 1990), chap. 4.

8. For the texts of the proclamations see Hourani, *Political Essay*, pp. 241–42.

9. Longrigg, *Syria and Lebanon*, p. 317.

10. Sasson, *Baderekh*, pp. 224–26.

11. Sasson reported that rumors of a British plan to annex Lebanon's Jebel Amal region to the Jewish national home prompted an offer from the Shi'a there to sell their land to the Zionists and move to Iraq. According to Sasson's report, Bishara al-Khoury encouraged Sasson to consider the proposition seriously, suggesting that the Zionists give Arida enough money to purchase the area from the Shi'a so that Maronites from America and elsewhere could settle there. Khoury argued that with the border area populated primarily by Maronites on one side and Jews on the other, the two peoples could cooperate without interference and one day stand as one against any Muslim/Arab threat (Sasson, *Baderekh*, pp. 224–25). If Sasson's account is accurate, this was a highly uncharacteristic position on Khoury's part. One is reminded, however, of Ya'akov Sharett's claim that a proposal for a joint Zionist-Maronite campaign to purchase Shi'a property in southern Lebanon and replace the Shi'a population with Maronite settlers along the Lebanon-Palestine border did reach the Agency (Ya'akov Sharett, interview with author, 1 April 1987, Tel Aviv).

12. Sasson, *Baderekh*, pp. 220–21.

13. For the text of Catroux's declaration, see Hourani, *Political Essay*, pp. 250–53, 378–81.

14. Sasson to Shertok, 4 January 1942, CZA, S25/4549 (Heb.). Sasson reported that when Naccache's government forbade the press to publish the patriarch's speech, the Maronite Church published and distributed his remarks at its own expense. Epstein added with concern that in his campaign against Catroux and Naccache, Arida was reaching out to Muslim, Druze, and even "pro-Nazi" extremists, all of whom opposed the current government and continuing French control in "independent" Lebanon (Epstein to Shertok, 21 January 1942, CZA, S25/5630 [Heb.]).

15. Epstein to Shertok, 21 January 1942, CZA, S25/5630 (Heb.). Epstein assured Naccache that he and Shertok would easily "find a common language."

16. Although Naccache never exploited his relationship with the Zionists while in office, British Intelligence reported that after his dismissal from the presidency, he traveled to Palestine as a guest of the Jewish Agency to discuss irrigation and industrial development plans of mutual interest to Lebanon and Palestine. The report concluded that nothing had happened so far but continued, "It is generally expected that the [Zionist] interests concerned, having once got their claws into the ex-President, will seek to pursue their ideas" (Lt. Col. G.W.F. [British Legation, Beirut], "Ex-President Naccache and the Jews," 15 May 1943, Public Record Office, London, fo22b/244 16482). I am grateful to Yossi Olmert of Tel Aviv University for providing me with this document.

17. Salibi, *Modern History*, pp. 186–87; Longrigg, *Syria and Lebanon*, p. 325; Roshwald, *Estranged Bedfellows*, chaps. 5–7. The bitter struggle between Britain and France and their respective clients in Lebanon is evident in Spears's memoirs, in which he mercilessly derides French supporters Naccache and Eddé. Naccache is characterized as a coward with a "strong dislike of any action" and overwhelming "personal timidity"; Eddé appears as "a notorious French stooge who had accumulated a not inconsiderable fortune largely by filching the land of villagers in the Bekaa valley by very questionable legal methods and who was favoured by the French in recognition of his fervent devotion to their administration" (Sir Edward Spears, *Fulfillment of a Mission: The Spears Mission to Syria and Lebanon, 1941–1944* [London: Cooper, 1977], pp. 168, 213).

18. Sasson, *Baderekh*, pp. 269–70.

19. Longrigg, *Syria and Lebanon*, pp. 329–31; Salibi, *Modern History*, p. 189; Hourani, *Political Essay*, pp. 286–88; Gaunson, *Anglo-French Clash*, pp. 123–44; Roshwald, *Estranged Bedfellows*, pp. 153–66.

20. Hourani, *Political Essay*, p. 287. J.C. Hurewitz agrees that the "French action so enraged every sectarian community that it provided for the first time an inner integration of sentiment, a consensus for preserving—at least for the time being—the Greater Lebanon" ("Lebanese Democracy in its International Setting," in *Politics in Lebanon*, ed. Leonard Binder [New York: Wiley and Sons, 1966], p. 228).

21. Longrigg, *Syria and Lebanon*, p. 331; Salibi, *Modern History*, pp. 189–90.

22. Sasson, *Baderekh*, p. 270; Catroux, quoted in Longrigg, *Syria and Lebanon*, pp. 332–33.

23. Hurewitz, "Lebanese Democracy," p. 228.

24. Eliahu Elath, "Hatziyonut Hafanikit Balevanon" [Phoenician Zionism in Lebanon], *Cathedra* 35 (April 1985): 124; idem, *Shivat Tzion Ve'arav* [Zionism and the Arabs] (Tel Aviv: Dvir, 1974), p. 312.

25. Salibi, *Modern History*, pp. 172–73.

26. Elath, *Shivat Tzion Ve'arav*, p. 313.

27. Salibi, *Modern History*, p. 173; Eliahu Elath, interview with author, 29 July 1986, Jerusalem; Barry Rubin, *The Arab States and the Palestine Conflict* (Ithaca: Syracuse University Press, 1982), p. 139.

28. Elath, interview with author, 29 July 1986; Aviezer Golan and Danny Pinkas, *Shem Tzofen: Hapeninah* [Code name: The pearl] (Tel Aviv: Zmora/Bitan, 1980), p. 111; Ya'akov Shimoni, lecture at the Shiloah Institute, Tel Aviv University, 7 December 1983.

29. *Bulletin*, Palestine Correspondence Bureau of Jerusalem (*Palcor*), 13 September 1944, Schwadran Collection (SC), Shiloah Institute, Tel Aviv University, vol. 7.1. Regarding an unproductive visit by Shertok to Khoury, see "Information," 4 February 1944, AD, MAN/ 806 (Fr.).

30. Avi, "A Letter from Beirut," 25 August 1944, CZA, S25/4556.

31. R. Trippon to Ben-Gurion, 10 October 1944, CZA, S25/4549 (Heb.). Trippon complained that the Jewish Agency should do more to counteract anti-Zionism among the Maronite youth and suggested enlisting the aid of the patriarch, whose recent remarks, Trippon claimed, "opened a wide door to joint [Maronite-Zionist] action."

32. Rubin, *Arab States and the Palestine Conflict*, p. 139; Epstein, "News from Syria and Lebanon," 3 February 1944, CZA, S25/4556 (Heb.).

33. Multiple reports and correspondence, 1944, AD, MAN/806 (Fr.).

34. "To Prevent the Sale of Property in Lebanon to Foreigners," *Ha'aretz*, 9 April 1944, (Heb.); "Zionist Capital Seeks To Invade Lebanon, Minister Alleges," *Palcor*, 17 September 1944, SC, vol. 7.1; Jewish Telegraph Agency, 14 August, 20 September, and 15 October 1945, SC, vol. 7.3.

35. Multiple correspondence, 1944, AD, MAN/808/7 (Fr.).

36. See M. Landau to Joseph Weitz, 6 April 1945; Joseph Weitz, 22 April 1945; and Sasson, 14 May 1945, all in CZA S25/4549 (Heb.).

37. "Disclaimer of Zionist Pretensions in Syria," *Digest Press and Events* (Jewish Agency), 21 November 1944, p. 7, copy in SC, vol. 7.1 (Shertok's press conference); "News from the Lebanon," 29 May 1945, CZA, S25/4556 (Heb.); "A Flood of Zionist Companies Sweeps the Country" (extracts from Lebanese newspaper *al-Hadaf* of 11 July 1945), 27 July 1945, CZA, S25/3179; Report of 17 October 1945, ISA, 2567/2.

38. Al-Sulh outlined the principles of the agreement in a speech before Parliament on 7 October 1943. See Salibi, *Modern History*, pp. 186–87; Clovis Maksoud, "Lebanon and Arab Nationalism," and Hassan Saab, "The Rationalist School in Lebanese Politics," both in *Politics in Lebanon*, ed. Leonard Binder; Walid Khalidi, *Conflict and Violence in Lebanon* (Cambridge: Center for International Affairs, Harvard University, 1979), pp. 23, 36, 162; Itamar Rabinovich, *The War for Lebanon, 1970–1983* (Ithaca: Cornell University Press, 1984), pp. 24–25; David C. Gordon, *The Republic of Lebanon: Nation in Jeopardy* (Boulder: Westview, 1983), pp. 20–21; Rubin, *Arab States and the Palestine Conflict*, p. 139.

39. Khalidi, *Conflict and Violence*, p. 162.

40. "What Is Going on in Lebanon?" *Hamashkif,* 6 July 1944 (Heb.).

41. Khalidi, *Conflict and Violence*, p. 36. See also Hourani, *Political Essay*, pp. 303–7.

42. Longrigg, *Syria and Lebanon*, pp. 351–52. He cites as examples Lebanese contributions to the Arab Offices that conducted pro-Arab (and anti-Zionist) propaganda in Europe and America and occasional demonstrations against continuing Jewish immigration to Palestine and in support of the Palestinian Arabs.

43. Young to Foreign Office, 23 September 1945, FO371/45380 E7183, held in ISA.

44. Quoted in Shone (Beirut) to Foreign Office, 18 March 1945, FO371/45392, E1883, held in ISA.

45. Sharett, *Yoman Medini*, 25 September 1937, vol. 2, p. 343; Sasson, *Baderekh*, p. 358.

46. For a description of the situation in the resort cities favored by Palestinian Jews, see A. Avi-Yoram, "In the Streets of Lebanon—in These Days," *Haboker,* 4 January 1946 (Heb.); "Lebanon, the Boycott's Only Sacrifice," *Davar,* 12 January 1946 (Heb.); "The Banning of Jewish Tourists Is a Blow to the Lebanon's Economy," *Ha'aretz,* 28 May 1946; "The End of the Desire to Travel to Lebanon," *Ha'aretz,* 17 July 1946 (Heb.); "The Lebanon's Farmers Demand Withdrawal from the Anti-Zionist Boycott," *Haboker,* 15 October 1946 (Heb.); A. Yakobi, "The People of the Levant Do Not have the Luxury of Concerning Themselves with the Problem of Eretz Yisrael," *al-Hamishmar,* 25 November 1947 (Heb.).

47. "Lebanon: Growth of the Phalangist Party," 20 September 1945, CZA, S25/8002 1.

48. "Le Manifeste de l'Association des Partis Libanais Antisionistes," 9 November 1945, ISA, 2567/2 (Fr.); Regarding Phalange involvement in the Bureau of the Struggle Against Zionism, see "Information," 17 August 1944, AD, MAN/806 (Fr.).

49. Naccache, quoted in E. Wallenstein, "Lebanon and the League of Arab States," *Ha'aretz,* 3 April 1945 (Heb.).

50. S. to Atarah [?], 12 December 1946, CZA, S25/3960 (Heb.). The Agency learned that the treaty Eddé envisioned entailed an end to Lebanon's participation in the anti-Zionist boycott, cooperation between the Jewish and Christian "national homes," and the transfer of southern Lebanon to the Yishuv. Activity along these lines depended upon Eddé's victory, which he insisted was "a question of money only."

51. Rubin, *Arab States and the Palestine Conflict*, p. 139.

52. "The Christian Minorities in the Lebanon and the Arab League," 14 November 1945, SC, vol. 7.3; this is an English account of Arida, interview with Habib Jamati, *Akhbar al-Yom,* 3 November 1945.

53. Eliahu Epstein, "The Rise of the Lebanon: Christian Refuge and Maronites' National Home," *Palestine and the Middle East*, March 1945, copy in SC, vol. 7.2.

54. T[uvia A[razi], "The Reactions of the Lebanese Christians to an Arab Union and to the Talks in Alexandria: The Maronite Patriarch's Declaration," 11 October 1944, CZA, S25/4556 (Heb.). Arazi quoted the text of a declaration by Arida in *al-Misri* on 8 October 1944. Arida spoke of Lebanon's right to establish friendly relations with "the neighboring nations" and in his report Arazi emphasized "note: 'neighbors' and not 'the Arab states.'" See also "The Maronite Patriarch's Speech at Bkerke" and "The Decisions Adopted at the Conference of Lebanese Delegations at Bkerke," 25 December 1941, CZA, S25/4549 (Heb.).

55. S. Schwartz, "Monsignor Arida's Forceful Deed," *Haboker*, 16 August 1945 (Heb.). The diminished Maronite position also attracted some attention in the American press. One observer noted that the withdrawal of French control in Lebanon also meant the withdrawal of French protection for the Christian minorities and opined that "in the interests of peace and humanity somebody is going to have to protect the various little religious groups and establishments" (Major George Fielding Eliot, "Outside Protection Held Vital to Levant's Divided Minorities," *New York Tribune*, 3 June 1945). Although traditional Maronite hegemony in Lebanon did seem to be waning, the Maronite community hardly constituted "a little religious group."

56. Salibi, *Modern History*, p. 188. A Protestant of Maronite stock, Thabit supported Eddé and served in his first government. According to a report of a 1941 meeting between Thabit and a Jewish Agency representative in Beirut, Thabit believed that it was "in the interest and desire of Christian Lebanon to have a strong Jewish state on its immediate borders." He counseled the Jewish Agency to eschew contact with Lebanese Muslims and asked to meet "responsible Jewish leaders and explain to them what good could be derived if both Jews and Christians collaborated" ("Meeting with Dr. Ayoub Tabit, Beirut," 20 October 1941, CZA, S25/10.372).

57. Arazi, "The Reactions of the Lebanese Christians to an Arab Union and to the Talks in Alexandria: The Maronite Patriarch's Declaration," 11 October 1944, CZA S25/4556 (Heb.). According to Arazi's report, the American Maronite community alone numbered 160,000.

58. Hourani, *Political Essay*, p. 297.

59. Avi, "A Letter from Beirut," 10 May 1944, CZA, S25/4556.

60. Michael Bar Zohar, *Ben-Gurion: The Armed Prophet* (Englewood Cliffs: Prentice Hall, 1968), p. 79.

61. Arazi to Shertok, 9 July 1945, CZA, S25/4949 (Heb.).

62. JAE meeting, 11 February 1945, CZA, vol. 31, p. 8 (Heb.). Abba Eban later repeated and explained the joke that Weizmann attributed to his grandfather. According to Eban, Weizmann used the same anecdote to decline an elephant offered by the king of Burma as a gift, saying that his grandfather had warned him never to accept a gift that had to be fed . . . and that could conceivably devour him (Abba Eban, lecture in Pittsburgh, Pennsylvania, 7 June 1989).

Perhaps the most telling point is that no one at the meeting even commented upon Weizmann's remarks, emphasizing again Lebanon's low priority in Agency planning. Conversation immediately resumed on those topics that dominated the meeting: Jewish immigration and the European Jews' desperate need of refuge, the Arab question within Palestine, and how to oppose British policies in Palestine without hurting the British war effort.

63. Arazi to Shertok, 9 July 1945, CZA, S25/4949 (Heb.); S. to Atarah [?], 12 December 1946, CZA, S25/3960 (Heb.).

64. Arida to British Foreign Minister Ernest Bevin, 2 October 1946, CZA, S25/6319 (Fr.); Mubarak to Bevin, 12 October 1946, CZA, S25/6319 (Fr.).

65. "Lebanon: Eddé Advocates United States as Protector of Lebanon," 15 September 1945, ISA, 2567/2.

66. Ya'akov Katz to Weizmann, 24 March 1946, WA. See also multiple letters from

Katz to Weizmann, WA; [Sharett?] to Katz, 12 May 1946, Ben-Gurion Archives (BGA), and CZA, S25/6319 (Heb.).

67. "Political Activity in the M[iddle] E[ast]," 16 September 1945, CZA, S25/4549. The writer made incredible proposals for both publicizing incidents of sectarian conflict within the Arab world and creating such incidents, all for the purpose of debunking and defusing pan-Arabism. He contended that there were many people ready to make trouble in the Arab world for the right price and singled out the Maronites as showing particular promise. Although he referred to "our Political Department," the writer clearly had no official affiliation with the department and apparently received no response to his proposals.

68. A. Bruzkus, "The Question of Possibilities for Activity Among the National and Religious Minorities in the Countries of the Near East," 26 March 1946, CZA, S25/9012 (Heb.). Bruzkus advocated the creation of a regional cultural association as a proxy through which the Jewish Agency could direct political activities among the region's minorities. The goal was to separate the religious and ethnic minorities from the Muslim Arab majority, thus splintering any anti-Zionist "Arab bloc" and creating a network of Zionist allies throughout the Middle East. Although Sasson's signature indicates that he read the memo, there is no evidence that he responded to the proposal.

69. *Encyclopaedia Judaica, Yearbook 1975–76* (Jerusalem: Keter, 1976), p. 262; Yehoshua Porath to author, 24 October 1989; idem, *Shelah ve'et Beyado* [The life of Uriel Shelah (Yonathan Ratosh)] (Tel Aviv: Machbarot Lesifrut, Zmora, 1989), pp. 81, 240; Miri Eliav-Feldon (Eliav's daughter and lecturer in history, Tel Aviv University) to author, 23 November 1989.

70. Elath, interview with author, 14 October 1986; "Extract from Eliahu Epstein's Messages, via I. Mireminski," 30 September 1945, CZA, S25/4556.

71. Epstein, "Rise of the Lebanon"; idem, "Demographic Problems of the Lebanon," 27 February 1945, CZA, S25/4556. That Epstein shared his Maronite friends' perception of an Islamic threat to the minorities in the region is clear from the following passage: "With [the Arab countries'] gaining independence [the minorities] are now given over to the mercy of the ruling Muslim Arab majority, which aspires to use its independence to renew the reign of 'dar al-Islam.' This [new reign] may be more fanatical, aggressive, and extremist in its social, economic, and political objectives than in the days of Turkish rule in the Arab east" (Eliahu Elath, *Hama'avak al Hamedinah* [The battle for statehood] [Tel Aviv: Am Oved, 1982], vol. 2, p. 29).

72. In 1945, Epstein wrote:

> The natural increase of the Christians in the Lebanon is roughly equal to that of the Yishuv in Palestine. . . . Against this, however, the Yishuv in Palestine has an incomparably more potential reserve in the way of immigration from abroad than that which is available to the Lebanese Christians through the return of emigrants. And just as the chief concern of Zionism in Palestine is the creation of possibilities for the absorption of fresh immigrants from abroad, so the Christians of Lebanon are faced first and foremost with the problem of preventing emigration from the country and, in consequence, the creation of opportunities for absorbing emigrants who do return. . . . In addition, attention is devoted to the creation of the opportunities for absorbing Christians who require a refuge ("Demographic Problems of the Lebanon," 27 February 1945, CZA, S25/4556).

73. Epstein to Shertok, 9 June 1942, CZA, S25/3580 (Heb.). In conversations with Sasson, Eddé similarly advocated Maronite-Zionist cooperation while insisting that talk of a practical plan was premature (Sasson, *Baderekh*, pp. 219–20).

74. Elath, interviews with author, 29 July and 14 October 1986; Moshe Sharett, Political Department Diary, 8 July 1936, CZA, S25/443 (Heb.); Epstein to Abba Hushi, 27 July 1939, CZA, S25/5580 (Heb.); Yoav Gelber, "Antecedents of the Jewish-Druze Alliance in

Palestine," *Middle Eastern Studies* 28, no. 2 (April 1992): 352–73. Elath contended that before he left for the United States, he had begun preliminary discussions on the idea with his contacts in the Maronite, Kurdish, Armenian, Druze, and Assyrian communities.

75. Under Corm's direction, the Lebanese exhibition, not surprisingly, stressed the Phoenician heritage of the country. Bernard Joseph noted that "they have been very careful to avoid creating the impression that they are Arabs" (Dr. Joseph's Office Diary, 6 November 1938, CZA, S25/1511; see also Corm to Epstein, 7 February 1939, CZA, S25/5580 [Fr.]).

76. Epstein to Corm, 29 March 1939, CZA, S25/5580; Epstein to Chaim Greenburg, 5 May 1939, CZA, S25/5580 (Heb.).

77. Shamoun's letter is reproduced in "Lebanese Americans Urge Open Door to Palestine: Ask President Roosevelt to Intercede," *Palestine Post*, 14 November 1938, p. 2.

78. Epstein to Eddé, 16 November 1938, CZA, S25/5581 (Fr.).

79. Sasson, *Baderekh*, p. 220.

80. Bernard Joseph, 28 December 1942, CZA, S25/4549.

81. "Letters from Beirut," 20 and 22 June 1945, compiled in a report composed in Jerusalem, 1 July 1945, CZA S25/4556 (Heb.).

82. Epstein and N. Goldmann, "Activities of Msgr. Akl in the U.S.A.," 17 October 1945, ISA, 2567/2. See also "Lebanon Priest Asks Aid: Msgr. Akl Seeks Protection for Catholics in His Country," *New York Times*, 20 August 1945; "For the Christians of Lebanon a Combination of Fears," *Davar*, 10 August 1945 (Heb.).

83. Epstein, "Lebanese Activities in the U.S.A.," 15 October 1946, CZA, S25/7488; ibid., December 1946, ISA, 2569/19; Elath, *Hama'avak*, vol. 2, p. 25.

84. Epstein, "Lebanese Activities in the U.S.A.," 15 October 1946, CZA, S25/7488; Elath, *Hama'avak*, vol. 2, p. 25.

85. For a detailed account of Harfoush's meeting with Epstein and Mokarzel at the Jewish Agency office in Washington and of Lebanese activities in the United States, see Elath, *Hama'avak*, vol. 2, pp. 22–31; Epstein, "Lebanese Activities in the U.S.A.," 15 October 1946, CZA, S25/7488.

86. Epstein and Arazi to Eddé, 27 June 1946, CZA, S25/9023.

87. Elath, *Zionism at the UN: A Diary of the First Days* (Philadelphia: Jewish Publication Society, 1976), pp. 198–200.

88. Epstein, "Conversation with Mr. Salloum A. Mokarzel, President of the Lebanese League in the United States and Editor of *al-Hoda* newspaper, New York," 3 February 1947, CZA, A263/18; Epstein, "Lebanese Activities in the U.S.A.," 15 October 1946, CZA, S25/7488; Epstein to Michael Clark, 1 February 1947, and Epstein to JAE, 10 July 1947, both in BGA, and CZA, S25/6319.

89. Arazi, "Meeting with Charles Malik, Lebanese Representative to Washington," 8 April 1945, CZA, S25/4549. Arazi recommended to the Political Department that they put Malik in touch "with our people in D.C. without delay before people like Philip Hitti hitch him to their wagon." Hitti, a historian of Lebanese origin, then at Princeton University, promoted Arab causes in academic circles. Amazingly, Arazi also contacted Naccache, Thabit, and Eddé and offered to introduce them to their fellow countryman Malik before he left for Washington, implying that they evidently did not know him.

90. Elath, *Hama'avak*, vol. 2, p. 89; idem, *Zionism at the UN*, pp. 48–49, 98–99.

91. Epstein, "Conversation with Dr. Charles Malik, Lebanese Minister to Washington, D.C.," 14 February 1946, CZA, S25/7488; Elath, *Zionism at the UN*, p. 102.

92. "Report of Y. Helman from His (Second) Trip to Beirut on Behalf of the Department," 24 March 1946, BGA.

93. William W. Haddad, "Christian Arab Attitudes Toward the Arab-Israeli Conflict," *Muslim World* 67, no. 2 (April 1977): 134.

94. Joseph P. Hutcheson's Diary, 21 March 1946, extracts reproduced in Allen H. Po-

det, "Husni al-Barazi on Arab Nationalism in Palestine," in *Zionism and Arabism in Palestine and Israel*, ed. Eli Kedourie and Sylvia Haim (London: Cass, 1982), pp. 178–79.

95. James Grover McDonald, "Diary, Interviews in Beirut, Thursday, March 21st [1946]," extracts in Podet, "Husni al-Barazi," pp. 180–81. See also Benny Morris, "The Phalange Connection," *Jerusalem Post Magazine*, 1 July 1983, p. 7; Bernard Joseph, *The Faithful City* (New York: Simon & Schuster, 1960), p. 210; Shimoni, lecture, Shiloah Institute, 7 December 1983; Yehoshua Porath, "History of a Friendship," *Jerusalem Post*, 22 May 1981, p. 7; Bartley C. Crum, *Behind the Silken Curtain* (New York: Simon & Schuster, 1947), p. 246; Longrigg, *Syria and Lebanon*, p. 352.

96. Gerold Frank, interview with Mubarak, *Palestine Post*, 21 March 1946; idem, "Beirut Archbishop Refutes Moslem Claims, Palestine Post, 21 March 1946," CZA, S25/9023. Mubarak declared that the Anglo-American Committee of Inquiry had not heard the true voice of Lebanese public opinion, else

it would have heard that voice declaring support of Jewish reconstruction in Palestine, support of Zionism as a symbol of progress and security for all the peoples of the Middle East. . . . [The] development of Lebanon is tied up with that of Palestine. We Christian Lebanese know that. We realize that Zionism is bringing civilization to Palestine and to the entire Middle East. I am very much in favor of Zionism because I have the good of Palestine at heart. . . . I tell you frankly that if you oppose Zionism in Palestine it means returning the people to the domination of savagery and the country to the state of anarchy and bribery in which it existed under the Ottoman Sultans. . . . You can be sure that in this country the great majority of these Christians—and that is the majority of the population—are against the reactionary Arab anti-Zionist opinion and support the Jews. . . . We realize that here is a struggle between civilization and regression, and that the Jews represent civilization. . . . In the Jews who are rebuilding Palestine there burns a very pure flame. We must not extinguish it. . . . I have been in Palestine thirty years ago, [and] it was an arid, forgotten land. I have seen it since. I tell you: we Lebanese are jealous of the good fortune Palestine has had. . . . Moslem Arabs in Palestine, Damascus, and Beirut sold land to the Jews at high prices, and now Moslem Arabs here want to regain those lands by ousting the Jews from Palestine.

In truth, Mubarak expressed the views of that tiny Maronite faction which had fallen from power, certainly not those of the majority of Lebanese Christians, as he asserted. And while technically Christians still outnumbered Muslims within Lebanon, Mubarak's own desperation was motivated by the imminent prospects of Muslim-Christian parity and, eventually, a Muslim majority. Although the interview does not serve Mubarak's stated purpose of expressing the real nature of Lebanese public opinion, it is an accurate portrayal of Mubarak's personal views. See also, McDonald, "Diary, Interviews in Beirut, Thursday, March 21st [1946]," extracts in Podet, "Husni al-Barazi," p. 180; Crum, *Behind the Silken Curtain*, pp. 245–46.

97. Itzhak Ben-Zvi, "The Fate of Christian Lebanon," *Ha'olam*, 25 April 1946 (Heb.).

98. Podet, "Husni al-Barazi," p. 172.

99. Ya'akov Shimoni to Bernard Joseph, "The Need for Our Action in Lebanon: Conversation with Tewfik Attieh, Beirut," 5 April 1946, CZA, S25/9023 (Heb.).

100. Joseph to David HaCohen, 12 April 1946, CZA, S25/4949 (Heb.).

101. Shimoni's account of meeting with HaCohen, in Shimoni to Joseph, 15 April 1946, CZA, S25/4949 (Heb.).

102. Joseph to Amos Landman, 15 April 1946, CZA, S25/4949 (Heb.).

103. Ya'akov Shimoni to Bernard Joseph, "The Need for Our Action in Lebanon: Conversation with Tewfik Attieh, Beirut," 5 April 1946, CZA, S25/9023 (Heb.).

104. Discussions with Awad reported by A. Latise to Bernard Joseph, 19 April 1946, CZA, S25/9023 (Heb.).

105. When an Agency operative did finally meet with Gemayel a year later, the Phalange leader acknowledged certain common Maronite-Zionist interests but declined to suggest any concrete cooperative ventures. See Avner Yaniv, *Dilemmas of Security: Politics, Strategy, and the Israeli Experience in Lebanon* (Oxford: Oxford University Press, 1987), pp. 29–30.

106. Discussions with Awad reported by A. Latise to Bernard Joseph, 19 April 1946, CZA, S25/9023 (Heb.).

107. Ibid. A. Latise witnessed the conversation between Awad and Sasson and reported its contents to Bernard Joseph.

108. Arida to Weizmann, 24 May 1946, BGA, (Fr.); Shimoni, lecture, Shiloah Institute, 7 December 1983; Shimoni, interview with author, 4 March 1987.

109. Treaty, 30 May 1946, CZA S25/3269, and BGA (Fr.).

110. Shimoni, lecture, Shiloah Institute, 7 December 1983.

111. Awad to Joseph, and Joseph to Awad, 30 May 1946, BGA (Fr); and Treaty, 30 May 1946, CZA S25/3269, and BGA (Fr.). See also Bernard Joseph, *Faithful City*, p. 210; Rabinovich, *War for Lebanon, 1970–1983*, p. 104; Shimoni, lecture, Shiloah Institute, 7 December 1983. The handful of people aware of the treaty kept its existence a secret for 14 years, until Joseph mentioned it in his book. Even then, the Central Zionist Archives did not declassify the treaty after the standard 30 years. The file was finally opened for the author in 1991. In the interim, scholars were permitted to mention the existence of the treaty but prohibited from revealing its provisions. See Porath, "History of Friendship," p. 7; Morris, "Phalange Connection," p. 7; Rubin, *Arab States*, p. 139.

112. Joseph to Tewfik Awad, n.d.; Wadia to [Joseph], 18 March 1947; and Joseph to [Wadia], 21 March 1947, all in CZA, S25/7488 (Arab.).

113. Latise to Joseph, 19 April 1946, CZA, S25/9023 (Heb.).

114. Eliahu Sasson to Moshe Shertok, 13 March 1947, CZA, S25/3960.

115. Eliahu Elath, interview with author, 14 October 1986, Jerusalem.

116. David Ben-Gurion to Antoine Pierre Arida, 3 June 1947, CZA, S25/3888 (Fr.). In this letter, Ben-Gurion thanks Arida for his letter of 30 May 1947, not found.

117. "Letter from A. Lutzky from the Lebanon," 12 July 1947, CZA, S25/4054 (Heb.).

118. Arida's letter reads in part:

> We see clearly that it is for the well-being of the Maronite sect that a committee of community notables in the diaspora be established . . . for the preservation of Lebanon's independence and Christian influence. . . . We entrust you with the formation of this committee and ask that when its incorporation is complete you inform us as to the suitable people who will begin their appointments to this project, so we can approve it. . . . It is true that our friends in the Jewish community are prepared to support this project both spiritually and materially. Contact the Jewish Agency and its director, Mr. Eliahu Epstein (Arida to Mokarzel, 9 July 1947, CZA, S25/4029 [Arab.]).

119. Lutzky worried that "in his role as private secretary to an old patriarch . . . in a church in which there is much corruption (they say it is possible to buy the bishops cheaply), [Awad] can do a lot of damage." Lutzky reported that Awad tried to persuade Arida to delete the section about the Jewish Agency from the letter to Mokarzel and prevent Lutzky from returning to the patriarch to raise the boycott issue as he was about to leave. In proofreading Arida's letter about the boycott, Lutzky discovered that Awad had deviated from the patriarch's oral dictation and openly confronted Awad in front of the patriarch, compelling Arida to have the letter retyped. Awad attempted to prevent the patriarch from signing and handing over to Lutzky copies of the two letters, but Lutzky again convinced Arida to disregard his secretary's advice. Lutzky emphasized that throughout their wrangling, both he and Awad maintained friendly demeanors, although he noted with some satisfaction, "[At the end of

the afternoon] I even gave him a ride in my car to one village and it seems to me that I drove in such a way that he'll never forget!" ("Letter from A. Lutzky from the Lebanon," 12 July 1947, CZA, S25/4054 [Heb.]). For Arida's letter about the anti-Zionist boycott, see Arida to Sheikh Nidra Aisi al-Khoury (representative of the Mount Lebanon), 9 July 1947, CZA, S25/ 4029 (Arab.).

120. Jorge Garcia Granados, *The Birth of Israel: The Drama as I Saw It* (New York: Knopf, 1948), pp. 198–99, 201–8.

121. Granados, *Birth of Israel*, p. 220; Aharon. H. Cohen, *Israel and the Arab World* (New York: Funk & Wagnalls, 1970), p. 377. The Lebanese elections of 25 May 1947 are widely acknowledged to have been marred by corruption and violence. See Salibi, *Modern History*, p. 193; David Gilmour, *Lebanon: The Fractured Country* (New York: St. Martin's, 1984), p. 49; Michael Hudson, *The Precarious Republic: Political Modernization in Lebanon* (New York: Random House, 1968), pp. 252–53. Hudson writes that "the elections of May 25, 1947 . . . stand above all the others before or since as a model for ingenious corruption."

122. "Letter from A. Lutzky from the Lebanon," 29 July 1947, CZA, S25/4054 (Heb.).

123. Ibid.

124. Lutzky, "Trip in Lebanon, 2 July 1947–2 August 1947," 4 August 1947, CZA, S25/ 3960 (Heb.). Lutzky reported that Eddé did express an interest in Zionist financial backing for his reelection bid in the next Lebanese elections, however.

125. Granados, *Birth of Israel*, p. 201; "Letter from A. Lutzky from the Lebanon," 29 July 1947, CZA, S25/4054 (Heb.).

126. Lutzky, "Trip in Lebanon, 2 July 1947–2 August 1947," 4 August 1947, CZA, S25/ 3960 (Heb.) and "Letter from A. Lutzky from the Lebanon," 29 July 1947, CZA, S25/4054 (Heb.). See also Sasson, *Baderekh*, p. 393. Lutzky claimed to have been instrumental in arranging Eddé's and Arida's meetings with UNSCOP. According to his reports, a third meeting scheduled between UNSCOP and the Phalange (the Phalange and Eddé's National Bloc refused to address the committee under the same roof) never took place. Lutzky noted that the Lebanese opposition was disorganized and that those groups who met with UNSCOP were those with the closest Zionist connections. He suggested to them that they needed to be more aggressive, show greater initiative, and tighten their relations with the Jews if they expected continuing Zionist assistance.

127. Matti Moosa, *The Maronites in History* (Syracuse: Syracuse University Press, 1986), p. 292. The statement he refers to is that of Anis Sayigh, *Lubnan al-Ta'ifi* (Beirut: Dar al-Sira al-Fikri, 1955), quoted in Michel Ghurayyib, *Al-Ta'ifiyya wa al-Iqta'iyya fi Lebanon*, 2d ed. (Beirut, 1964), p. 78 (Arab.).

128. Eliahu Epstein to JAE, 10 July 1947, BGA, and CZA, S25/6319.

129. Mubarak to Judge Sandstrom (president of the Commission of Inquiry of UN-SCOP), 5 August 1947, CZA, S25/5436 (Fr.).

130. Lutzky, "The Mubarak Affair, According to the Press and Internal Information," 7 October 1947, ISA, 2567/12 (Heb.). Mubarak's letter appeared in *al-Diyar* in Arabic translation and then in the original French on 27 and 28 September 1947. Most of the other Beirut papers followed suit.

131. Michael Sasson to author, 23 June 1987; Lutzky, "The Mubarak Affair, According to the Press and Internal Information," 7 October 1947, ISA, 2567/12 (Heb.).

132. A. Grinblat, "Aftermath of the Publication of Archbishop I. Mubarak's Memorandum to UNSCOP in the Beirut Daily *al-Diyar* on 27 September 1947," 16 October 1947, SC, vol. 7.5; Lutzky, "The Mubarak Affair, According to the Press and Internal Information," 7 October 1947, ISA, 2567/12 (Heb.); Haddad, "Christian Arab Attitudes," pp. 129–30. Haddad cites the resolution in part: "We strongly disavow Mubarak's memorandum. . . . Archbishop Mubarak has no right to speak for the Maronite community, . . . especially not on political matters. . . . [The Christian Lebanese position and that of all of Lebanon is] rejection

of the partition of Palestine." The Maronite representative of Eddé's National Bloc party in parliament joined in the condemnation of Mubarak.

133. Michael Sasson to author, 23 June 1987.

134. A. Grinblat, "Aftermath of the Publication of Archbishop I. Mubarak's Memorandum to UNSCOP in the Beirut Daily *al-Diyar* on 27 September 1947," 16 October 1947, SC, Vol. 7.5; Lutzky, "The Mubarak Affair, According to the Press and Internal Information," 7 October 1947, ISA, 2567/12 (Heb.).

135. A. Grinblat, "The American Arab Press on Zionism and Lebanese Affairs" and "The Maronite Patriarch on Zionism and Lebanese Affairs," 10 November 1947, SC, vol. 7.5. Grinblat discusses the treatment of the patriarch's *al-Hayat* interview in the 21 October issue of *al-Hoda* and translates much of the interview from the 8 October issue of *al-Hayat*. In light of his mutual assistance treaty with the Jewish Agency, Arida's alleged comment that with their own political influence and material resources, the Jews in Palestine did not need the support of any Lebanese individual or group, is particularly interesting.

136. Lutzky, "The Mubarak Affair, According to the Press and Internal Information," 7 October 1947, ISA, 2567/12 (Heb.).

137. Haddad, "Christian Arab Attitudes," p. 130; Cohen, *Israel and the Arab World*, p. 377; contrast Shimoni, interview with author, 4 March 1987.

138. Handbill, "From the Bishop Mubarak to the Honorable Lebanese People," 24 August 1947, ISA, 2569/19 (Arab.); Lutzky, "Trip in Lebanon, 2 July 1947–2 August 1947," 4 Aug. 1947, CZA, S25/3960 (Heb.); Eliahu Epstein to JAE, 10 July 1947, BGA, and CZA, S25/6319.

139. Rabinovich, *War for Lebanon*, p. 104; Shimoni, lecture, Shiloah Institute, 7 December 1983; Shimoni, interview with author, 4 March 1987.

140. Haddad, "Christian Arab Attitudes," p. 128.

141. France was torn between the security that a Jewish state might offer Christian interests in Lebanon and a fear of antagonizing those Muslims under French control in North Africa. Sachar attributes the French decision to vote in favor of partition to a phone call from Weizmann to former prime minister Léon Blum. See Howard M. Sachar, *A History of Israel* (New York and Oxford: Knopf and Oxford University Press, 1981–87), vol. 1, p. 294. See also Cohen, *Israel and the Arab World*, p. 390; M. Fischer to M. Shertok, 9 February 1948, and notes of a meeting between H. Berman and R. Neuville, 24 April 1948, in *Te'udot Limediniyut Hakhutz shel Medinat Yisrael* [Political and diplomatic documents, December 1947–May 1948], ed. Gedalia Yogev (Jerusalem: Central Zionist Archives, 1979), vol. 1, pp. 26, 322–23.

142. Gideon Rafael, lecture, Shiloah Institute, Tel Aviv University, 21 December 1983; Hudson, *Precarious Republic*, p. 325.

143. Weizmann to Mubarak, 5 December 1947, in *LCW*, vol. 23, letter 87.

144. Elath, *Shivat Tzion Ve'arav*, p. 314.

145. Regarding the hostility between Arida and Khoury, see General Beynet to Minister of Foreign Affairs, 1 December 1944, AD, MAN/755 (Fr.).

146. Shimoni remarks upon the strange fact that the Agency did not have much contact with Mubarak, its most faithful and outspoken supporter, in this later period. He suggests that since Mubarak was so genuinely pro-Zionist, the Agency did not need to encourage him, instruct him, or coordinate activities with him. As for Mubarak's exclusion from the treaty, it is likely that Arida purposely avoided involving the archbishop because he could not count on him to adhere to the patriarch's strict demand for secrecy. Shimoni, lecture, Shiloah Institute, 7 December 1983; Shimoni, interview with author, 4 March 1987.

CHAPTER 6

1. Ya'akov Shimoni, interview with author, 4 March 1987, Jerusalem; Yehoshua Porath, interview with author, 10 March 1987, Jerusalem; Yehoshua Palmon, interview with au-

thor, 26 March 1987, Kfar Shmariyahu, Israel; Ya'akov Sharett, interview with author, 1 April 1987, Tel Aviv. See also, e.g., Moshe Sharett, *Yoman Medini*, 22 July 1936, vol. 1, p. 217. Sharett notes that in meeting with Epstein, he had him "skip over his conversation with Arida because I wanted to hear about events in Damascus."

2. Shimoni, interview with author, 4 March 1987. A complete copy of the treaty exists among Ben-Gurion's personal papers as well as in the Central Zionist Archives. See Treaty, 30 May 1946, BGA, and CZA S25/3269 (Fr.).

3. Itamar Rabinovich, *The Road Not Taken: Early Arab-Israeli Negotiations* (New York: Oxford University Press, 1991), pp. 42–43.

4. Yoav Gelber, "Antecedents of the Jewish-Druze Alliance in Palestine," *Middle Eastern Studies* 28, no. 2 (April 1992): 370.

5. Ian Black, "Zionism and the Arabs, 1936–1939," Ph.D. diss., University of London, 1979, pp. 415–16.

6. Glenn E. Perry, "Israeli Involvement in Inter-Arab Politics," *International Journal of Islamic and Arabic Studies* 1, no. 1 (1984): 24–25.

7. Gideon Raphael, lecture at the Shiloah Institute, Tel Aviv University, 21 December 1983; David Ben-Gurion, *Zikhronot* [Memoirs] (Tel Aviv: Am Oved, 1974), 27 July 1937, vol. 4, p. 331.

8. Ben-Gurion, *Zikhronot*, 27 and 29 July 1937, vol. 4, pp. 331, 367; idem, *Yoman Hamilchamah* [War diary] (Tel Aviv: Misrad Habitachon, 1982), 24 May and 18 June 1948, vol. 2, pp. 454, 533, and 19 December 1948, vol. 3, p. 887.

9. William W. Haddad, "Christian Arab Attitudes Toward the Arab-Israeli Conflict," *Muslim World* 67, no. 2 (April 1977): 130.

10. "Conversation with Hamid Franjieh," 15 December 1949, ISA, 2531/12 (Heb.).

11. Black, "Zionism and the Arabs," p. 418.

12. Kenneth Stein, *The Land Question in Palestine, 1917–1939* (Chapel Hill: University of North Carolina Press, 1984), p. xvi.

13. Eliahu Elath, interview with author, 29 July 1986, Jerusalem.

14. See, e.g., Itzhak Ben-Zvi to JAE, 23 August 1938, CZA, S25/3500 (Heb.).

15. Itamar Rabinovich, *The War for Lebanon, 1970–1983* (Ithaca: Cornell University Press, 1984), p. 165.

16. "Conversation with Hamid Franjieh," 15 December 1949, ISA, 2531/12 (Heb.).

17. Walid Khalidi, *Conflict and Violence in Lebanon* (Cambridge: Center for International Affairs, Harvard University, 1979), p. 147.

18. Elath, interview with author, 29 July 1986.

19. Black, "Zionism and the Arabs," p. 311.

20. Sasson to Shimoni, 28 November 1948, ISA, 3749/1 (Heb.).

21. Raphael to Walter Eytan, 28 December 1950, ISA, 2408/16 (Heb.).

22. Ya'akov Shimoni, "A Conversation with Emile Eddé, 3 July 1948," 13 July 1948, ISA, 2565/12 (Heb.); Middle East Department to Foreign Minister, "Sectarian Agitation in Lebanon," 26 August 1948, ISA, 2565/12 (Heb.); "A Meeting with an Emissary of the Archbishop Mubarak," 28 February 1949, ISA, 2563/23 (Heb.). Shimoni, interview with author, 4 March 1987; idem, lecture, Shiloah Institute, 7 December 1983; [Levy-Brohl?], "Israeli Assistance for the Organization of a Coup in Lebanon," n.d., ISA, 163/5/A (Fr.). For lingering Mubarak-Israel relations, 1948–51, see multiple correspondence, ISA, 163/5, 2563/3, 2563/23 (Eng., Fr., Heb.). Regarding Phalange overtures to Israel, see David Ben-Gurion, *Min HaYoman* [From Ben-Gurion's diary—the war of independence], eds. G. Rivlin and E. Oren (Tel Aviv: Misrad Habitachon, 1986), 5 June 1949, p. 444; and Benny Morris, "Israel and the Lebanese Phalange: The Birth of a Relationship, 1948–51," *Studies in Zionism* 5, no. 1 (Spring 1984): 125–44.

23. Rabinovich, *War for Lebanon*, p. 105.

BIBLIOGRAPHY

Archival Sources

Israel

Ben-Gurion Archives (BGA), Sede Boqer, Israel.
Central Zionist Archives (CZA), Jerusalem, Israel.
   Record Groups:
      JAE   Minutes of the Meetings of the Jewish Agency Executive
      S2   Education Department, Jewish Agency
      S20   Department for Jews of the Middle East, Jewish Agency
      S25   Political Department, Palestine Zionist Executive/Jewish Agency
      Z2   The Central Zionist Office (1905–11)
      Z4   Zionist Organization/Jewish Agency Executive, London (1917–55)
Haganah Archives (HA), Tel Aviv, Israel.
Israel State Archives (ISA), Jerusalem, Israel.
   Record Groups:
     Israel Foreign Ministry Papers
     Ministry of Minority Affairs
     Prime Minister's Office
Weizmann Archives (WA), Rehovot, Israel.
Archive for Jewish Education in Israel (ED), Tel Aviv University, Ramat Aviv, Israel.

France

Archives Diplomatiques du Ministère des Affaires Étrangères (AE), Paris, France.
   Série E - Levant 1918–29 (LE 18–29)
   Série E - Levant 1918–40 (LE 18–40)
     Sous-série Syrie-Liban
     Sous-série Palestine (PAL)

Série Société des Nations (SDN)
  Sous-série Mandats
Centre des Archives Diplomatiques de Nantes (AD), Ministère des Affaires Étrangères, Nantes, France.
  Série Mandat Syrie-Liban (MAN)
    Fonds "Beyrouth"
    Archives du Haut Commissariat de France en Syrie et au Liban

PUBLISHED DOCUMENT COLLECTIONS

Yogev, Gedalia, ed. *Te'udot Limediniyut Hachutz shel Medinat Yisrael* [Political and diplomatic documents, December 1947-May 1948]. Jerusalem: Central Zionist Archives, 1979.

INTERVIEWS

Aharon Amir, Jerusalem, 30 March 1987
Yonah Ben-Azar, Kibbutz Hanita, Israel, 9 April 1987
Itamar Ben-Barak, Kibbutz Hanita, Israel, 9 April 1987
Gamliel Cohen, Tel Aviv, Israel, 7 May 1993
Shula Cohen-Kishik, Jerusalem, 20 May 1986
Abba Eban, Pittsburgh, Pennsylvania, 24 October 1993
Eliahu Elath, Jerusalem, 29 July and 14 October 1986
Miri Eliav-Feldon, correspondence with author, 23 November 1989
Walter Eytan, Jerusalem, 6 March 1987
Shalom Fein, Metulla, Israel, 28 April 1987
Yossi Goldberg, Metulla, Israel, 28 April 1987
Nahum Hurwitz, Kibbutz Kfar Giladi, Israel, 27 April 1987
Achiam Kroll, Kibbutz Kfar Giladi, Israel, 27 April 1987
Chaim Levkov, Holon, Israel, 11 May 1987
Elchanan Oren, Ramat Gan, Israel, 4 March 1987
Yehoshua Palmon, Kfar Shmariyahu, Israel, 26 March 1987
Yehoshua Porath, Jerusalem, 10 March 1987, and correspondence with author, 24 October 1989
Dina Rudalinski, Metulla, Israel, 28 April 1987
Kamal Salibi, Portland, Oregon, 31 October 1992
David Sandler, Metulla, Israel, 28 April 1987
Michael Sasson, correspondence with author, 24 April and 23 June 1987
Arye Shalav, Tel Aviv, 31 March 1987
Amnon Shamosh, Kibbutz Ma'ayan Baruch, Israel, 29 April 1987
Ya'akov Sharett, Tel Aviv, 1 April 1987
Ya'akov Shimoni, Jerusalem, 4 March 1987
Yossi Vogel, Kibbutz Ein Gev, Israel, 26 April 1987
Amnon Yonai, Netanya, Israel, 12 May 1987

NEWSPAPERS

Hebrew

Davar
Ha'aretz
Haboker
Hamashkif
al-Hamishmar

Ha'olam
Hatzofeh

English

Herald Tribune
Jerusalem Post
New York Times
New York Tribune
Palestine Post
Washington Post

Arabic

al-Diyar
al-Hoda
al-Nahar

BOOKS

Abraham, Antoine J. *Lebanon at Mid-Century: Maronite-Druze Relations in Lebanon 1840–1869.* Lanham: University Press of America, 1981.

Ajami, Fouad. *The Arab Predicament.* Cambridge: Cambridge University Press, 1981.

Allon, Yigal. *Masakh Shel Chol* [A curtain of sand]. Tel Aviv: Hakibbutz Hameuchad, 1959.

Almog, Samuel. *Zionism and the Arabs.* Jerusalem: Zalman Shazar Center, 1983.

Amir, Aharon, ed. *Levanon: Eretz, Am, Milchamah* [Lebanon: Land, people, war]. Tel Aviv: Hadar, 1979.

Antonius, George. *The Arab Awakening.* Philadelphia: Lippincott, 1939.

Arlosoroff, Chaim. *Yoman Yerushalayim* [Jerusalem diary]. Tel Aviv: Mifleget Poale Eretz Yisrael, 1941.

Bar Zohar, Michael. *Ben-Gurion: The Armed Prophet.* Englewood Cliffs: Prentice Hall, 1968.

Ben-Gurion, David. *Min Hayoman* [From Ben-Gurion's diary—the war of independence]. G. Rivlin and E. Oren, eds. Tel Aviv: Misrad Habitachon, 1986.

———. *Pegishot im Manhigim Arviyim* [Meetings with Arab leaders]. Tel Aviv: Am Oved, 1967. English translation: *My Talks with Arab Leaders.* Trans. Aryeh Rubinstein and Misha Louvish. Jerusalem: Keter, 1972.

———. *Yoman Hamilchamah* [The war of independence: Ben Gurion's diary]. 3 vols. Tel Aviv: Misrad Habitachon, 1982.

———. *Zikhronot* [Memoirs]. 6 vols. Tel Aviv: Am Oved, 1971–87.

Binder, Leonard, ed. *Politics in Lebanon.* New York: Wiley, 1966.

Brecher, Michael. *The Foreign Policy System of Israel.* New Haven: Yale University Press, 1972.

Caplan, Neil. *Futile Diplomacy.* 2 vols. London: Cass, 1983–86.

———. *Palestine Jewry and the Arab Question, 1917–1925.* London: Cass, 1978.

Cohen, Aharon. *Israel and the Arab World.* New York: Funk & Wagnalls, 1970.

Cohen, Michael J. *Palestine 1936–1945: Retreat from Mandate: The Making of British Policy 1936–1945.* New York: Holmes & Meier, 1978.

Crum, Bartley C. *Behind the Silken Curtain.* New York: Simon & Schuster, 1947.

Dayan, Moshe. *Avnai Derekh* [The story of my life]. Tel Aviv: Dvir, 1976.

Dayan, Shmuel. *Biyemai Chazon Umatzor* [In days of vision and siege]. Tel Aviv: Massada, 1953.

Dictionnaire de Biographie Francaise. Paris: Librairie Letouzey et Ane, 1961.

Elath, Eliahu. *Hama'avak al Hamedinah* [The battle for statehood]. Tel Aviv: Am Oved, 1982.

———. *Shivat Tzion Ve'arav* [Zionism and the Arabs]. Tel Aviv: Dvir, 1974.

———. *Zionism at the U.N.: A Diary of the First Days.* Trans. Michael Ben-Yitzhak. Philadelphia: Jewish Publication Society, 1976.

Elon, Amos. *The Israelis: Founders and Sons.* New York: Bantam Books, 1972.

Encyclopaedia Judaica Yearbook, 1975–1976. Jerusalem: Keter, 1976.

Esman, Milton J., and Itamar Rabinovich, eds. *Ethnicity, Pluralism, and the State in the Middle East.* Ithaca: Cornell University Press, 1988.

Ettinger, Shmuel, ed. *Hatziyonut Vehashealah Ha'aravit* [Zionism and the Arab question]. Jerusalem: Zalman Shazar Center, 1979.

Evron, Yair. *War and Intervention in Lebanon.* London: Croom Helm, 1987.

Gaunson, A. B. *The Anglo-French Clash in Lebanon and Syria, 1940–1945.* London: Macmillan, 1987.

Gilmour, David. *Lebanon: The Fractured Country.* New York: St. Martin's, 1984.

Golan, Aviezer, and Danny Pinkas. *Shem Tzofen: Hapeninah* [Code name: The Pearl]. Tel Aviv: Zmora/Bitan, 1980. English translation: *Shula: Code Name The Pearl.* New York: Delacorte, 1980.

Gordon, David C. *The Republic of Lebanon: Nation in Jeopardy.* Boulder: Westview, 1983.

Granados, J. Garcia. *The Birth of Israel: The Drama as I Saw It.* New York: Knopf, 1948.

Haddad, Heskel M. *Jews of Arab and Islamic Countries.* New York: Shengold, 1984.

Haim, Sylvia, ed. *Arab Nationalism.* Berkeley: University of California Press, 1962.

Hof, Frederic C. *Galilee Divided: The Israel-Lebanon Frontier, 1916–1984.* Boulder: Westview, 1985.

Hourani, Albert. *Arabic Thought in the Liberal Age, 1798–1939.* London: Oxford University Press, 1962.

———. *Minorities in the Arab World.* London: Oxford University Press, 1947.

———. *Syria and Lebanon: A Political Essay.* London: Oxford University Press, 1946.

Hudson, Michael. *The Precarious Republic: Political Modernization in Lebanon.* New York: Random House, 1968.

Hurewitz, J. C. *The Struggle for Palestine.* New York: W. W. Norton, 1950.

Joseph, Bernard. *The Faithful City.* New York: Simon & Schuster, 1960.

Kaufmann, Yehezkel. *The Biblical Account of the Conquest of Canaan.* Jerusalem: Magnes and The Hebrew University of Jerusalem, 1953.

Kedourie, Elie. *The Chatham House Version and Other Middle-Eastern Studies.* Hanover: University Press of New England, 1984.

Kedourie, Elie, and Sylvia Haim, eds. *Zionism and Arabism in Palestine and Israel.* London: Cass, 1982.

Khalidi, Walid. *Conflict and Violence in Lebanon.* Cambridge: Center for International Studies, Harvard University, 1979.

Kimche, Jon. *There Could Have Been Peace.* New York: Dial, 1973.

Kisch, Frederick H. *Palestine Diary.* London: V. Gollancz, 1938.

Klieman, Aaron S. *Israel and the World after Forty Years.* Washington: Pergamon-Brassey's and International Defense, 1990.

Kurzman, Dan. *Genesis 1948.* Cleveland: New American Library, 1970.

Laqueur, Walter. *A History of Zionism.* New York: Schocken Books, 1976.

Lissak, Moshe, and Daniel Horowitz. *The Origins of the Israeli Polity: Palestine Under the Mandate.* Chicago: University of Chicago Press, 1978.

Litvinoff, Barnet, ed. *The Essential Chaim Weizmann.* New York: Holmes & Meier, 1982.

Longrigg, Stephen. *Syria and Lebanon Under French Mandate.* London: Oxford University Press, 1958.

McLaurin, R. D., ed. *The Political Role of Minority Groups in the Middle East.* New York: Praeger, 1979.

Mandel, Neville J. *The Arabs and Zionism Before World War I.* Berkeley: University of California Press, 1976.

Mattar, Philip. *The Mufti of Jerusalem: Al-Hajj Amin al-Husayni and the Palestinian National Movement.* New York: Columbia University Press, 1988.

Moosa, Matti. *The Maronites in History.* Syracuse: Syracuse University Press, 1986.

Nisan, Mordechai. *Minorities in the Middle East.* Jefferson, NC: McFarland, 1991.

Owen, Roger, ed. *Essays on the Crisis in Lebanon.* London: Ithaca, 1976.

Pearlman, Moshe. *Ben-Gurion Looks Back in Talks with Moshe Pearlman.* New York: Simon & Schuster, 1965.

Perlmutter, Amos. *Israel: The Partitioned State.* New York: Charles Scribner's Sons, 1985.

Porath, Yehoshua. *The Emergence of the Palestinian Arab National Movement, 1918–1929.* London: Cass, 1974.

———. *The Palestinian Arab National Movement, 1929–1939.* London: Cass, 1977.

———. *Shelah ve'et Beyado* [The life of Uriel Shelah (Yonathan Ratosh)]. Tel Aviv: Machbarot Lesifrut, Zmora, 1989.

Rabinovich, Itamar. *The Road Not Taken: Early Arab-Israeli Negotiations.* Oxford: Oxford University Press, 1991.

———. *The War for Lebanon, 1970–1983.* Ithaca: Cornell University Press, 1984.

Rey, Alain, ed. *Dictionnaire Universel des Noms Propres.* Paris: Dictionnaires Le Robert, 1986.

Roshwald, Aviel. *Estranged Bedfellows: Britain and France in the Middle East During the Second World War.* New York: Oxford University Press, 1990.

Rubin, Barry. *The Arab States and the Palestine Conflict.* Syracuse: Syracuse University Press, 1981.

Sachar, Howard M. *A History of Israel.* 2 vols. New York and Oxford: Knopf and Oxford University Press, 1981–87.

Said, Amin. *Al-Thawra al-Arabiya al-Kubra* [The great Arab revolt]. Vol. 3. Cairo: Matba'a Issa al-Babi al-Halabi, 1934.

Salibi, Kamal S. *A House of Many Mansions: The History of Lebanon Reconsidered.* Berkeley: University of California Press, 1988.

———. *The Modern History of Lebanon.* New York: Praeger, 1965.

Sasson, Eliahu. *Baderekh el Hashalom* [On the road to peace]. Tel Aviv: Am Oved, 1978.

Sharett, Moshe. *Yoman Medini* [Political diary]. 5 vols. Tel Aviv: Am Oved, 1968–79.

Sheffer, Gabriel. *Resolution Versus Management of the Middle East Conflict: the Confrontation Between Ben-Gurion and Moshe Sharett.* Jerusalem: Magnes, 1980.

Sitton, David. *Kehilot Yehudai Sefarad Vehamizrach Ba'olam Beyamainu* [Jewish communities of Spain and the East in the world in our days]. Jerusalem: Ahva Cooperative, 1974.

Spears, Edward. *Fulfillment of a Mission: The Spears Mission to Syria and Lebanon, 1941–1944.* London: Cooper, 1977.

Stein, Kenneth. *The Land Question in Palestine, 1917–1939.* Chapel Hill: University of North Carolina, 1984.

Stillman, Norman A. *The Jews of Arab Lands in Modern Times.* Philadelphia: Jewish Publication Society, 1991.

Sykes, Christopher. *Crossroads to Israel, 1917–1948.* Bloomington: Indiana University Press, 1973.

Teveth, Shabtai. *Ben-Gurion and the Palestinian Arabs.* Oxford: Oxford University Press, 1985.

Tidhar, David. *Entziklopedia Lechalutzai Hayishuv Ubonav* [Encyclopedia of the Yishuv's pioneers and its builders]. 19 vols. Tel Aviv: Sifriyat Rishonim, 1947–71.

Weinberg, Moshe. *Yomano Shel Shlomo Kostika* [Shlomo Kostika's Diary]. Tel Aviv: Yad Tabenkin and Hakibbutz Hameuchad, 1989.

Weizmann, Chaim. *The Letters and Papers of Chaim Weizmann.* 23 vols. London and Jerusalem: Oxford University Press and Israel Universities Press, 1968–80.

————. *Trial and Error: The Autobiography of Chaim Weizmann*. New York: Harper & Brothers, 1949.

Wolecki, Eli, ed. *May'ah Siporai Aliyah* [One hundred aliyah stories]. Tel Aviv: Misrad Habitachon, 1987.

Yaniv, Avner. *Dilemmas of Security: Politics, Strategy, and the Israeli Experience in Lebanon*. Oxford: Oxford University Press, 1987.

Zamir, Meir. *The Formation of Modern Lebanon*. London: Croom Helm, 1985.

Zeine, Zeine N. *The Struggle for Arab Independence*. Beirut: Khayat's, 1960.

ARTICLES

Avramski-Bleiyi, Irit. "Yehudai Suriya Velevanon Takhat Shilton Vishi" [The Jews of Syria and Lebanon under Vichy rule]. *Pa'amim* 28 (1986): 131–57.

Bar-Ayal, Avi. "Gvulot Eretz Yisrael Batfisato Shel David Ben-Gurion" [David Ben-Gurion's Perception of the Borders of the Land of Israel]. *Kivunim* 21 (November 1983): 5–15.

Bar-Simon-Tov, Ya'acov. "Ben-Gurion and Sharett: Conflict Management and Great Power Constraints in Israeli Foreign Policy." *Middle Eastern Studies* 24 (July 1988): 330–56.

Black, Ian. "Zionism and the Arabs, 1936–1939." Ph.D. diss., University of London, 1978.

Caplan, Neil. "Negotiation and the Arab-Israel Conflict, 1918–1948." *Jerusalem Quarterly* 6 (Winter 1978): 3–19.

Caplan, Neil, and Ian Black. "Israel and Lebanon: Origins of a Relationship." *Jerusalem Quarterly* 27 (Spring 1983): 48–58.

"Defenders of the Middle East." *Economist*. 24 June 1950, pp. 1390–91.

Elath, Eliahu. "Hatziyonut Hafanikit Balevanon" [Phoenician Zionism in Lebanon]. *Cathedra* 35 (April 1985): 109–24. English translation: "Phoenician Zionism in Lebanon." *Jerusalem Quarterly* 42 (Spring 1987): 38–56.

Flinder, Alexander. "Is This Solomon's Seaport?" *Biblical Archeology Review* 15, no. 4 (July/August 1989): 30–43.

Gelber, Yoav. "Antecedents of the Jewish-Druze Alliance in Palestine." *Middle Eastern Studies* 28, no. 2 (April 1992): 352–73.

Haddad, William W. "Christian Arab Attitudes Towards the Arab-Israeli Conflict." *Muslim World* 67, no. 2 (April 1977): 127–45.

————. "The Christian Arab Press and the Palestine Question: A Case Study of Michel Chiha of Bayrut's *Le Jour*." *Muslim World* 65, no. 2 (April 1975): 119–30.

Hourani, Albert. "Ideologies of the Mountain and the City." In *Essays on the Crisis in Lebanon*, ed. Roger Owen. London: Ithaca, 1976.

Katz, Joseph. "Tokhniyot Tziyoniyot Lerekhishat Karka'ot Balevanon Batchilat Hamay'ah Ha'esrim" [Zionist plans for purchasing properties in Lebanon in the early twentieth century]. *Cathedra* 35 (April 1985): 53–57.

Khalaf, Tewfik. "The Phalange and the Maronite Community: From Lebanonism to Maronitism." In *Essays on the Crisis in Lebanon*, ed. Roger Owen. London: Ithaca, 1976.

Kupperschmidt, Uri M. "Tmikhat Hapatriarch Hamaroni Arida Bayehudim Nirdafai Hanatzim" [The Maronite Patriarch Arida's support for Jews persecuted by the Nazis]. *Pa'amim* 29 (1986): 72–80.

Morris, Benny. "Israel and the Lebanese Phalange: The Birth of a Relationship, 1948–1951." *Studies in Zionism* 5, no. 1 (Spring 1984): 125–44.

————. "The Phalange Connection." *Jerusalem Post Magazine*, 1 July 1983, pp. 7–8.

Nachmani, Amikam. "Middle East Listening Post: Eliahu Sasson and the Israeli Legation in Turkey, 1949–1952." *Studies in Zionism* 6, no. 2 (Autumn 1985): 263–85.

Perry, Glenn E. "Israeli Involvement in Inter-Arab Politics." *International Journal of Islamic and Arabic Studies* 1, no. 1 (1984): 11–31.

Podet, Allen H. "Husni al-Barazi on Arab Nationalism in Palestine." In *Zionism and Arabism in Palestine and Israel.* Elie Kedourie and Sylvia Haim, eds. London: Cass, 1982.

Shavit, Ya'akov. "Hebrews and Phoenicians: An Ancient Historical Image and Its Usage." *Studies in Zionism* 5, no. 2 (Autumn 1984): 157–80.

Shlaim, Avi. "Conflicting Approaches to Israel's Relations with the Arabs: Ben-Gurion and Sharett, 1953–1956." *Middle East Journal* 37, no. 2 (Spring 1983): 180–202.

Stoakes, Frank. "The Super Vigilantes: The Lebanese Kataeb Party as Builder, Surrogate, and Defender of the State." *Middle Eastern Studies* 11, no. 3 (October 1975): 215–36.

Zamir, Meir. "Emile Eddé and the Territorial Integrity of Lebanon." *Middle Eastern Studies* 14, no. 2 (May 1978): 232–35.

———. "Smaller and Greater Lebanon—the Squaring of a Circle?" *Jerusalem Quarterly* 23 (Spring 1982): 34–53.

INDEX

Aaronsohn, Aaron, 41
Abdullah (Emir of Transjordan), 20, 149–50
al-Ahdab, Khayr al-Din (Lebanese prime minister): and the mufti, 110–11, 191 n.99, 191 n.100
Ajami, Fouad: on Maronite-Zionist rivalry, 34
Ajami, Marie, 73
Akhbar al-Yom, 127
Akl, Monsignor Paul, 133
al-Diyar, 143
Alexandria Protocol of 1944, 125
al-Hayat, 143
al-Hoda, 133
Aliyah, 22
Alliance Israelite Universelle, 52, 82
Alliance of minorities. *See* Minority alliance concept
al-Makshouf, 103
Anglo-American Committee of Inquiry, 117, 134–36
Antonius, George, 190 n.91
Arab conference at Bludan (1946), 125
Arab Higher Committee, 95, 98
Arab nationalism: role of Lebanese Christians, 34, 173 n.50

Arab Revolt (1936–1939), 88, 95–97, 102; Druze opposition to, 110; effect on Zionist policy, 149, 150; pan-Arabization of, 150, 152
Arazi, Tuvia, 129, 198 n.89; and Charles Malik, 134
Arida, Antoine Pierre, 31, 52; *al-Hayat* interview, 202 n. 135; distrust of Arab League, 127; fear of Muslim majority rule, 109; and German-Jewish settlement in Lebanon, 78–79; letter to Ben-Gurion, 140; letter to Chaim Weizmann, 163; and Maronite-Jewish business proposals, 67–68; opposition to Catroux and Naccache, 120, 121, 193 n.14; opposition to Khoury government, 126, 127; pro-Zionism, 61–62; quarrel with Tewfik Awad, 143–44; reaction to Mubarak's U.N. letter, 143; and shared Lebanese-Zionist border, 100; support for independent Christian Lebanon, 62; U.N. testimony on Palestine, 141, 142; understanding of Arab solidarity, 150–51; and Zionist-Maronite treaty, 136–42